PENTECOST
TO THE
PRESENT

PENTECOST
TO THE
PRESENT

BOOK THREE: *WORLDWIDE REVIVALS AND RENEWAL*

JEFF OLIVER

Newberry, FL 32669

Bridge-Logos
Newberry, FL 32669

Pentecost to the Present:
The Holy Spirit's Enduring Work in the Church
by Jeff Oliver

Printed in the United States of America.

Editing services by ChristianEditingServices.com

Cover/Interior design by Kent Jensen | knail.com

Cover photo: The Apostolic Faith Gospel Mission on Azusa Street in 1928. Source: Flower Pentecostal Heritage Center.

International Standard Book Number: 978-0-91210-636-6

VP 03-03-17

DEDICATION

To the Spirit of God, whose tireless work through the centuries has gone largely unnoticed.

To Pastor Reggie Scarborough of Family Worship Center in Lakeland, Florida—the man who taught me "progressive Pentecost."

To my beautiful wife, Faith, without whose love and support I could not have completed this work.

And to our West Highland Terrier, Gracie Lou, who lay at my feet or on my lap through most of this writing.

A special thanks to Karen Burkett, Harold Helms, Glenn Gohr, Craig Keener, Douglas Jacobsen, Mark Nickens, Edward Harding, and all who contributed to the editing process.

CONTENTS

FOREWORD

After many years of study and research, Jeff Oliver has now published the fruits of his labor. *Pentecost to the Present: The Holy Spirit's Enduring Work in the Church* is a very readable and accurate history of charismatic Christianity from the days of the apostles to the present day. As Jeff said, he wrote this book to show the world that Pentecostalism has deep "roots in historic Christianity" contrary to what many have thought. He also shows that such spiritual gifts as speaking in tongues has recurred over the centuries before the advent of modern Pentecostalism.

This book is a popular history, "written in plain language" as a resource for Pentecostal and charismatic leaders and lay persons who may not know or understand their own heritage. *Pentecost to the Present* is useful for those who want to seek a better and deeper understanding of their own Pentecostal faith. Jeff has covered all the bases in the Pentecostal tradition from the New Testament church through the church fathers, the Reformation, the Wesleyan Holiness revival, the classical Pentecostal churches, and the charismatic movement in the mainline churches. Along the way he has included short biographies of most of the leaders he covers along with many wonderful portraits of them all.

This book is well written, easy to read, and tells the Pentecostal story in a narrative form that is easy to grasp. The questions at the end of each chapter will make this book useful in adult small groups, youth groups, family discussions, and as a classroom text in college classes.

Jeff Oliver knows whereof he speaks. Coming into Pentecostalism in the days of the charismatic renewal, he joined a number of Pentecostal and charismatic churches. Before writing this book he attended Rhema Bible Training College in Broken Arrow, Oklahoma, and served as a Christian Education Director and senior pastor for thirteen years. Most recently, he has joined the International Church of the Foursquare Gospel where he was ordained to the ministry, and is now helping to plant a Foursquare congregation in Charlotte, North Carolina. His desire is to help the many "Christian adults and youth who are unaware of their rich spiritual heritage in Christ dating back to Pentecost." He has done a great job.

VINSON SYNAN, PH.D.

DEAN EMERITUS, REGENT UNIVERSITY SCHOOL OF DIVINITY

INTERIM DEAN, ORAL ROBERTS UNIVERSITY
COLLEGE OF THEOLOGY AND MINISTRY

INTRODUCTION

Without knowing the Holy Spirit's work in history, we cannot possibly understand what He is doing today, much less prepare for what He will do.

This third book in a series of three books brings us up to the present day, sparked by the 1904-05 Welsh Revival and the Azusa Street Revival in 1906, followed by the global rise of Pentecostalism and the charismatic renewal.

Book One: Early Prophetic and Spiritual Gifts Movements covers the period from the early church through the Middle Ages, when much of Northern Europe was converted through miracle-working missionary monks.

Book Two: Reformations and Awakenings covers the period from the Middle Ages to the early twentieth century, including the Renaissance and the Enlightenment and how they affected Christianity both in Europe and in the New World.

This third and final installment, *Book Three: Worldwide Revivals and Renewal*, illustrates how:

- Evan Roberts gained worldwide attention through the 1904-05 Welsh revival.

- Charles Parham founded the modern Pentecostal baptism with speaking in tongues.

- William Seymour spearheaded an international Pentecostal movement from Azusa Street in Los Angeles in 1906.

- Pentecostalism spawned new denominations, national and international ministries, global renewal movements, and inspired innovators to take modern revivalism to a whole new level.

- Pentecostalism penetrated American Middle-class Protestantism, as many observers began speaking of a "third force" in Christianity.

- Revolutionary changes in the Catholic Church opened the door for the Catholic Charismatic Renewal.

- The charismatic movement went global with charismatic mega churches, Bible schools, and television networks taking the message of renewal to the world.

- The twenty-first century has witnessed a dramatic shift in Christianity to the Southern Hemisphere fueled, in part, by the global rise of Pentecostalism, with many new movements on the horizon.

PENTECOST . . . AGAIN

(C. 1901–1910)

General Booth's Salvation Army reported from London in 1890: 2,000 dead, 2,000 suicides, 30,000 prostitutes, 160,000 arrests for drunkenness, and nearly a million paupers—welcome to the Modern Age![1] By the turn of the twentieth century, dreams of a Christian society were quickly fading. The world was changing too fast and society was becoming too big and complex for the church to do much about it. Wesley's idealism only a generation before ("I look upon all the world as my parish") was quickly being replaced by Moody's realism ("I look on the world as a wrecked vessel. God has given me a lifeboat and said, 'Save all you can.'")[2]

---

1   William Booth, *In Darkest England and the Way Out* (London: Funk & Wagnalls, 1890): Bruce L. Shelley, *Church History in Plain Language, Third Edition* (Nashville: Thomas Nelson, 2008), 411 [hereafter CH].

2   Wesley, *Journal of John Wesley: Christian Classics Ethereal Library: www.ccel.org/ccel/wesley/journal.vi.iii.v.html* (Accessed 5 February 2013); D.L. Moody, "Secret Power: 32: The Gospel Sermon on the Blessed Hope" January 5, 1877: CH 432.

Catholics and Protestants alike increasingly felt the futility of trying to solve the world's problems by any conventional means, while the two schools of Christian thought—liberal and conservative—seemed further apart than ever toward reaching an agreeable solution. But what both camps failed to consider was the possibility of a third factor in that equation—God. The Spirit of God had intervened before in the affairs of men, and he would do it again.

Americans, perhaps above all, were feeling the effects of radical social and cultural changes. Even now, it is mindboggling to consider just a few of the changes that were taking place around the turn of the twentieth century—mass production, mass communication, mass media, mass transit, free postal delivery, bicycles, automobiles, airplanes, ocean liners, paved roads, truss bridges, skyscrapers, electric lights, telephones, radios, vacuum cleaners, baseball, amusement parks, vaudeville, jazz, and motion pictures. Fearing such overwhelming changes, many clung to the old ways. Others looked forward to the future with a renewed interest in eschatology, Bible prophecy, and end-times events. A.J. Gordon held two major prophetic conferences before the turn of the century—one in New York in 1878 and the other in Chicago in 1886—each mapping out strategies for the coming century and predicting the world would continue its decline into sin before the premillennial return of Christ. Property at Dowie's Zion City in 1900 could not be purchased, only leased for 1,100 years (allowing a thousand years for Christ's millennial reign and no more than a hundred for Christ's return).

CHARLES FOX PARHAM

One man deeply interested in "later day movements" was Charles Fox Parham (1873–1929), who had visited Zion City in 1900. Parham's family had moved from Iowa to Kansas when he was ten. Sickly through much of his youth, he was often confined to his bed for months at a time where he began reading and studying the Bible and sensing a call to ministry. After his mother died when he was only twelve, his father remarried the daughter of a Methodist circuit rider a year later. By fifteen, Parham had already preached his first sermon, and by sixteen, he was studying for ministry at Southwestern Kansas College. However, being a young man exposed to peer pressure and not wanting to become a "beggarly preacher," he decided he could serve God just as well by being a physician. The only problem was, as he began studying medicine, he developed rheumatic fever and became bedridden. Again, the situation motivated him to study the Scriptures—particularly divine healing scriptures. Parham believed God wanted to heal him but was chastening him for not going into the ministry and that it was the Devil who had convinced him not to go in the ministry. Parham promised the Lord that if he could go somewhere where he would not have to beg or take up collections, he would preach. As he neared death, he cried out, "If Thy will is done in me, I shall be whole."[3] Suddenly every organ and joint in his body was made whole—except his ankles. Believing that all formal education was a hindrance to ministry, Parham vowed to quit college and immediately reenter itinerant ministry if God would heal his ankles.

---

3   Mrs. Charles Parham, *The Life of Charles F. Parham*, (Birmingham: Commercial Printing, 1930), 6–9: Roberts Liardon, *God's Generals: Why They Succeeded and Why Some Failed* (New Kensington, Penn.: Whitaker, 1996), 112 [hereafter GG].

Instantly, he felt "a mighty electric current" going through his ankles and making them whole.

PARHAM'S HEALING MINISTRY

At nineteen, Parham was asked to pastor the Methodist Church of Eudora, Kansas, where he met his future wife, Sarah Thistlewaite—a Quaker. But Parham found the denominational church too confining for his inspirational style of ministry and left after only two years, returning again to itinerant ministry. While on the road, he proposed to Sarah, they were married in a Quaker church, and two years later, she gave birth to a son, Claude. But then Parham fell sick again, this time with heart disease, and young Claude developed a fever as well. While in his weakened state, Parham was asked to go pray for another man who was ill when the scripture "Physician, heal thyself" suddenly erupted inside him.[4] As Parham prayed for the other man, he felt the power of God also going into him and was instantly healed. Parham rushed home to tell his wife what had happened and then prayed for his son, who also was healed. From that moment, Parham would renounce all dependency on medicine and commit his life to preaching divine healing and praying for the sick. Then in 1898, the Parhams moved to Topeka, Kansas, and opened Bethel Healing Home—a place for the sick and infirm to come and receive prayer in an atmosphere of faith. He also began publishing *Apostolic Faith* magazine while offering classes for those preparing for ministry. The home was operated entirely "by faith" as each resident trusted God to provide for his or her own funds.

---

4   Luke 4:23

A FACT-FINDING MISSION

A new fact.

In 1900, "deciding to know more fully the latest truths restored by the later day movements," Parham set out on a fact-finding mission to study other ministries.[5] Among others, he visited Dowie's ministry in Chicago, A.B. Simpson's Christian Alliance in Nyack, New York, A.J. Gordon's work in Boston, and Frank Sandford's "Holy Ghost and Us Bible School" in Durham, Maine. Parham was especially struck by some Bible students in Maine whom he witnessed coming down out of their prayer tower speaking in tongues and one in particular, Jennie Glassey, who claimed to speak an African dialect and to be called to missions in Africa. At some point, Parham had also been exposed to B.H. Irwin's Fire-Baptized Holiness groups and, though he agreed with their "third work" doctrine on the baptism in the Holy Ghost, he did not like the emotionalism that so often accompanied it. Parham returned home convinced God had something more "to meet the challenge of a new century," stating, "I returned home fully convinced that while many had obtained real experience in sanctification and the anointing that abideth, there still remained a great outpouring of power for the Christians who were to close this age."[6]

Charles Fox Parham was a forward-thinking minister who wanted "to know more fully the latest truths restored by the later day movements." Known as the "Father of Pentecostal theology," he became one of the principal founders of the modern Pentecostal movement by articulating its principal doctrines, including speaking in tongues as the "introductory sign" and "gift first bestowed upon the baptized." Source: Apostolic Archives International Inc.

---

5   Mrs. Charles Parham, *The Life of Charles F. Parham* (Baxter Springs, KS: Apostolic Faith Bible College, 1930), 48: *Great Commission Bible College: gcbcedu.us/TheLifeOfCharlesFParham470pages.pdf* (Accessed 8 February 2013).

6   Ibid.

BETHEL BIBLE COLLEGE

In October 1900, the Parhams opened Bethel Bible College in a beautiful rented castle-like facility in Topeka called "Stone's Folly," so called because its builder, Erastus Stone, ran out of money before completing it. The house even had an observatory and adjacent room that was perfect for a prayer tower. As they dedicated the building, one man looked out from the prayer tower and saw a vision of a "vast lake of fresh water about to overflow, containing enough to satisfy every thirsty need."[7] The school was opened for "all ministers and Christians who were willing to forsake all, sell what they had, give it away, and enter the school for study and prayer." Forty students responded. Subjects included repentance, conversion, consecration, sanctification, healing, and the imminent return of Christ. Convinced that the true model for the Spirit's outpouring was the upper room experience in Acts 2, Parham told his students that the true Spirit baptism, which would foreshadow any current revival, had not yet arrived, and gradually, the student body came to accept his vision.

Erastus Stone, a man intent on building his family of five the largest mansion in the state of Kansas, eventually ran out of funds. Two years later, Rev. Parham rented the building from its new owners for his Bethel Bible College. It would soon become the site of the twentieth century's "upper room." Source: Flower Pentecostal Heritage Center.

7   Ibid., 57.

A NEW CENTURY DAWNS

By late December, as each regularly scheduled course was taught, a consensus had been reached on repentance, conversion, sanctification, healing—even the second coming—but the question of evidence for Holy Spirit baptism had proved much more difficult. So as Parham was about to leave to preach in Kansas City, he gave the students a special assignment: study the Bible, particularly Acts, to learn more about biblical evidence for the baptism in the Holy Spirit. When Parham returned on New Year's Eve, he was amazed at what the students reported: "To my astonishment they all had the same story, that while there were different things occurred when the Pentecostal blessing fell, that the indisputable proof on each occasion was that they spoke with other tongues."[8] That evening at the New Year's Eve Watch Night Service, the Spirit manifested with unusual intensity. Then at 11:00 p.m. on December 31, 1900, just as the new century was about to dawn, one of the students—a Holiness preacher named Agnes Ozman—asked Parham to pray for her that she might receive the baptism in the Holy Spirit. Parham hesitated, then "humbly in the name of Jesus, I laid my hand upon her head and prayed. I had scarcely repeated three dozen sentences when a glory fell upon her, a halo seemed to surround her head and face, and she began speaking in the Chinese language and was unable to speak in English for three days. When she tried to write in English to tell us of her experience she wrote . . . Chinese."[9]

---

8   Ibid., 52.
9   Ibid., 52–53.

THE PENTECOSTAL BLESSING

For the next three days, all regular activities at Bethel were suspended as the students prayed and waited in the "upper room" for their personal Pentecost. On January 3, Parham left for another speaking engagement, fully expecting that when he returned later that evening, the entire student body would be caught up in the Pentecostal experience. Parham entered the building around 10:00 pm. As he reached the top of the stairs, he saw a flicker of light brighter than the light coming from the coal oil lamps in the room. Then as he entered the room, he was overwhelmed by what he saw. Some were sitting, others kneeling, and still others were standing with hands raised in the air, but all were singing beautifully, as if led by an invisible conductor, Charles Wesley's hymn "Jesus, Lover of my Soul"—in tongues! One student told Parham, "Just before you entered, tongues of fire were sitting above their heads," perhaps explaining the flicker of light he had seen.[10] Then, finding his own place of prayer behind a table, Parham knelt and asked God to also give him the Pentecostal blessing. The Lord told him if he was willing to undergo the persecution, hardships, trials, slander, and scandals that would go along with it, the blessing was his. Parham said, "Lord, I will. Just give me this blessing." He recorded, "Right then there came a slight twist in my throat, a glory fell over me and I began to worship God in the Swedish tongue, which later changed to other languages and continued so until the morning."[11]

---

10 Ibid., 53.
11 Ibid., 54.

THE INITIAL EVIDENCE

Soon newspaper reporters, language professors, and government interpreters converged on the school to investigate the phenomenon. Experts concluded that the students had spoken in twenty-one different languages from around the world. Topeka newsboys shouted in the streets, "Pentecost, Pentecost, read all about the Pentecost!" The headline in the *Topeka Capitol* read, "A Queer Faith, Strange Acts . . . Believers Speaking in Strange Languages." The *Kansas City World* wrote, "These people have a faith almost incomprehensible at this day."[12] Parham told a reporter for the *Kansas City Times* that the students had never studied those languages and that language speakers from those countries had also been brought in to authenticate the languages. Parham said those who spoke in foreign languages had been equipped by God as missionaries to those countries and that missionaries would no longer need to learn languages—just receive the baptism in the Holy Spirit. Though this aspect would not hold true, Parham's school had essentially articulated one of the principal doctrines of Pentecost—speaking in tongues—as the "introductory sign" or "gift first bestowed upon the baptized," earning Parham the title "Father of Pentecostal theology."[13] J. Roswell Flower, founding secretary of the Assemblies of God, described Parham's laying his hands on Ozman as the "touch

---

12   These articles were reprinted in Parham's *Apostolic Faith*, Nov. 1927, 2–5: Vinson Synan, *"The Holiness-Pentecostal Tradition: Charismatic Movements in the Twentieth Century* (Grand Rapids, Mich.: Eerdmans, 1971), 91-92 [hereafter HPT].

13   Dorries, "Edward Irving and the Standing Sign," Gary B. McGee, ed., *Initial Evidence: Historical and Biblical Perspectives on the Pentecostal Doctrine of Spirit Baptism* (Eugene, Oregon: Wipf & Stock, 1991), 49 [hereafter IE]: Eddie L. Hyatt, *2000 Years of Charismatic Christianity* (Lake Mary, Fla.: Charisma, 2002), 141 [hereafter CC]; Douglas Jacobsen, ed., *A Reader in Pentecostal Theology: Voices from the First Generation* (Bloomington: Indiana University, 2006), 31.

felt round the world" that "made the Pentecostal movement of the twentieth century."[14]

Shortly after midnight on January 1, 1901, Agnes Ozman, in a "shot heard round the world," asked Charles Parham to lay hands on her that she might receive the gift of the Holy Ghost. Ozman later said, "It was as hands were laid upon my head that the Holy Spirit fell upon me and I began to speak in tongues, glorifying God." Her colleagues reported that a halo had surrounded both her face and head. Later, Parham and thirty-four other students also began speaking in unknown languages. Source: Flower Pentecostal Heritage Center.

Later that year, Stone's Folly was sold out from under them and the residents dispersed. Parham warned the new owners that since the building had been dedicated to the Lord's use, if it was used for secular purposes, it would be destroyed. They ignored him, and within a few months, it had burned to the ground. Parham soon closed his Topeka operations and set out on a whirlwind revival tour to preach the baptism in the Holy Spirit with tongues as the initial evidence.

EVAN ROBERTS

Meanwhile, in Britain a Welsh minister had requested that a Keswick conference be held in Wales. In 1903, word from the first Welsh Keswick came that "a revival would soon be witnessed." In 1904, a unified prayer was made at the second Welsh Keswick: "to raise up someone to usher in the revival."[15] At the same time, a twenty-six-year-

---

14   J. Roswell Flower, "Birth of the Pentecostal Movement" *Pentecostal Evangel* (26 Nov. 1950), 3: CC 141.

15   Mrs. Jessie Penn-Lewis, *The Awakening in Wales* (London: Marshall Bralters, Keswick, Paternoster, 1905), 58: Wesley Duewel, *Revival Fire* (Grand Rapids, Mich.: Zondervan, 1995), 182 [hereafter RF].

old coal miner named Evan Roberts (1878–1951) had been praying for years, "O God, fill me with your Spirit" and "O God, send mighty revival."[16] Evan was a bit of a modern mystic who prayed all day long, often skipping meals. When he was not praying, he was reading or studying his Bible, a commentary, or a theology book. At age fifteen, Evan was teaching Sunday school at the Calvinist Methodist Moriah Chapel in Loughor, Wales, where he soon became superintendent and wrote hymns and poetry, and played the piano and organ. Longing to further his ministerial studies but lacking the prerequisites for college, Evan joined a preparatory school in 1904 but soon found even that to be too constraining because of his constant burden to pray. Then two weeks into his schooling, both of Evan's lifetime prayers were answered as he became one of twenty young people invited by Rev. Seth Joshua to accompany him on his evangelistic meetings in Blaenannerch as part of the Calvinistic Methodist forward movement in Wales. On the way to one of the meetings, they sang, "It is coming; it is coming; the power of the Holy Ghost. I receive it; I receive it; the power of the Holy Ghost."[17] The next day, Rev. Joshua closed the 7:00 a.m. meeting praying, "Lord . . . bend us."[18]

As they returned to Rev. Joshua's house for breakfast, Evan could only pray, "O Lord, bend me." He heard the Spirit say, "That is what you need."[19] Then at the 9:00 a.m. service, the Spirit came mightily on Evan as he fell to his knees with sweat pouring down his face and tears

16 Wesley L. Duewel, *Heroes of the Holy Life* (Grand Rapids, Mich.: Zondervan, 2002), 135 [hereafter HHL].

17 RF 185.

18 Efion Evans, *The Welsh Revival of 1904* (Bryntirion, Wales: Evangelical Movement of Wales/Bryntirion, 1969), 70: RF 186; *here* bend means to bind; constrain [to do God's will].

19 Ibid.

streaming down his cheeks, crying, "Bend me; bend me; bend me! Oh! Oh! Oh! Oh!"[20] Evan knew he had been filled with the Spirit. He wrote, "I felt ablaze with a desire to go through the length and breadth of Wales to tell of the Savior."[21] God gave him a vision of 100,000 souls being won to Christ. Now absolutely certain that God was getting ready to send revival, Evan began telling everyone he knew to "pray, obey, and surrender totally to the Spirit." Upon returning home, Evan requested a leave of absence from school, telling his family, "You shall see there will be a great change in Loughor in less than a fort-night. We are going to have the greatest revival that Wales has ever seen."[22] That Monday, a revival did break out at Moriah Chapel in Loughor that would soon sweep the entire country.

On Monday evening, October 31, 1904, Evan Roberts, full of the Holy Ghost, commenced a series of prayer meetings at which he made urgent appeals for people to repent of their sinful state and confess Jesus Christ as their Savior and Lord. The Great Welsh Revival was under way, and before it closed, hundreds of thousands were affected—not only in Wales but also across the world. Source: welshrevival.org.

1904–05 WELSH REVIVAL

During the first week of revival, Evan instructed the people, "Now, we must believe that the Spirit will come; not think He will come; hope He will come; but firmly believe He will come."[23] The following

---

20 Ibid.

21 Ibid.

22 D.M. Phillips, *Evan Roberts* (London: Marshall Brothers, Keswick, Paternoster Row, 1923), 171: HHL 139.

23 Ibid., 227–228: RF 189.

Monday, the church was crowded and many were crying aloud in prayer when suddenly a powerful sound in the distance was heard as God's presence entered and filled the building.[24]

Evan himself led many of the meetings, which were often characterized by cries of mercy, weeping, laughing, dancing, joy, singing, praying, brokenness, and lying prostrate on the floor. Local newspapers reported 20,000 conversions within the first five weeks and 85,000 within four months. The meetings were especially well attended by men and children. One newspaper reported that two-thirds of the participants were men, and half of those were young men. In some meetings, the children and youth outnumbered the adults. Many people also began arriving by train from all over the British Isles, India, China, Japan, Germany, France, America, and Russia. Even in Catholic nations like France, Italy, and Portugal, the foreign press covered the revival.

One firsthand witness wrote, "A sense of the Lord's presence was everywhere. It pervaded, nay, it created the spiritual atmosphere. It mattered not where one went, the consciousness of the reality and nearness of God followed. Felt, of course, in the Revival gatherings, it was by no means confined to them; it was also felt in the homes, on the streets, in the mines and factories, in the schools, yea, and even in the theatres and drinking-saloons. The strange result was that wherever people gathered it became a place of awe, and places of amusement and carousal were practically emptied."[25] Another individual described it as "the universal, inescapable sense of the presence of God."[26]

24 RF 190.
25 R.B. Jones, *Rent Heavens* (London: Stanley Martin, 1930), 43–44: RF 183–184.
26 Ibid., 43: RF 183.

Interestingly, many of the revival's participants who could not ordinarily speak Welsh had supernatural experiences during the revival in which they were able to pray, testify, or sing at length in fluent Welsh. William F.P. Burton, who would become a Pentecostal pioneer in Great Britain and cofounder of the Congo Evangelistic Mission in Zaire, reported hearing speaking in tongues for the first time at the Welsh Revival.[27] This gift of tongues was also related to a popular preaching phenomenon known in the Scottish Highlands as the "Highland wail" and in Wales as the "Welsh Hwyl." During communion season among the Scottish Highlands Presbyterians, preachers would use a high, intensive singsong Gaelic to induce a spirit of joy and repentance among their parishioners, which often approached ecstasy. The Welsh Hwyl was similarly used to describe the "divine gust" or "mighty wind" that would inspire preachers and descend on congregations, often filling them with the power and presence of God. Both were evident in the Welsh Revival and helped provide a hunger and stimulus for worldwide Pentecostalism.[28]

THE REVIVAL MEETINGS

One local reporter wrote that though a thousand or two would often attend the services, order reigned: "The meetings . . . were absolutely without any human direction or leadership. 'We must obey the Spirit' is the watchword of Evan Roberts. Three-fourths of the meeting consists of singing. No one uses a hymnbook. No one gives out a

27   Burton, "My Personal Pentecost," *World Pentecost*, I (1973), 19; Ramon Hunston, "The Welsh Revival 1904–05," Awstin, *The Religious Revival in Wales, 1904* (Cardiff, Wales, 1905), 10–11; Evans, *Welsh Revival*: Michael P. Hamilton, ed. *The Charismatic Movement* (Grand Rapids, Mich.: Eerdmans, 1975), 96 [hereafter CM].
28   H.I. Bell, *Development of Welsh Poetry* (Oxford, 1936): CM 96–97.

interesting

hymn. . . . People pray and sing; give testimonies; exhort as the Spirit moves them. . . . I have seen nothing like it."[29] Another wrote, "The revival is born along by the billowing waves of sacred songs. . . . It is the singing, not the preaching that is the instrument which is most efficacious in striking the hearts of men."[30]

Evan always sought the Spirit's leading for a service, often remaining quiet and in the background unless prompted by the Spirit to speak, exhort, pray, or lead. Most of the time, he simply urged the people to "obey the Spirit" and then remained silent, letting others break in one after another. One time, he interrupted the singing only to say, "We may sing all night without saving. It is prayer that tells, that saves, and that brings heaven down among us. Pray, friends, pray."[31] The Spirit always kept the meetings peaceful and orderly. Evan also depended on the Spirit to guide him in accepting invitations, knowing where to speak, and which meetings to attend. Once he cancelled a meeting where thousands were waiting on him because he felt checked by the Spirit. If he felt he would be placed on a pedestal or that Christ would not get all the glory, he would not go. At another time, when asked to reveal his revival secrets, Evan replied, "I have no secret, ask and ye shall receive." Then later, when asked again, he replied, "It is certainly beyond my power to instigate a fresh revival, for revival can alone be given by the Holy Spirit of God when the conditions are fulfilled. . . . Bend the church and save the world."[32]

---

29   Phillips, *Evan Roberts*, 303: RF 196–197.
30   Ibid., 299–302: RF 196.
31   Evans, *Welsh Revival*, 141: RF 201.
32   Ibid., 171–173: RF 202.

REVIVAL SPREADS

Newspaper reports of the Welsh Revival were similar to that of Finney's revivals, with some eighty percent reportedly continuing to live Christian lives some six years later.[33] By the fall of 1905, however, Evan's ministry and influence were waning. Feeling exhausted, he suffered a complete physical breakdown and soon retired completely to a life of prayer. Though he made a brief comeback in 1928 that included some prophecies, healings, and deliverance, he quickly retreated again to prayer. He later wrote, "My work is confined to prayer, and it is such that I have devoted myself for the last twenty-five years. . . . I work as hard at prayer as if I had undertaken any other form of religious work. . . . By preaching I would reach the limited few—by and through prayer I can reach the whole of mankind for God."[34] Evan's prayers must have worked because when news of the Welsh Revival reached other nations, it swept from country to country until some five million were reportedly converted. Yet none was quite like the revival about to hit America.

An Evan Roberts' revival meeting in Anglesey, Wales, July 4, 1905. The revival's staggering success was not due to man's wisdom but to the power of God. Exhausted from a formidable schedule of meetings, Evan eventually suffered from extreme overtiredness and retired as an intercessor, spending up to eighteen hours a day in prayer. Source: encyclopedia.christian. by. Photo: Wikimedia/Slivkov vitali.

33 Ibid., 202.
34 Evans, *Welsh Revival*, 180–182: RF 203.

THE APOSTOLIC FAITH MOVEMENT

When Charles Fox Parham set out on his whirlwind tour, he quickly discovered that support for his newfound experience would be much more difficult than originally thought. However, finally in 1903, while Parham was preaching at a popular health resort in El Dorado Springs, Missouri, Mary Arthur, the wife of a prominent citizen of Galena, Kansas, was miraculously healed. She and her husband then invited Parham to preach in Galena through the winter of 1903–1904, and thousands came to the meetings. The *Joplin Herald* reported it was the greatest demonstration of power and miracles since the time of the apostles with 1,000 being healed and 800 converted.[35] After Galena, Parham gained a strong following and began recruiting young men and women to join his crusade team. Unlike other Holiness preachers though, Parham encouraged his staff to dress stylishly, believing Christianity ought to be attractive to the world. In 1904, the first Apostolic Faith Assembly was built in Keelville, Kansas, and the movement quickly spread into Kansas, Oklahoma, and Texas. In 1905, Parham held a series of meetings at Bryan Hall in Houston, Texas. Parham loved to exhibit his collection of Holy Land artifacts at the meetings, and the press loved to report on them. Sometimes Parham's crusade team would even dress up in Holy Land garb after the meetings and parade down the street with their Apostolic Faith movement banner to drum up support for the meetings. But Parham was not always welcomed. Once while preaching, he took a drink of water and doubled over in pain, then prayed and the pain went

---

35 Parham, *Life of Parham*, 97; Edith L. Blumhofer, *Restoring the Faith: The Assemblies of God, Pentecostalism, and American Culture* (Urbana & Chicago: University of Illinois, 1993), 53.

away. After the meeting, someone examined the water and found it contained enough poison to kill a dozen men.[36] Undeterred, Parham moved his headquarters to Houston, and in January 1906, opened a Bible Training School. According to his wife, Sarah, twenty-five students enrolled, including "one colored man."[37] Despite the "Jim Crow" segregation laws in force in Texas at the time, this particular student was so humble and so determined to learn God's Word that Parham obliged him.

Rev. Charles Parham (front center) and his Apostolic Faith crusade team held a series of revival meetings in Bryan, Texas, in the summer of 1905. From there, Parham would hold a ten-week training session in Houston, which would soon fan the flames of Pentecost around the world. Source: Flower Pentecostal Heritage Center.

WILLIAM JOSEPH SEYMOUR

William Joseph Seymour (1870–1922) was the son of former African slaves from Centerville, Louisiana. Though raised Catholic, his parents, Simon and Phillis, occasionally attended a Baptist church while continuing to work on the plantation after they were freed. Like many African Americans in those days, Seymour had only a Bible for reading and for education prior to enrolling in school. As a young man determined to get a new start in life, Seymour traveled north to Memphis and St. Louis, taking whatever odd jobs he could find as a porter, truck driver, or bartender. At twenty-five, Seymour

36 Parham, *Life of Parham,* 134.
37 Ibid., 137.

again traveled north to Indianapolis, where he received salvation at the Simpson Chapel Methodist Episcopal Church. Seymour was particularly fond of Wesley's teachings and the church's outreach to all classes of people. Yet, dissatisfied with how far it seemed the Methodists had strayed from their Wesleyan roots, he soon joined the Evening Light Saints—a "come-outer" Holiness group that would later become the Church of God (Anderson, Indiana).

In 1900, Seymour went to Chicago, where he sat under John Alexander Dowie's ministry for a time before moving on to Cincinnati and attending Martin Wells Knapp's "God's Bible School," which taught missions, holiness, healing, and the imminent return of Christ, all of which helped form a foundation for Seymour's beliefs. Also during this time, Seymour received a call to ministry but had many doubts and reservations. Shortly thereafter, he contracted smallpox, which was often fatal in those days. Seymour managed to pull through, but the illness left him facially scarred and blind in his left eye. He felt the disease had been God's judgment on him for refusing to accept his call and immediately set out as an itinerant preacher. Like many preachers in those days, Seymour supplemented his income as a traveling salesman rather than receiving offerings.

SEYMOUR IN HOUSTON

In 1903, Seymour moved to Houston to stay with relatives while continuing to preach throughout Texas and Louisiana. In 1905, Seymour felt led to go to Jackson, Mississippi, to meet with a "significant colored clergyman," believed to be C.P. Jones—one of the founders of the Church of God in Christ.[38] While in Houston, Seymour also befriended Mrs. Lucy Farrow, the niece of famous abolitionist Frederick Douglass, a pastor of a small Holiness mission, and a worker in Charles Parham's ministry. Mrs. Farrow was known to the Parhams simply as "Auntie," having worked closely with them in ministry and serving as a caretaker for their children. In 1905, the Parham's asked "Auntie" to come watch their children during their move from Kansas to Texas. Mrs. Farrow agreed, asking Seymour if he would pastor her church in her absence and Seymour also agreed. Mrs. Farrow had also spoken with Seymour about receiving the baptism in the Holy Spirit, but Seymour was reluctant. Later, however, after attending Parham's meetings, he was convinced.

PARHAM'S BIBLE SCHOOL

When Parham announced he was opening a Bible school, Mrs. Farrow insisted that Seymour attend. However, since Texas segregation laws at the time did not permit blacks and whites to be in the same school together, Seymour could not become a resident. But that did not stop Seymour. Sarah Parham wrote, "He was so humble and so deeply interested in the study of the word that Brother Parham could not refuse him. So he was given a place in the class and eagerly drank in the truths which were so new to him and found for his hungry soul."[39] (Though some accounts place Seymour in the hallway, an adjacent room, or out on the veranda, several historical eyewitnesses saw Seymour in

---

38 "Pentecost Brings Healing," (2009) Healing and Revival Press: *healingandrevival. com/BioWSeymour.htm* (Accessed 10 February 2013).

39 Parham, *Life of Parham*, 137.

the classroom along with the others).[40] Regardless, Seymour sat under Parham's ministry, "drinking in" the truths concerning the baptism in the Holy Spirit with the evidence of speaking in other tongues.

William Joseph Seymour, the son of former African slaves from Louisiana, sat in Parham's Bible School in Houston, Texas, in 1906, where "he was given a place in the class and eagerly drank in the truths which were so new to him and found for his hungry soul." Source: Mrs. Charles Parham, *The Life of Charles F. Parham* (1930), p. 137. Photo: Flower Pentecostal Heritage Center.

THE LOS ANGELES CONNECTION

Another friend of Lucy Farrow's, who was living with relatives in Houston at the time, was Miss Neely Terry of Los Angeles. She also attended Farrow's church (including during Seymour's pastorate) and had served as the Parhams' cook. Miss Terry returned to Los Angeles

---

40   Howard Goss, *The Winds of God*, 73: "A negro Baptist preacher from Houston was selected—a Brother Seymour, who had often attended the morning session of the school"; Rev. Pauline Parham, lecture given in 1989, "William Seymour humbly asked Bro. Parham if he could sit outside and take in the lessons, but Bro. Parham gave him a place in the class-room with the other students to learn the truths about the Pentecostal message," The *Apostolic Faith Report*, May, 1921; "One negro man by the name of Seymour, became a regular attendant, taking his seat in the classes: and it was here that he gained the full knowledge of the Full Gospel message," Research Center, Section 2, *Apostolic Archives International: www.apostolicarchives.com/ps3.html* (Accessed 11 February 2013); Eddie L. Hyatt, "Across the Lines: Charles Parham's Contribution to the Inter-Racial Character of Early Pentecostalism" from the Fall 2004 issue of the Pneuma Review, Pauline Parham, "Dad Parham, being from Kansas, was not used to such laws and customs and he welcomed Seymour into the classroom . . . The account I heard from those present was that he was welcomed into the class along with everyone else," *Pneuma Foundation: www.pneumafoundation.org/article.jsp?article=EHyatt-AcrossTheLines.xml* (Accessed 11 February 2013).

after learning that her friends and family had been kicked out of their Baptist church for professing Holiness doctrine and had begun a small Holiness mission in her cousins' home—Richard and Ruth Asberry. Sister Julia Hutchins had been elected their interim pastor until a permanent replacement could be found. When Miss Terry arrived in Los Angeles, she told the group about Pastor Seymour's strong and gentle leadership, and they immediately sent for him. Parham, however, had plans for Seymour to do mission work there in Houston. But when the invitation arrived from Los Angeles, Seymour believed it to be a "divine call," and Parham obliged him, even helping to pay for his train fare.[41]

SEYMOUR IN LOS ANGELES

When Seymour arrived in Los Angeles on February 22, 1906, the city was already racially diverse, free of segregation laws, and in revival mode. Joseph Smale, pastor of the First Baptist Church of Los Angeles, was fired up, having just returned from a three-week tour with Evan Roberts in Wales. Immediately, he ordered cottage prayer meetings to be held throughout the city in preparation for the coming revival and began hosting interdenominational Spirit-led meetings at his church. However, unwilling to let believers from other denominations lead their meetings, the church elders shut them down after only four months. So Smale and a group from the church founded the First New Testament Church of Los Angeles. Frank Bartleman, who had been working with various Holiness missions throughout the city, also began corresponding with Evan Roberts in hopes of sparking a similar

---

41 James S. Tinney, *In The Tradition of William J. Seymour*, (Spirit Press, 1978), 15: quoted from "Father of Modern-Day Pentecostalism," in *Journal of the Interdenominational Theological Center* (Fall 1976): GG 145.

revival in Los Angeles. Evan replied to one of his letters stating, "I pray God to hear your prayer, to keep your faith strong, and to save California."[42] Convinced now more than ever that a Los Angeles revival was imminent, Bartleman wrote in *Way of Faith* magazine, "Los Angeles seems to be the place and this the time, in the mind of God, for the restoration of the Church."[43]

Best known for his chronicles of the 1906 Los Angeles Revival, Frank Bartleman eventually authored 6 books, 4 pamphlets, some 500 published articles, and over 100 tracts, many of which covered the events leading up to and surrounding the revival and the subsequent worldwide Pentecostal movement. Source: Flower Pentecostal Heritage Center.

Meanwhile, after arriving in Los Angeles, Seymour felt a greater burden to pray for Los Angeles, stating, "Before I met Parham, such a hunger to have more of God was in my heart that I prayed for five hours a day for two and a half years. I got to Los Angeles, and there the hunger was not less but more. I prayed, 'God, what can I do?' The Spirit said, 'Pray more.' 'But Lord, I am praying five hours a day now.' I increased my hours of prayer to seven, and prayed on for a year and a half more. I prayed to God to give what Parham preached, the real Holy Ghost and fire with tongues with love and power of God like the apostles had."[44]

42   Frank Bartleman, *Azusa Street* (Plainfield, N.J.: Logos, 1980), 33: GG 144.

43   Wayne E. Warner, "The Miracle of Azusa," *Pentecostal Evangel*, vol. 22 (Sept. 1996), 11: Vinson Synan, *The Century of the Holy Spirit: 100 Years of Pentecostal and Charismatic Renewal* (Nashville: Thomas Nelson, 2001), 45 [hereafter CHS].

44   John G. Lake, *Spiritual Hunger—The God-Men* (Dallas: Christ for the Nations, 1980), 60: CC 144.

Seymour was turning the church of the pastors is

SEYMOUR LOCKED OUT

By the time Seymour arrived at the Holiness mission two days after arriving in Los Angeles, it had already outgrown the Asberrys' home on Bonnie Brae Street and moved to a small building on the corner of Ninth and Santa Fe. Since Miss Terry had been closely associated with Parham's ministry in Texas, Seymour assumed they wanted to hear more of the same and chose for his first Sunday morning text Acts 2:4: "And they were all filled with the Holy Ghost, and began to speak with other tongues, as the Spirit gave them utterance." After admitting that he himself had not yet received the gift, Seymour emphatically taught that a person had to speak in tongues or they were not baptized in the Holy Spirit. Though some received this new teaching with enthusiasm, others vehemently opposed it. After the service, church members Edward and Mattie Lee invited Seymour to their home for Sunday dinner, but when they all returned for the evening service, they found that Sister Hutchins had padlocked the doors!

Since Seymour was now without a job or a place to live, the Lees felt obligated to bring him home with them. Undaunted, Seymour simply continued to pray daily, often inviting the Lees to pray with him. Though unsure at first of their new houseguest, the Lees grew to like him, as did several other members of the church who joined them for prayer. When Sister Hutchins learned of this, she called for a meeting between Seymour and the officials of the Southern California Holiness Association with which they were affiliated. When confronted, Seymour simply and matter-of-factly restated Acts 2:4 and the premise that no one had received the baptism in the Holy Spirit until they spoke in tongues. As far as Seymour was concerned, their problem was not with him but with the Word of God. One of the officials later conceded, "The contention was all on our part. I have never met a man who had such control over his spirit. No amount of confusion and accusation seemed to disturb him. He would sit behind that packing case and smile at us until we were all condemned by our own activities."[45] This would not be the first or last time Seymour's calm leadership skills would be noticed.

214 NORTH BONNIE BRAE STREET

After only a week, the prayer meetings outgrew the Lees' home, and Richard and Ruth Asberry again offered their home on Bonnie Brae Street. Though the Asberrys did not yet agree with Seymour's teachings, they felt bad about what had happened and Seymour obliged them. At first, the Bonnie Brae meetings were primarily attended by "negro washwomen" and a few of their husbands.[46] However, as news spread throughout the area, a number of believers from the Holiness Church on Hawthorne Street, Arthur Osterberg's Full Gospel Church, as well as Frank Bartleman and a number of white believers from the Peniel Holiness Mission began joining them. All that was missing now was the baptism in the Holy Spirit, and since Seymour had yet to receive it himself, he was having difficulties leading others in the experience. One night when Edward Lee asked Seymour to lay hands on him to receive the baptism, he fell into a trance and his wife Mattie panicked, immediately calling for an end to the proceedings. Then in late March,

---

45   C.M. McGowan, *Another Echo From Azusa* (Covina, Calif.: Oak View Christian Home), 3: GG146.

46   Robert Mapes Anderson, *Vision of the Disinherited*, (Peabody, Mass.: Hendrickson, 1992), 65.

Seymour told the group about his good friend Lucy Farrow in Houston who had not only received the Holy Spirit but as one of Parham's altar workers was also quite successful in leading others into the experience. Immediately, they took up an offering and sent for Lucy Farrow.

312 AZUSA STREET

Now fully aware of the growing number of people attending the evening meetings and needing a place to meet for prayer in the daytime as well, Seymour began searching for a building. About two and a half miles away in the old downtown industrial district was an abandoned two-story 4,800 square-foot building on a dead-end street. Originally home to the Stevens African Methodist Episcopal Church, the church had relocated in 1903 to a better part of town. Since then, it had been used as a wholesale house, warehouse, lumberyard, stockyard, tombstone shop, and most recently, a stable with rooms for rent upstairs. About the only clue left that it had once been used as a church was the Gothic style window over the front entrance. The building was completely trashed, its doors and windows broken, and it was desperately in need of repairs. But the rent was only eight dollars a month and Seymour had a building. Now all he needed was the money.

312 Azusa Street as it appeared before Seymour rented it from its original occupants, the First AME Church (c. 1906). The "FOR SALE" sign is visible in the upper left corner. Below it is the door through which most parishioners entered the building. In the foreground is the rear of the "tombstone" shop—Brown and Ford Marble and Granite Works. Source: Flower Pentecostal Heritage Center.

THE PASADENA CONNECTION

That night Seymour prayed and received his answer: the following night, after the meeting, he was to take a trolley to Pasadena. Though it was illegal for a black man to be in Pasadena after dark in those days, Seymour did not argue—he simply obeyed. The next night after the meeting, he rode the trolley to Pasadena until the Lord instructed him to get off. Then the Spirit led him to an apartment where a Sister Julia Carney and several of her friends from the First Baptist Church were praying for revival and for the baptism in the Holy Spirit. Sister Carney had received the baptism experience herself two years earlier after a Brother Lankford had returned from Parham's school in Topeka. When Brother Lankford shared his experience with Dr. Finis Yoakum, founder of the Pisgah Home rescue mission in Los Angeles where Sister Carney attended, Dr. Yoakum immediately embraced it and shared the experience with his church, and Sister Carney received. Though only fifteen at the time and married, Sister Carney felt led to move to Pasadena and share her experience with her friends. When Seymour walked up to her apartment, it was 10:30 p.m. Normally, if a black man knocked on a door in Pasadena at 10:30 at night in 1906, the door was slammed and the police were called. But this night the Spirit was in charge and the owner simply greeted him at the door: "Can I help you?" Seymour replied, "You're praying for revival, right?" Astonished, the ladies inside unanimously replied, "Yes!" Seymour said, "I'm the man God has sent to preach that revival." Immediately, the ladies invited Seymour in, and after some excited chatter, he preached and received an offering. The offering was more than enough to rent the warehouse. And there "in a barn-like room on the ground floor of an old Methodist Church . . . about a dozen congregated each day, holding meetings on Bonnie Brae in the evening."[47]

DIVINE BLESSINGS

When Lucy Farrow arrived from Houston, her testimony immediately inspired others to receive the baptism in the Holy Spirit, so on Friday, April 6, Seymour announced a ten-day fast to tarry for the blessing of baptism—but ten days would not be needed. On Monday, April 9, the third day of the fast, Seymour was getting ready to leave for prayer at the Bonne Brae House when Mr. Lee, feeling weak and sick from the fast, asked if Seymour would pray for him so he could attend the meeting. Seymour anointed Mr. Lee with oil, prayed, and he was healed. Then Mr. Lee again asked Seymour to lay hands on him to receive the baptism in the Holy Spirit. This time he immediately began speaking in other tongues! The two rejoiced as they walked together to the meeting. (According to other accounts, Mr. Owen "Irish" Lee was first to receive the baptism).[48]

---

47 J. Edward Morris and Cindy McCowan, Tom Welchel, narrator, *Azusa Street: They Told Me Their Stories: The Youth and Children of Azusa Street Tell Their Stories*, First Revised Edition (Mustang, Okla.: Dare2Dream Books, 2010), 27–29 [hereafter TMTS]; The Apostolic Faith, vol. 1 no. 1 (Sept., 1906) Amos Morgan, "The Azusa Street Mission Time Line," Chap. 1 "About April 1, 1906," *Azusa Books: www.azusabooks.com/ time.shtml#1* (Accessed 13 February 2013).

48 Various conflicting accounts were given on who first received the baptism in the Holy Spirit. Some placed Seymour at the home of Irish-American immigrant Owen "Irish" Lee (not Edward Lee) during this time. Owen Lee had recently joined the Bonne Brae group from the Penial Holiness Mission. According to some accounts, Owen Lee, a former Catholic, had a vision of the Twelve Apostles and was first to have Seymour lay hands on him. Others placed Lucy Farrow at the home of Owen Lee stating that she was the one who laid hands on him. Regardless, Owen Lee later took his Pentecostal experience back to Ireland.

When they arrived at the Bonnie Brae House, every room in the house was packed with people praying. Seymour led the group in singing, testimonies, and more prayer. Then choosing again for his text Acts 2:4, Seymour shared Mr. Lee's testimony of how he had received healing and the baptism in the Holy Spirit prior to the meeting. But before Seymour could finish, Mr. Lee raised his hands up in the air and began shouting aloud in other tongues! Everyone instantly fell to the floor and began praying for the baptism. Soon six or seven others began speaking in tongues—including Jennie Evans Moore, who would later become Seymour's wife. Others rushed out on the front porch prophesying and preaching. Still others ran out in the street speaking in tongues. Then the Asberrys' young daughter came in the living room to see what the commotion was, and she and her brother also ran out in the street screaming and yelling as neighbors began gathering in the street to see what was happening. Then Jennie Moore climbed back up on the piano bench from where she had fallen and began singing and playing the piano in a beautiful melody of tongues and interpretation. But that was not the strangest part—Jennie had never played piano before! The meeting lasted well past 10:00 p.m.

THE BONNIE BRAE REVIVAL

The next night, the crowds grew so large they had to build a makeshift pulpit on the front porch for Seymour and others to preach from as the porch became their pulpit and the street their pews. Day and night the revival continued for three days. Sometimes shouts of excitement could be heard coming from the house. Other times it would fall silent.

Those who entered the house often fell under the power and lay on the floor for three to five hours. Even Sister Hutchins came with her entire congregation and spoke in tongues. On Thursday, April 12, the third day of the revival, Seymour was preaching when suddenly the foundation gave way, sending the porch crashing into the steep bank in the front yard, but miraculously, no one was injured. One eyewitness wrote, "They shouted three days and nights. It was Easter season. The people came from everywhere. By the next morning there was no way of getting near the house. As people came in they would fall under God's power; and the whole city was stirred. They shouted until the foundation of the house gave way, but no one was hurt."[49]

The Asberry home on 214 North Bonnie Brae Street as it appeared in 1907. Source: Flower Pentecostal Heritage Center.

The police were emphatic: "Either shut it down or rent a place like a regular church or auditorium. You have gotten too big to continue to meet at this home."[50] Seymour had been warned several times before. After many had left on the last night, Seymour was praying inside when a white man came and knelt beside him to pray. After much praying and seeking for the Holy Ghost, his white friend said wearily in exhaustion, "It is not the time." Seymour replied, "Yes it is, I am not going to give up." Now continuing to pray alone, suddenly

---

49   *Pentecostal Evangel*, vol. 6, no. 4 (1946) 6: Walter J. Hollenweger, *The Pentecostals* (London: SCM, 1972), 23: CHS 49.

50   TMTS 27.

a sphere of white-hot brilliance seemed to appear, draw near, and fall upon him. Divine love melted his heart as he sank to the floor. Soon he heard unutterable words as from a great distance. Then he slowly realized the indescribably lovely language belonged to him. It poured from his innermost being. Seymour had finally received his Pentecostal blessing! At length, he arose happily with a broad smile on his face and embraced those around him.[51]

OPENING NIGHT ON AZUSA STREET

Though Sister Carney and her friends had raised enough money to rent the warehouse, much work remained with little time or money left to do it. Arthur Osterberg, pastor of the Full Gospel Church and timekeeper for the McNeil Construction Company, donated the labor to replace the doors and windows. Mr. McNeil, owner of the construction company and a devout Catholic, donated the lumber and supplies. Sister Carney and her friends volunteered to help remove some of the clutter that had accumulated over the years. Sister Carney recalled how Brother Seymour assigned each volunteer an area to clean and mentioned how grateful she was for being assigned the task of cleaning up after the goats with their little droppings instead of the horses or cattle![52] After clean up, the volunteers gathered wooden fruit crates found behind a nearby grocery store and nailed 2x12 planks to the crates, which served as benches, before finally spreading sawdust on the floor. Seymour set two empty shoebox crates in the center of

---

51 Douglas J. Nelson, "For Such a Time as This: The Story of Bishop William J. Seymour and the Azusa Street Revival" (PhD diss., University of Birmingham, UK, 1981), 191–192: Stanley M. Burgess, ed., *Christian Peoples of the Spirit* (New York Univ. NY, 2011), 237 [hereafter CP].

52 TMTS 32.

the room for a makeshift pulpit with altar benches running around it and seating for thirty to forty people—it would not be enough. The second floor was also cleared of debris, creating a large "upper room" for candidates to "tarry" for the Holy Ghost, with several smaller rooms that doubled as sleeping quarters for Seymour and the staff and for laying hands on the sick. On Saturday, April 14—just two days after the porch collapsed—the first meeting was held at Azusa Street.

THE PRESS

On Tuesday, April 17, the *Los Angeles Daily Times* sent a reporter to the evening meeting to investigate what was going on down at the old warehouse. The next morning, the following headline and article appeared on the front page: "WEIRD BABEL OF TONGUES ... New Sect of Fanatics is Breaking Loose ... Wild Scene Last Night on Azusa Street ... Gurgle of Wordless Talk by a Sister ... Meetings are held in a tumble-down shack on Azusa Street, near San Pedro Street, and the devotees of the weird doctrine practice the most fanatical rites, preach the wildest theories and work themselves into a state of mad excitement in their peculiar zeal. Colored people and a sprinkling of whites compose the congregation, and night is made hideous in the neighborhood by the howlings of the worshippers, who spend hours swaying back and forth in a nerve racking attitude of prayer and supplication. They claim to have the 'gift of tongues' and to understand the babel."[53] This article, intending to slander them, had the opposite effect.

---

53 *Los Angeles Daily Times* (April 18, 1906), 1.

Front page of the *Los Angeles Times*, Wednesday morning, April 18, 1906. Source: *Los Angeles Times*. Photo: Wikimedia/Magnus Manske.

THE EARTHQAKE

That same morning as many Los Angeles residents were receiving the news of this "new fanatical sect," another seismic event occurred that sent shockwaves up and down California's coast. At 5:12 a.m., an estimated 8.2 earthquake—one of the most devastating in history—rocked the city of San Francisco. The quake resulted in equally devastating fires that lasted for several days as 3,000 people died and about 80 percent of San Francisco was destroyed. Buildings shook as far south as Los Angeles, where two more aftershocks were felt just before noon, leaving many to wonder if the San Francisco quake had some sort of connection to the spiritual quake taking place in Los Angeles. Certainly earthquakes had been recorded in Acts and in New England preempting the Great Awakening, but not many had occurred simultaneously with a revival.[54] Spiritual fervor in Los Angeles would soon reach an all-time high. The only difference was, whereas in times past religious zeal resulting from a natural disaster would quickly wane, this spiritual ferment would last for several years! And while the San Francisco quake was felt up and down the west coast, shockwaves from this Los Angeles revival would soon be felt

54   Acts 4:31, 16:26

around the world. Bartleman wrote, "I found the earthquake had opened many hearts. . . . It was used mightily in conviction, for the gracious after revival. In the early 'Azusa' days both heaven and hell seemed to have come to town."[55]

THE MEETINGS

A typical meeting at Azusa Street would open with one of the elders explaining the order of service (there was no order and there was no typical service): "We have no planned program, nor are we afraid of anarchy or crooked spirits. God the Holy Spirit is able to control and protect His work. If any strange manifestations come, trust the Holy Spirit, keep in prayer, and you will see the word of wisdom go forth, a rebuke, an exhortation that will close the door on the enemy and show the victory won. God can use any member of the body, and He often gives the more abundant honor to the weaker members."[56]

The service would then begin with someone singing a song or sharing a testimony. Then, like in early Quaker services, anyone who felt led could get up and preach or sing in English or in tongues with interpretation. Meanwhile, as with Finney's revivals, prayer was taking place continually on the second floor. And like in the camp meetings of old, anyone could be seen shouting, dancing, jerking, shaking, weeping, laughing, falling into trances, or speaking or singing in tongues. When the power of God hit, one or two would fall down, or a hundred at a time would fall like dominoes. But mostly,

---

55 Bartleman, *Azusa Street*, 53.
56 Stanley M. Horton, "A Typical Day at Azusa Street," Assemblies of God *Heritage* Vol. 2 No. 3 Fall 1982, 3, 6, *Flower Pentecostal Heritage Center: http://ifphc.org/pdf/Heritage/1982_03.pdf* (Accessed 16 February 2013).

everyone just prayed and trusted God to direct the meetings. Altar calls were also Spirit led. Sometimes a group of people would suddenly or spontaneously rush to the altar to seek God. Bartleman wrote, "Someone might be speaking. Suddenly the Spirit would fall upon the congregation. God himself would give the altar call. Men would fall all over the house, like the slain in battle, or rush for the altar en masse, to seek God. The scene often resembled a forest of fallen trees. Such a scene cannot be imitated. I never saw an altar call given in those early days. God himself would call them. And the preacher knew when to quit. When He spoke we all obeyed. It seemed a fearful thing to hinder or grieve the Spirit. The whole place was steeped in prayer. God was in His holy temple. It was for man to keep silent."[57]

If anyone stood and spoke out of their intellect or without being "anointed" by God to speak, the Spirit would soon convict them and they would sit down. If not, they may have heard wailing sobs coming from the audience. Or worse, Mother Jones would get up and look the speaker straight in the eye. That meant, "You're not anointed. Go sit down!" If the speaker did not understand by her look, then she would proceed to tell them. Meetings began at 10:00 a.m. and often lasted for hours or days. No one ever grew tired because the Spirit seemed to energize not only the meetings but also all who attended them. Even the curious and eager would come and sit for hours, listening to strange sounds, songs, and exhortations. Sounds of shouting and rejoicing could be heard and a "supernatural atmosphere" felt from blocks away.

---

57 Bartleman, Azusa Street, 59–60: Lee A. Howard *Manifestations Throughout Church History: Examining the Physical Evidence of Revival* (April 15, 2012), Kindle Edition. Kindle Locations 458–463 [hereafter MCH].

THE DELUGE

By the summer of 1906, meetings were continuous day and night as thousands from all classes, races, and walks of life began crowding inside and outside the tiny 40x60 warehouse. Bartleman wrote, "The color line was washed away in the blood."[58] By September, the first issue of *The Apostolic Faith* was going out to nearly 20,000 and eventually to over 50,000 subscribers. The train station a half mile away continually unloaded passengers arriving from all over the continent as news of the revival spread through both the religious and secular press. Among the visitors were many seasoned Holiness ministers and missionaries who would soon spread the Pentecostal message around the world. Some reportedly fell out in the Spirit or spoke in tongues as soon as they walked across the platform, exiting the train. One train station worker said this was a regular occurrence. Others could be seen falling in the streets and speaking in tongues within blocks of the mission, while still others reported being healed before reaching the building.

The sign on the building read, "Apostolic Faith Gospel Mission. Whoso-ever Will, May Come. Let Brotherly-love Prevail." Source: Flower Pentecostal Heritage Center.

Before long, a number of spiritualists, hypnotists, charlatans, and anyone else who felt they needed to bring "correction" to the movement also began converging on the meetings and trying their influence.

58　Frank Bartleman, *How Pentecost Came to Los Angeles* (1925), 54, *Christian Classics Ethereal Library: www.ccel.org/ccel/bartleman/los.i.html* (Accessed 17 February 2013).

However, whenever Seymour or one of the elders tried to step in and take control, that only drew more attention to the enemy, causing fear, and the Spirit would stop moving. So they learned to just back off, pray, and continue to let the Spirit lead the services. Again Bartleman wrote, "Presumptuous men would sometimes come among us. Especially preachers who would try to spread themselves in self-opinionation. But their effort was short-lived. Their minds would wander, their brains reel. Things would turn black before their eyes. They could not go on. We simply prayed. The Holy Ghost did the rest."[59]

PARHAM'S QUANDARY

Seymour began writing urgent appeals to Parham, his spiritual father, asking him to come quickly to help discern between the real and the false. Unfortunately, Parham had another equally urgent request on his desk at the time begging him to come to Zion, Illinois, where Wilbur Voliva had recently replaced John Alexander Dowie, creating much bitterness, strife, and confusion. Both needs were urgent, but after seeking God, Parham urged Seymour to continue his meetings while he went to Zion before all was lost.

When Parham arrived in Zion, he was immediately met with opposition from Voliva. However, when Zion's grand hotel manager invited Parham to hold meetings in the hotel basement, hundreds began attending. Voliva was vehement. Parham was "winning some of our most faithful people," he cried.[60] Local newspapers described

---

59 Bartleman, *Azusa Street*, 59–60.

60 *North Chicago News*, 26 September 1906: Blumhofer, "Christian Catholic Apostolic Church": Cecil M. Robeck, Jr., ed., *Charismatic Experiences in History* (Peabody, Mass.: Hendrickson, 1985), 136 [hereafter CE].

Parham as having "a pleasant and convincing manner that makes his discourse almost irresistible."[61] Parham's messages also sounded much like Dowie's: "Old-time Religion, Christ's Soon Coming, Repentance, Salvation, Healing, Sanctification, Baptism of the Holy Ghost."[62] Voliva shut down the hotel meetings and proceeded to rent every auditorium in the city, so Parham had nowhere to go. However, convinced now more than ever that Zion needed Pentecostal blessings to bring peace and restoration, Parham split up his crusade team by scheduling multiple concurrent cottage meetings in large homes throughout the city. In one such meeting, F.F. Bosworth, John G. Lake, and Marie Burgess Brown—future founder of Glad Tidings Tabernacle in New York City—were all baptized in the Holy Spirit. Audiences reportedly spilled out onto the porches and lawns as thousands attended the cottage meetings. Hundreds were released from bitterness and despair after receiving the baptism in the Holy Spirit and speaking in tongues. Hundreds of others saw visions and responded to the call to full-time ministry.

Many have criticized Parham over the years for going to Zion instead of Azusa. However, in so doing, Parham not only permanently merged the streams of Pentecostalism and divine healing but also, by tapping into Dowie's worldwide ministry, some five hundred independent Spirit-baptized healing ministries were launched into a worldwide harvest, essentially creating a second global thrust of Pentecostalism concurrent with Azusa. Commenting

---

61   *Waukegan Daily Gazette*, 15 October 1906: Blumhofer, "Christian Catholic Apostolic Church": CE 136.

62   Toronto *Evening Telegram*, 19 January 1907: Blumhofer, "Christian Catholic Apostolic Church": CE 136.

on Parham's decision, one author wrote, "His decision to go to Zion City precipitated one of the most important religious events of the twentieth century."[63] Historian Edith Blumhofer, agreed: "In the fall of 1906, two restorationist teachings converged briefly in Zion City, Illinois. The two subsequently fragmented but their brief union resulted in the emergence of a third creative force that would survive as one of the formative influences in American Pentecostalism."[64]

PARHAM IN LOS ANGELES

By the time Parham arrived in Los Angeles in October 1906, he had already heard reports about "all the stunts common in old camp meetings among colored folks" that were happening there, including "white people imitating unintelligible, crude negroisms of the Southland, and laying it on the Holy Ghost."[65] Of course, this was disturbing to Parham, who understood tongues not as ecstatic languages but as unlearned foreign languages and who regarded emotionalism as extreme and fanatical. Parham wrote, "I hurried to Los Angeles, and to my utter surprise and astonishment I found conditions even worse than I had anticipated . . . manifestations of the flesh, spiritualistic controls, saw people practicing hypnotism at the altar over candidates seeking baptism."[66]

So after being warmly introduced by Seymour as his "Father in this gospel of the Kingdom," Parham spoke only two or three times before

---

63 Gordon P. Gardiner, *Out of Zion Into All the World*, (Shippensburg, Pa.: Destiny Image, 1990), 3: CC 154.
64 Blumhofer, "Christian Catholic Apostolic Church": CE 126.
65 Parham, *Life of Parham*, 160–163.
66 Ibid., 163–170.

he began denouncing what he called "hypnotists" and "spiritualists" who had taken over the meetings.[67] Then after being told by two of Seymour's elders that he was "not wanted in that place," Charles Fox Parham, the "father" of the "Apostolic Faith Gospel Mission," was not allowed to speak again. Now thoroughly disgusted, and much as he had done in Zion City, Parham went a few blocks away to the Women's Christian Temperance Union and began holding meetings of his own. Though Parham claimed that "between two and three hundred who had been possessed of awful fits and spasms and controls in the Azusa Street work were delivered, and received the real Pentecost teachings and spake with other tongues,"[68] this time the meetings were short-lived, while the Azusa Street Revival would continue for several more years.

PARHAM IN ZION

After only two months in Los Angeles, Parham returned to Zion, this time moving his family and publication. He was again met with opposition from Voliva and again found success in his revival meetings—so much so that some urged him to begin a new movement. But Parham stated he wished to bring only peace to Zion, not more confusion and division. Though Parham moved back to Kansas in 1907, he left a thriving Pentecostal ministry in Zion consisting of many former leaders from Dowie's ministry. Even Seymour, who had visited Zion in June of that year, said it reminded him of "Old Azusa, ten months ago," saying "people here receive the baptism in their pews while the service is going on, sometimes scores of them receive

67   Ibid.
68   Ibid.

it. . . . There are little children from six years and on up who have the baptism with the Holy Ghost."[69] In the end though, it was Dowie's ministry that had, in large part, allowed Pentecostalism to flourish, and it was in Pentecostalism that "the real significance of Dowie's message was preserved and expanded."[70] Even as late as the 1930s, Dr. Lilian B. Yeomans, who had once been healed under Dowie's ministry, said, "Some people say that Dr. Dowie's work is dead. No! It is more alive today than ever."[71]

Later that year, Parham was preaching in San Antonio, Texas, when news hit the wires that he had been arrested on sodomy charges. Though he was soon released and nothing was ever proven, Parham immediately accused Voliva of creating an "elaborate frame" to destroy his ministry. Nevertheless, the incident would leave a permanent mark on Parham's ministry, causing many Pentecostals to this day to distance themselves, some even refusing to recognize him as a founder. But then the Lord did forewarn him that his Pentecostal blessing would be accompanied by "persecution" and "scandal."

Over the years, Parham has also been accused of being a racist. But that's a pretty tough accusation for a Southern white man living in an era of racism who broke local laws to accept a black student, invited a black woman (Lucy Farrow) to preach at his meetings, and often preached in black churches. Parham did make some racist comments like labeling the extremes at Azusa Street as "darky camp meeting

---

69   The *Apostolic Faith* 1 (June-Sept., 1907), 1: Blumhofer, "Christian Catholic Apostolic Church": CE 138–39.

70   Blumhofer, "Christian Catholic Apostolic Church": CE 140.

71   Gordon P. Gardiner, "The Apostle of Divine Healing," *Bread of Life* 6 (March, 1957), 15: Blumhofer, "Christian Catholic Apostolic Church": CE 138–39.

stunts" and later commending the Ku Klux Klan for their promotion of religion and moral values—which they allegedly displayed at the time. Nevertheless, in perspective, Parham was likely neither a civil rights activist nor a rabid racist but as a principal founder of the Pentecostal movement helped set the tone for interracial relations—both bad and good. Parham died in 1929.

PARHAM AND SEYMOUR PART WAYS

While Parham would spend the rest of his life denouncing Seymour and the Azusa Street Revival as a case of "spiritual power prostituted" to the "awful fits and spasms" of "holy rollers and hypnotists," Seymour felt it his duty as leader of the revival to protect the movement of God at all costs—even if that meant overriding his father in the faith.[72] Seymour had learned that whenever he tried to limit God to a certain form, culture, expression, or mode, the Spirit would invariably stop moving. Parham argued, "The Holy Ghost does nothing that is unnatural or unseemingly, and any strained exertion of the body, mind or voice is not the work of the Holy Spirit, but of some familiar spirit, or other influence. The Holy Ghost never leads us beyond the point of self-control or the control of others, while familiar spirits or fanaticism leads us both beyond self-control and the power to help others."[73] Seymour, on the other hand, refused to say anything negative about his mentor, stating in his newsletter two months later, "We thought of having him to be our leader . . . before waiting on the Lord. We can be rather hasty, especially when we are very young in the power of the Holy Spirit. We are just like a baby—full of love—and were willing to

72 Parham, *Life of Parham*, 164–202.
73 Ibid.

accept anyone that had the baptism with the Holy Spirit as our leader. But the Lord commenced settling us down, and we saw that the Lord should be our leader."[74]

AZUSA CRITICS

Like every other movement of God, the Azusa Street Revival had more than its share of critics. Some of the local Holiness churches had lost so many members that they had to close their doors and join the revival by default. Others, disturbed by the growing trend, warned their members to stay away. Some even called the police, asking them to shut down the meetings. Others reported them to the Child Welfare Agency, claiming there were unsupervised children in and around the building at all hours of the day and night. Still others complained to the health department of cramped quarters and unsanitary conditions, which they felt represented a danger to public health. Pastor Smale of the First New Testament Church originally supported and joined the movement but later denounced it, closing their church's doors to the "tongue-talkers." Phineas Bresee, founder of the Pentecostal Church of the Nazarene, declared it to be a false revival—apparently without even visiting—and in 1919 had "Pentecostal" removed from their name so as not to be mistakenly associated with the likes of Azusa. However, many intending to bring ridicule or correction to the meetings after visiting gained a completely new perspective. Some were knocked to the floor where they seemed to wrestle with unseen opponents for hours only to rise up later convicted of their sin and error. One foreign reporter who was asked to write a humorous story on the

---

74 *The Apostolic Faith* (December, 1906): Cecil M. Robeck, Jr. and Amos Yong, ed., *The Cambridge Companion to Pentecostalism*, (Cambridge University Press, 2014), 29.

"circuslike" atmosphere at Azusa met a young woman at the meeting who told him how she had received the Holy Spirit and then spoke to the reporter in other tongues. After the meeting, the reporter asked the woman how she had learned the language of his native country. She told him she did not have a clue what she was saying. He then told her she had given an accurate account of his entire sinful life in his native tongue. He immediately renounced his sins and accepted Jesus. But when he returned home and told his boss he could not write a false story ridiculing the movement and offered to write a truthful report instead, he was fired.

ERASING THE LINES

The Azusa Street Mission was the first totally integrated church in America. The painted sign on the side of the building aptly read, "Whoso-ever Will, May Come. Let Brotherly-love Prevail." Most of the criticisms launched against the revival had to do with the blurring or erasing of lines. Since Seymour believed the Spirit of God resided in every believer, leading and guiding them and not just the leaders, he allowed anyone to speak during the services, thus erasing the traditional lines between clergy and laity. Having "Spirit-led" services also erased the boundaries of established ecclesiastical order, structure, and liturgy. They did not even collect an offering. Instead, a sign on the wall over a box read, "Settle with the Lord." Virtually everything was left to the spontaneous move of God. Because speaking in tongues as ecstatic languages was allowed, all lines of human constraint and sophistication were also set aside. One critic wrote, "[they sang] in a faraway tune that sounded very unnatural and repulsive."[75] Another wrote that "some of the brightest and best" members of the church had fallen into the "fearful delusion" of speaking in tongues.[76] Bringing revival to the streets and marketplace also blurred the lines between religious and secular space. Many sang and preached on street corners, while others knocked on doors, witnessing and praying for the sick. Others carried their witness into the workplace and community, where they fed and cared for the poor. There was a blurring of all economic and social barriers as rich and poor, educated and uneducated, worshiped together. The mere fact that some were illiterate was considered conclusive evidence by others of their blatant error. The age barrier was also broken as youth as young as twelve years old ministered to the sick. Ultimately, it was the blurring of the races and sexes that drew the most criticism. Blacks and whites mixing and men and women kissing and hugging one another were considered repulsive to many. One woman reported being incensed at the sight of a colored woman with her arms around a white man's neck while "praying for him."[77] However, for every one person who criticized the movement, it seemed a thousand more came and believed in their work—and it's no wonder after hearing the countless stories and testimonies that occurred over a span of several years. One firsthand eyewitness wrote, "I would have rather lived six months at that time than fifty years of ordinary life."[78]

---

75   Josephine M. Washburn, *History and Reminiscences of the Holiness Church Work in Southern California and Arizona* (South Pasadena: Record Press, 1912), 383–389; Alma White, *Demons and Tongues* (Zerapath, N.J.: 1949), 71–73, Frank J. Ewart, *The Phenomenon of Pentecost* (Hazelwood: Word Aflame Press, 1975), 45: HPT 101.

76   Ibid.

77   Ibid.

78   Bartleman, *Azusa Street*, 59–60.

Early leaders of the Azusa Street Mission in 1907. William Seymour seated front, third from right, with Clara Lum to his left; Jennie Evans Moore (Seymour) standing back, third from left, with Glenn A. Cook and Florence Crawford to her left. The girl in front is Florence Crawford's daughter. Source: Flower Pentecostal Heritage Center.

THE YOUTH OF AZUSA

Some of the most amazing stories were told by the youth of Azusa who were privileged to pray daily for the sick before the meetings. Many appreciated the fact that they did not have to watch all the older people do all the work and have all the fun. Liberty was given to anyone who wanted to pray for the sick, and God seemed to honor that by healing nearly everyone who was prayed for. Many of the youth were used by God in ways that most seasoned adults and ministers only dream about. One said, "Anyone who attended Azusa very long had great miracles—especially if a person attended at least once a week—you had miracles!"[79] Another said, "When you came into Azusa, you got healed. The more you attended, the more faith you had, and the more things would happen. Because your faith was building up as you saw other people believing and you believed, soon you had no doubt when you walked up to someone that they were going to get healed. After a while it was easy to have boldness to walk up to someone and proclaim 'God is going to heal you tonight!'"[80] Azusa was a hands-on workshop for the miraculous led by God himself. Tommy Welchel, who heard and recorded many of their stories, said, "No wonder they had such a

79 TMTS 96.
80 Ibid., 105.

revival, no wonder this thing went worldwide. Yes, they received the speaking in tongues and that was great, but many of the miracles that were performed were not done by big preachers. Many of those being used by God were just ordinary teenagers and young people doing extraordinary works for God."[81]

EVERYDAY HEALINGS

Sister Carney from Pasadena, who was seventeen at the time, told of a woman who came in appearing to be in a lot of pain and holding a bloody bandage at the side of her head. When she asked the woman what had happened, she said she had caught her husband with another woman. When she and the other woman got in a fight, the woman bit her ear off, but she did not have the ear with her. So Sister Carney pulled the bandage away slightly to confirm she had no ear and without hesitation began to pray. Immediately the pain left, and this time when she pulled the bandage away, she saw a new ear growing right before her eyes![82] She said those kinds of miracles happened two to three times a day through her alone. Brother Lankford, who had been one of Parham's students in Topeka and was twenty at the time, was praying for a man in a wheelchair who had been paralyzed from his waist down for two years when Sister Carney broke in: "No, no, no, that's not faith!" Then she went over to the man, picked up his legs, and put the footrests up so he could stand up. Brother Lankford continued praying for him and suddenly they could hear bones cracking. The man straightened up, rose out of his wheelchair, and took off running, leaping, shouting, and dancing, as others ran with him![83]

---

81   Ibid., 75.
82   Ibid., 32–33.
83   Ibid., 74.

Brother Fox, who was eighteen, remembered a sign language teacher who brought his entire class of thirty-five deaf students to a meeting. Brother Fox said to the man, "If you want to teach them to sign, why did you bring them to a place where they could get healed? You're going to be out of a job!" The teacher replied, "You're talking like they're all going to get healed." "They are!" said Brother Fox. Brother Fox then gestured to the students to join hands in a circle. Looking at the teacher, he said, "Evidently, you don't have much faith, so stand off to the side." Then, forgetting they were deaf, he instructed the students: "Now, I'm going to lay hands on this man and start with him." The teacher started laughing at him. Undeterred, Brother Fox whispered in the first man's ear and told the spirit to come out and he was immediately healed. Then the man who was healed became excited and, seeing his excitement, the others started getting healed one by one until all were healed within a few minutes. Yet Fox had only laid hands on one of them. From then on, whenever a group joined hands in a circle touching each other, Brother Fox said all were healed.[84]

Other testimonies sounded like stories from the Gospels. When Brother Bill Brown, who was sixteen, saw a man lying on a cot, he asked, "Do you want to be healed? Do you want to take up your cot and carry it home?" The man smiled and said, "Yes." Brother Bill prayed for him, and immediately he got up, folded up his cot, and began worshiping God.[85]

---

84   Ibid., 116–117.
85   Ibid., 125.

THE HEAVENLY CHOIR

During the meetings, letters and testimonies were often read about people in other parts of the world who had received the baptism in the Holy Spirit and spoke in tongues after hearing of the Azusa Street Revival. Praise would often erupt as the letters were being read, leading to spontaneous worship and singing in other tongues, which Seymour called "the Heavenly Choir." Whenever "the Heavenly Choir" began to sing, the power of God would increase and an anointing would fall on the service. The Heavenly Choir was described as "not something that could be repeated at will, but supernaturally given for each special occasion and . . . one of the most indisputable evidences of the presence of the power of God."[86] At other times, Brother Seymour would ask Brother Sines to begin singing a certain song or hymn. Brother Sines was a concert pianist who brought his piano and could sing and play any song Seymour wanted without sheet music or a hymnal. Later, Brother Christopher, who owned a Stradivarius violin, accompanied Sines on the piano. He and Sines were great friends, having played together in concerts, but Brother Christopher said when he played his violin "in the Spirit," he played at a level he could never have achieved even at his greatest concert.[87]

THE BOX

Whenever Brother Seymour came downstairs to join a service (usually already in progress), he would put a shoe crate, which everyone

---

86   A.W. Orwig, "Apostolic Faith Restored," *Weekly Evangel*, 18 March 1916, 4; A.G. Osterberg, interview by Jerry Jensen and Jonathan E. Perkins, tape recording, March 1966; Transcription by Mae Waldron, Assemblies of God Archives, Springfield, Tape one, 1293, 075; Horton, "A Typical Day at Azusa Street," Assemblies of God *Heritage*, 6; CHS 57.

87   TMTS 55, 58.

referred to as "the box," over his head. From a natural standpoint, it looked silly and ridiculous, but for Seymour, it was an act of humility that was highly critical to the power of God being displayed. Sometimes Seymour would sit like a statue with the box on his head for ten minutes. Other times, he would sit like that for an hour. But invariably, whenever Seymour removed the box from his head, the greatest miracles would take place. In fact, "the box" became so sacred and significant that nobody dared touch it—even when Seymour was not in the room. Brother Sines noticed a glow around the box when it was on Seymour's head. He asked Seymour once what was going on inside the box when it was on his head. He said he was meditating and waiting on God. He also said whenever he spoke to God inside the box, it was a whisper in tongues, and though he could hear himself speaking in tongues, he could understand every word he was saying.[88] Sister Carney said the miracles "stopped when Brother Seymour stopped putting that box over his head. When he quit coming down and putting the box on his head, it started dying."[89]

Really would like verification?

THE SHEKINAH GLORY

Another fascinating feature of the Azusa Street Revival was the constant, abiding, and visible presence of God, which many said was like breathing in pure oxygen. One observer said that when Seymour came down and the Heavenly Choir started singing, the "Shekinah Glory" would "rise and fill the whole room, and you could breathe so much better—as if the room were filled with pure oxygen."[90] Others

88 Ibid., 57.
89 Ibid., 36.
90 Ibid., 91.

said it was like heaven coming down. Sometimes the visible mist was only a foot high in the room and people would lie down in it just so they could breathe in God's glory. One woman, who was only a toddler at the time, later told how she loved to attend the meetings with her mother and crawl under the pew to take a nap, only to awaken later and play with the thick mist that filled the room.[91] Sometimes Seymour would wave his foot and play with the mist. Other times, the mist would become so thick that it would rise and fill the whole building like when Solomon's priests in the Old Testament praised God with one unified sound and the cloud of the Lord filled the temple.[92] Many at Azusa Street walked in the mist, sat in it, ran their hands through it, and breathed it into their lungs, but no one could capture it. Brother Christopher tried to bottle it and bring it home, but to his dismay, the bottle was empty the next morning.[93] Some said that whenever the Spirit started moving, the smoke-like substance began to glow even brighter. Others believed it to be the other way around—whenever God's glory manifested, miracles happened.

THE ROOFTOP FLAMES

The flames that often appeared outside the building were as captivating as the glory of God inside. Many confirmed that when the greatest miracles were happening inside, flames could be seen above the building outside. The fire department was called on several occasions as passers-by reported flames leaping from the rooftop. Some said the flames could be seen as far away as Grand Central Station. One said, "It looked like

---

91   Ibid., 21.
92   1 Kings 8:10–11, 2 Chron 5:13–14.
93   TMTS 58.

flames about fifty feet in the air coming down and was also going up out of the roof to meet, merge, and go through the flame coming down."[94] Sister Carney once went outside to investigate when she saw John G. Lake and asked him to explain to her what was happening. He said, "Fire was coming down from heaven into the building, and fire was going up from the building and meeting the fire coming down."[95] Then she walked about a half a block and saw the awesome sight for herself.

A caricature of the rooftop flames at Azusa Street by Joyce C. Edwards, from *Like as of Fire: Newspapers from the Azusa Street World Wide Revival*, collected by Fred T. Corum and Rachel A. Harper Sizelove (Washington, D.C.: Middle Atlantic Regional Press, 1991), p. 1. Source: Dupree Holiness and Pentecostal Center. Photo: University of Southern California Digital Library. Pentecostal and Charismatic Research Archive.

THE MIRACLES

On one occasion when the flames were dancing on the rooftop, Seymour approached a man with a wooden leg and asked, "What did you come here for?" The man replied, "I want you to pray for my leg. It is starting to get gangrene where the wooden leg attaches." Seymour replied, "I'm just upset because you have the wooden leg on. It would be a challenge for God to grow a leg out when the wooden leg is attached." The man immediately removed the wooden leg and stood before Seymour on his one good leg. Seymour laid hands on the man and proclaimed, "Let Thy Name be Glorified. In the Name of Jesus, I command this leg to grow out." Then he said to the man,

94   Ibid., 50.
95   Ibid., 37.

"The gangrene is gone; you are healed." Suddenly, now with two legs, the man ran up on the platform and around the room and the crowd went wild! No one could get him to stop rejoicing and praising God. Needless to say, Seymour did not have to preach that night.[96]

Another time when the flames were on the roof, Seymour approached a man who had lost his arm ten years earlier in a work-related accident. The arm was totally severed at the shoulder. Brother Seymour asked the crowd, "Would you like to see God have a wonderful time here tonight? Some of you may remember the man's leg that grew out about a year ago." Seymour then asked the one-armed man, "Can you work with just one arm?" "I'm just given minimal paying jobs and I barely make enough money to even eat," he replied. Seymour shook his head and responded, "That's not good. Are you married?" "Yes." "Got kids?" "Yes." Then turning to the crowd, he said, "This man needs to be able to make a living. This man needs to work and he needs to be able to pay his tithe." Then turning back to the man Seymour asked teasingly, "Will you tithe if I pray for you and God gives you your arm back?" "Yes!" he exclaimed. Seymour burst out laughing. "I'm just having fun." Then he slapped his hands on the man's shoulder and commanded the arm to grow out—and almost instantly, it grew out. The man stood in total shock, then started moving his new arm around and feeling it with his other hand, awed by the miracle. A few weeks later, the man returned, bringing two hundred people with him and telling everyone at the meeting he had gotten his old job back. Many who came with him also needed healing and were fully restored as different ones from the crowd prayed and laid hands on them.[97]

96 Ibid., 77.
97 Ibid., 78.

MASS HEALINGS

Often Seymour would go to a section where everyone was in wheelchairs or on cots carried from the hospital and point to them, saying, "Everyone on the cots or wheelchairs, you're healed in the Name of Jesus." Then everyone would get up and walk around fully healed![98] One time there were about a dozen cripples who looked as though they had rheumatoid arthritis. Seymour pointed to them and said, "You want to see a miracle over there? Every one of you within a few minutes are going to be up and walking in the Name of Jesus." Suddenly, bones could be heard popping everywhere as everyone rose up shouting with legs, arms, and hands totally straight.[99] Such mass healings were so frequent that the youth of Azusa Street had a name for it and often tried to mimic it, but were rarely successful. They called it "doing a Seymour."

BROTHER SEYMOUR

Everyone at Azusa Street loved Brother Seymour. Since he never took a salary, he could often be seen walking through the crowd with five or ten dollar bills sticking out of his pants pockets which people had placed there unbeknownst to him. One brother described Seymour as "one of the sweetest men I have ever met."[100] Another said he was "the meekest man I had ever met."[101] John G. Lake said, "It was God in him that attracted people."[102] Even in social settings, one could feel

---

98   Ibid., 35.
99   Ibid., 48.
100 Ibid., 47.
101 Vinson Synan, "William Seymour," *Christian History*, (Issue 65), 17–19.
102 John G. Lake, *Adventures in God* (Tulsa: Harrison House, 1981), 18–19.

the anointing on Seymour. Others reported that when they touched him, a kind of electricity would shock them. Lake wrote, "God had put such a hunger into that man's heart that when the fire of God came it glorified him. I do not believe any other man in modern times had a more wonderful deluge of God in his life than God gave to that dear fellow, and the glory and power of a real Pentecost swept the world."[103]

SEYMOUR'S PREACHING

Seymour did not have to preach often because the miracles frequently spoke for themselves, but when he did preach, he usually emphasized salvation or one's need to renounce sin and accept Jesus as Savior. He often hurled challenges at his audience, urging them to turn from the world or leave their rigid traditions behind and seek salvation, sanctification, and the baptism in the Holy Spirit. Because speaking in tongues was such a novelty at Azusa Street, Seymour often tried to downplay its role, saying, "Now, do not go from this meeting and talk about tongues, but try to get people saved."[104] Seymour believed salvation to be the grand purpose of Pentecost as he wrote in his first newsletter, "God has been working with His children mostly, getting them through to Pentecost, and laying the foundation for a mighty wave of salvation among the unconverted."[105] Like Finney, Moody, Torrey, and many others before him, Seymour preached that the real purpose of the baptism in the Holy Ghost was "to be flooded with

---

103 Lake, *Spiritual Hunger—The God-Men*, 14: CC 145.
104 Stanley H. Frodsham, *With Signs Following: The Story of the Latter-Day Pentecostal Revival* (Springfield: Gospel, 1946), 38: Grant McClung ed., *Azusa Street & Beyond* (Gainesville, Fla.: Bridge-Logos, 2006), 3.
105 *The Apostolic Faith*, (September, 1906).

the love of God and power for service."[106] Tongues would follow. But above all, Seymour preached love. He declared, "If you get angry, or speak evil, or backbite, I care not how many tongues you may have, you have not the baptism with the Holy Spirit. You have lost your salvation."[107] Lake said Seymour "had the funniest vocabulary. But, I want to tell you, there were doctors, lawyers, and professors, listening to the marvelous things coming from his lips. It was not what he said in words, it was what he said from his spirit to my heart that showed me he had more of God in his life than any man I had ever met up to that time."[108]

Azusa Street Pilgrims in 1907. William Seymour and John G. Lake (front), John A.D. Adams, F.F. Bosworth, and Thomas Hezmalhalch (back). Hezmalhalch co-founded with Lake the Apostolic Faith Mission of South Africa. Adams became president of the Apostolic Faith Mission of Australia and New Zealand. Bosworth toured throughout North America. All four were influenced by Dowie and Seymour. Source: Flower Pentecostal Heritage Center.

THE PILGRIMS OF AZUSA STREET

The many ministers who attended the Azusa Street Revival became part of a worldwide network of Pentecostal missionaries. Florence Crawford, one of Seymour's staff members, went to Portland, Oregon, and started her own Apostolic Faith movement in the Pacific Northwest. William H. Durham returned to his North Avenue Mission in Chicago

106 "William J. Seymour's Doctrine and Discipline," Article K, *River of Revival Ministries: azusastreet.org/WilliamJSeymourDiscipline.htm* (Accessed 18 February 2013).

107 *The Apostolic Faith*, (June, 1907).

108 Lake, *Adventures in God*, 18–19.

to found the Pentecostal movement in the Midwest and Canada. Elder Sturdevant left Los Angeles in 1906 to establish the first Pentecostal church in New York City on his way to Africa. C.H. Mason took the Pentecostal message back to Tennessee and the Deep South. G.B. Cashwell brought Azusa back to North Carolina and also toured the South. F.F. Bosworth, John G. Lake, and an entourage from Zion City made the spiritual pilgrimage to Azusa Street in 1907. Bosworth would eventually take Pentecost to major cities in North America through his healing revivals. Lake would take Pentecost to South Africa and later to the Pacific Northwest. Lucy Farrow and Sister Hutchins went to Liberia, Africa. T.B. Barratt, a Methodist pastor from Norway, heard about the Los Angeles revival while touring America, received the baptism in the Holy Spirit from his New York hotel room while corresponding with Seymour, and then brought it back to northern Europe. Alexander Boddy, who would make his church in Sunderland, England, a center for British Pentecostalism, came and visited Azusa Street after its glory days. Frank Bartleman circled the globe once and Europe twice. Others went to India, China, Japan, Hong Kong, and the Philippines. Some founded Pentecostal churches; others founded entire denominations. Actually, nearly all Pentecostal groups today—directly or indirectly—can trace their lineage back to Azusa Street. In time, anyone who visited Azusa Street became part of an honorary class of citizens called "the pilgrims of Los Angeles"—a sort of "Who's Who" in Pentecost and was treated with veneration and respect in Pentecostal circles worldwide.[109]

---

109 Carl Brumback, *Suddenly . . . from Heaven* (Springfield, Missouri: Gospel Publishing, 1961), 64–87; Bartleman, *How Pentecost Came to Los Angeles*, 54–60: HPT 103.

THE DECLINE

The factors leading up to the decline and ultimate demise of the Azusa Street Revival were not much different from any other historical revival. A stricter order was eventually imposed on the services, limiting the flow of the Spirit. Unity among the various races, classes, and ideologies began to wane. Measures to formalize were introduced: purchasing the building, becoming incorporated, putting an official name on the building—even setting up a "throne" for Elder Seymour. Wholesale rejection by the Christian community—especially the Holiness movement—finally caught up with them. Plus, much as the Holiness movement had once been perceived by the Methodists, many early Pentecostals saw themselves or were perceived by others as being part of a spiritual aristocracy.

The biggest blow came after Seymour married Jennie Evans Moore in 1908. Jennie, who was on staff, suggested it was the Lord's will for them to marry and Seymour agreed. Clara Lum, who was also on staff, did not agree. Lum, along with Florence Crawford and many other early Pentecostals, believed that Christ's return was imminent and there was no time for marriage. To them, Seymour's marriage meant he had fallen into disbelief. So as ministry secretary, Lum left to join Crawford in Portland, Oregon, apparently taking the entire ministry publication including 50,000 subscribers with her! The next issue of *The Apostolic Faith* went out exactly as before, only with a different return address, so no one questioned it and began sending their donations to Oregon. Literally overnight Seymour had lost his worldwide influence and support. His plans to build churches, rescue missions, foreign missions, schools, and colleges were all gone. Though

Seymour attempted to recover the publication, first by traveling to Portland and speaking directly to Crawford and Lum, and later, by sending his wife and an entourage to Portland's postmaster with proof that the publication had belonged to them, both attempts failed.

THE SECOND SHOWER

By late 1909, numbers had dropped so dramatically that Seymour was forced to go on a cross-country preaching tour just to keep his now dwindling mission afloat. Leaving his wife and two young men in charge, he traveled from Maine to San Diego, preaching the Pentecostal message. Then in 1911, William Howard Durham (1873–1912), a white evangelist from Chicago who had visited the Azusa Mission in its heyday, decided to relocate his ministry to Los Angeles—the birthplace of modern Pentecostalism. After holding several successful meetings there, the two young men Seymour had left in charge decided to invite Durham to come and speak. Suddenly, it was like old times again. Hundreds attended with hundreds more being turned away. Many visiting ministers who had come during the "glory days" returned for a second visit. Bartleman called it "the second shower of the Latter Rain," saying, "the fire began to fall at old Azusa as at the beginning."[110] Durham was a "pulpit prodigy" who could easily induce his audiences into fits of shouting and jerking known as "the Durham jerks" but with one glaring doctrinal difference.[111] Durham vehemently opposed the Wesleyan-Holiness "second work" doctrine of sanctification, stating there was only salvation and the baptism in the Holy Spirit. Durham believed Christ's work on the cross was a "Finished Work" and that sanctification was something

---

110 Bartleman, *Azusa Street*, 150.
111 Ibid., 150–152.

to be progressively worked out over the course of one's life, not some instantaneous experience. Though welcomed like a breath of fresh air by those in the Holiness camp who often felt alienated or backslidden, the two men, troubled by the popularity of this new teaching, contacted Seymour, who immediately returned home. After meeting with Durham and being unable to reach an agreement, Seymour again padlocked the door. Like Parham, Durham went across town to a larger facility, but this time, the crowds of Azusa followed as thousands were reportedly saved, baptized, and healed, while the Azusa Mission lay virtually deserted. Nevertheless, Durham's meetings did not last long as he soon contracted pneumonia and died two months later.

When William Howard Durham returned home after visiting Azusa Street, he transformed his North Avenue Mission, the city of Chicago, and the Midwest into a center for Pentecostalism. Finding the three-step Pentecostal doctrine of salvation, sanctification, and Spirit baptism difficult to accept, he began preaching a two-step "Finished Work" doctrine of salvation and Spirit baptism instead. The doctrine quickly spread through the movement. Source: Flower Pentecostal Heritage Center.

AZUSA'S LEGACY

The two men who had tried to take over Seymour's ministry—Parham and Durham—were both white. The two women who had apparently succeeded in taking Seymour's ministry away—Lum and Crawford—were also white. In 1915, citing growing racism, Seymour regrettably changed the church's constitution, stating that all its officers must be people of color and that he looked forward to a day when such restrictions would no longer be necessary. Sadly, Seymour spent the last ten years of his life struggling to keep the small mission afloat while occasionally traveling and attending ministers' conferences without any notice or recognition. Seymour died in 1922.

After Seymour's death, his wife Jennie continued pastoring the church until 1930, when some of the remaining church members tried to take it from her. Tired of the legal battle that ensued, the Los Angeles courts declared the building a fire hazard and offered it to the Assemblies of God. But at the time, the Assemblies declined, stating, "We are not interested in relics."[112] It was demolished in 1931. Today the property is a parking lot, part of the Japanese-American Cultural and Community Center in Naguchi Plaza. In 1997, the Church of God in Christ refurbished the Bonnie Brae House and opened it to the public. That same year, the Azusa Street Memorial Committee erected a plaque at the site of the old mission that reads, "This plaque commemorates the site of the Azusa Street Mission, which was located at 312 Azusa Street. Formally known as the Apostolic Faith Mission, it served as a fountainhead for the international Pentecostal movement from 1906–1931. Pastor William J. Seymour oversaw the 'Azusa Street Revival.' He preached a message of salvation, holiness, and power, welcomed visitors from around the world, transformed the congregation into a multicultural center of worship, and commissioned pastors, evangelists, and missionaries to take the message of 'Pentecost' (Acts 2:1–41) to the world. Today, members of the Pentecostal-charismatic movement number half a billion worldwide."[113]

---

112 Assemblies of God *Heritage*, Vol. 25, No. 4, Winter 2005–06, "The Azusa Street Revival: Celebrating 100 Years," *Flower Pentecostal Heritage Center: ifphc.org/pdf/Heritage/2005_04.pdf* (Accessed 19 February 2013).

113 Cecil M. Robeck Jr., "Azusa Street Revival," Stanley M. Burgess, ed. and Eduard M. Van Der Maas, ed., *The New International Dictionary of Pentecostal and Charismatic Movements* (Grand Rapids, Mich.: Zondervan, 2002), 349 [hereafter DPCM].

The Apostolic Faith Gospel Mission on Azusa Street in 1928. After being declared a fire hazard, the building was demolished in 1931. Many scholars and historians agree that something happened here that changed the face of Christianity worldwide. Source: Flower Pentecostal Heritage Center.

SEYMOUR'S LEGACY

Today many believe that "barn-like" "tumble-down shack" on Azusa Street to be the birthplace of modern Pentecostalism, earning Seymour the title "Father of modern Pentecostalism."[114] But perhaps Sydney Ahlstrom—the acclaimed church historian from Yale—summed it up best when he described Seymour as "the most influential black leader in American religious history."[115] Ahlstrom wrote in his 1972 award-winning book *A Religious History of the American People*, "Seymour exerted a greater influence upon American Christianity than any other Black Leader" and *Christian History* magazine named Seymour, along with Billy Graham, C.S. Lewis, Mother Teresa, and Martin Luther

---

114 Ashley Sample, "William Joseph Seymour: The Father of Pentecostalism, Azusa Street: The Impact," Last Updated April 17, 2001, HIS 338 Student Website Page *Georgetown College: spider.georgetowncollege.edu/htallant/courses/his338/students/asample/WJSASIMP.htm* (Accessed 20 February 2013).

115 Sydney E. Ahlstrom, spoken in a 1972 lecture: Vinson Synan, "The Origins of the Pentecostal Movement," Last Updated: April 17, 2006, Holy Spirit Research Center, *Oral Roberts University: www.oru.edu/library/special_collections/holy_spirit_ research_center/pentecostal_history.php* (Accessed 22 February 2013).

King Jr., as one of the top ten Christians of the twentieth century.[116] Pentecost began in a stable . . . again.

---

116 Sydney E. Ahlstrom, *A Religious History of the American People*, (New Haven, Conn.: Yale University, 1972): The Azusa Street Revival: *www.theazusastreetrevival.com/home.html* (Accessed 22 February 2013); Vinson Synan, "Pentecostalism: William Seymour," (January 1, 2000) *Christianity Today/Christian History & Biography: www.ctlibrary.com/ch/2000/issue65/3.17.html* (Accessed 22 February 2013).

STUDY QUESTIONS

1. What conditions around the turn of the twentieth century led many Christians to cling to the old ways, while others looked to the future with a renewed interest in eschatology, Bible prophecy, and end-times events? Explain.

2. What "later day movements" did Charles Parham visit during his fact-finding mission in 1900, and how might they have influenced his beliefs? His ministry? His Bible schools?

3. Explain what happened at Charles Parham's Bethel Bible College in Topeka, Kansas, at the turn of the twentieth century? How did these events shape modern Pentecostalism?

4. Name some features of the 1904–05 Welsh Revival. What similarities did this revival have with Finney's Rochester revival? With the Azusa Street Revival?

5. How would you describe the spiritual atmosphere of Los Angeles when William Seymour arrived in 1906?

6. What circumstances led to the Bonnie Brae revival? What led to its abrupt shutdown?

7. What connection does 312 Azusa Street have with Jesus' birthplace in Bethlehem? Why do you think that is?

8. Do you see any connection among the earthquakes of Acts 4:31 and 16:26, the one that rocked New England in 1727 prior to America's First Great Awakening, and the one that rocked California in 1906 concurrent with the Azusa Street Revival?

9. Explain the significance of Charles Parham's visit to Zion City, Illinois, in 1906. How did this contrast with Parham's visit to Los Angeles later that year?

10. What do you believe was the most outstanding feature of the Azusa Street Revival? What was your personal favorite?

11. What circumstances led to the decline and ultimate demise of the Azusa Street Revival?

12. What is the legacy of the Azusa Street Revival?

13. William Seymour has been called the "Father of modern Pentecostalism," "the most influential black leader in American religious history," and one of the Top Ten Christians of the twentieth century. How would you describe William Seymour?

2

THE PENTECOSTAL MOVEMENT

(c. 1906–1945)

The first half of the twentieth century saw what one historian called "the replacement of the great world religions by three post-Christian ideologies: nationalism, communism, and individualism."[1] (Post-Christian meaning Christianity was no longer the dominant ideology.) After Christianity divided Europe between Catholics and Protestants and then retreated, it was replaced by other ideologies—nationalism and communism—which resulted in two world wars. In North America, Christianity was replaced by individualism as its dominant ideology. But in either case, much like first-century Christians, twentieth-century Christians suddenly found themselves a subculture within a greater political, social, and economic world.

---

1   Arnold Toynbee: CH 419.

67

EUROPEAN NATIONALISM

By the early twentieth century, the dominant ideology of Europe was nationalism. A young Serbian nationalist assassinated the Crown Prince of the Austro-Hungarian Empire in 1914, and within months, Europe had been plunged into its First World War. What began as a conflict between the empires of Germany and Austria and the allies of France, Russia, and Britain eventually involved twenty-seven nations, including the United States. Also, after years of discontent over Russian Czar Nicholas II's mishandling of the economy now exacerbated by war, the Bolsheviks overthrew their thousand-year monarchy in 1917, replacing it with a classless, socialist, atheistic regime called communism. Then Germany, feeling more like a victim of war than instigator, rejected the 1919 Treaty of Versailles, giving birth to yet another nationalist-socialist regime called Nazism. Adolph Hitler, its undisputed leader, envisioned a "Third Reich" that would restore the first two (Charlemagne's Holy Roman Empire and the German Empire recently destroyed in World War I). Thus, World War II was mostly about the unfinished business of World War I. But more than just an ideology, Nazism was also a religion of racism and hatred. Hitler believed the white Aryan race, which descended from ancient Persians, was to be a "master race" whose strength and purity could be maintained only by exterminating Jews, Gypsies, the weak, infirm, blacks, homosexuals, Jehovah's Witnesses, and anyone else who opposed his agenda. Hitler blamed everything from Bolshevism to capitalism on the Jews, declaring even Christianity to be part of a Jewish plot to take over the world. Six million Jews and 11 million other prisoners and civilians were exterminated by the Nazis, while over 100 million served in military units from over 100 nations,

A bitter understanding of Nazism. It was not just the Jews as so much history presents.

leaving more than 73 million dead by casualty of war between 1939 and 1945.

AMERICAN INDIVIDUALISM

In 1873, retired Yale president Theodore Woolsey spoke of a Christian America when he said "that the vast majority of the people believe in Christ and the Gospel, that Christian influences are universal, that our civilization and intellectual culture are built on that foundation."[2] Some fifty years later in 1924, journalist H.L. Mencken, speaking of the same America, said, "If any man stands up in public and solemnly swears that he is a Christian, all his auditors will laugh."[3] Something had gone terribly wrong. A century of European liberalism being taught in America's public schools and universities had taken its toll as individualism—the stepchild of liberalism—replaced Christianity as America's dominant ideology. No longer were Americans living by a Christian standard of consideration for others, their society, or the world. Instead, most Americans began demanding their rights to serve their own selfish interests. And, since America had been founded mostly by Separatists and rugged individualists, it was an easy sell. America's isolationist policies of the 1930s reflected this new ideology, which enabled many Americans to turn a blind eye and deaf ear to the wars raging around them, that is until it was struck blind-sighted by the Empire of Japan on December 7, 1941.

Meanwhile, many Protestant, evangelical, and fundamentalist churches began following the Catholic Church down a path toward isolationism by retreating into their "lifeboat" churches, holy-huddle

---

2   CH 393.

3   Ibid.

prayer meetings, Bible studies, and spiritual revivals in what one church historian labeled "The Great Reversal."[4] In contrast with early European and American Protestants who led the charge in reforming society through their welfare and missionary societies, now suddenly in the twentieth century after one liberal coined the term "social gospel," many churches began forsaking Christ's salt and light imperative to pursue personal faith, salvation, and holiness instead.[5]

In the highly publicized Scopes "Monkey" Trial of 1925, William Jennings Bryan fought to "protect the Word of God against the greatest atheist or agnostic in the United States" by outlawing teaching on evolution in American public schools.[6] Though Bryan won, five days later, he died, and in many ways, the Christian effort to transform American culture died with him. But by turning its back on society and attempting to transform individuals instead, without realizing it, the American church had succumbed to American individualism becoming exactly what those in the Enlightenment Age had hoped the church would become: "a private system of piety which doesn't impinge on the public world."[7] What's worse, many Christians bought

---

4   The phrase "Great Reversal" was coined by Timothy L. Smith in *Revivalism and Social Reform* (New York: Abingdon, 1957): David O. Moberg, *The Great Reversal: Evangelism Versus Social Concern: An Evangelical Perspective* (Philadelphia: Lippincott, 1972) Book Review by Katie Funk Wiebe, *Direction Journal* Vol. 2 No. 1 (April, 1974), 185–186: *www.directionjournal.org/3/1/great-reversal-evangelism-versus-social.html* (Accessed 26 February 2013).

5   Walter Rauschenbusch, *Theology for the Social Gospel*, (New York: Abingdon, 1917), 1.

6   CH 437.

7   N.T. Wright, *What Saint Paul Really Said: Was Paul of Tarsus the Real Founder of Christianity?* (Grand Rapids, Mich.: Eerdmans, 1997), 154: "Wanted: Churches that Engage in Reforming & Transforming their Nation! (Part 3)" (Dec 10, 2012) *Catalyst Ministries: www.catalystmin.org/kingdom-mission/2012/12/10/wanted-churches-that-engage-in-reforming-transforming-their.html* (Accessed 27 February 2013).

into the lie, thinking if they could no longer shape their culture, at least they could keep their own spirituality in shape by retreating into a religious subculture. But while many churches were retreating inward, a new force in Christianity was expanding outward and going global.

A NEW FORCE IN CHRISTIANITY

The first issue of *The Apostolic Faith* printed at Azusa Street made this clarion call: "The Apostolic Faith Movement . . . . Stands for the restoration of the faith once delivered unto the saints–the old time religion, camp meetings, revivals, missions, street and prison work and Christian unity everywhere."[8] Subsequent issues declared, "Beginning of a Worldwide Revival," "Pentecost Both Sides the Ocean."[9] Outbreaks of tongues were reported in London, Stockholm, Oslo, Calcutta, Africa, Canada, Hawaii, China, Denmark, Australia, and Jerusalem. Many who initially responded to the call thinking they were gifted to speak in a foreign language returned home disillusioned. Others adapted, learned languages in conventional ways, or simply became "missionaries of the one-way ticket" by successfully carrying the torch of Pentecost to the ends of the earth.[10]

INDIA

At least one Pentecostal revival, however, did not wait for Azusa Street. Noting the timeline, Frank Bartleman wrote, "The present

---

8   *The Apostolic Faith* 1, No. 1 (September, 1906), 2.
9   *The Apostolic Faith*, (January 1907), 1: HPT 130; *The Apostolic Faith*, (Feb-Mar, 1907).
10 HPT 129.

world-wide revival was rocked in the cradle of little Wales . . . brought up in India" and became "full grown in Los Angeles."[11] India had had a rich Pentecostal heritage dating back to the apostle Thomas, but widespread reports of prophecy, tongues, interpretation, visions, dreams, heavenly signs, praying for the sick, shaking, falling under the power, and such had continued since the 1857 worldwide prayer revival. In 1898, Minnie Abrams (1859–1912), a Methodist missionary from the U.S., joined Pandita Ramabai's (1858–1922) world-famous Mukti Mission about a hundred miles southeast of Bombay (Mumbai). The mission included a school and home for young widows and orphaned girls. News of the Wesleyan-Holiness and Higher Life movements had aroused interest in the power and working of the Holy Spirit, but when word of the Welsh Revival arrived in January 1905, Ramabai spoke urgently of the need for revival, organizing some 550 young women and girls to meet twice daily for prayer.

In June, a matron from one of the girls' dorms reported to Administrator Abrams that one of the girls had been baptized with "fire" in the middle of the night. She said, "I saw the fire, and ran across the room for a pail of water, and was about to pour it on her, when I discovered that she was not on fire."[12] Immediately, revival spread as others reported seeing visions and dreams, visible tongues of fire, and signs in the heavens and experiencing burning sensations, being slain in the Spirit, and speaking in other tongues. Later that month, Ramabai was teaching when the Holy Spirit fell and everyone in the room began praying and weeping aloud. Soon many more were

---

11   Bartleman, *Azusa Street*, 19.

12   Minnie F. Abrams, "The Baptism of the Holy Ghost and Fire," *Indian Witness* (April 26, 1906), 261: CHS 84.

repenting, singing, dancing, and speaking in tongues and all regular school activities were suspended.

One visiting Methodist missionary from the U.S. reported, "Presently I heard someone praying near me very distinctly in English. Among the petitions were 'O Lord, open the mouth. . . . O Lord, open the heart. . . . O Lord, open the eyes! Oh, the blood of Jesus! . . . Oh, give complete victory! Oh, such a blessing! Oh, such glory!' I was struck with astonishment, as I knew that there was no one in the room who could speak English, besides Miss Abrams." Later, attempting to ascertain why they spoke in English, he said, "I have an idea that it is in mercy to us poor missionaries from Europe and America who, as a class, seem to be Doubting Thomases, in regard to gifts and workings of the Spirit, and not receiving the power of the Holy Spirit as we ought."[13] Soon Abrams' "praying bands" of women evangelists went with her to other missions to hold revival meetings. At one Anglican mission in Bombay, another revival broke out among the students there, and one student was heard by an interpreter praying for the conversion of Libya in a language she did not know. In 1906, Abrams wrote the book *Baptism of the Holy Ghost and Fire* telling about the Indian revival and urging Christians around the world to pray for the fullness of the Spirit. She wrote, "The best preparation for a revival is not a committee but a praying band."[14] But when reports from the Azusa Street Revival arrived, Ramabai and Abrams realized there was a still deeper outpouring they had not received and immediately began tarrying anew for the Spirit and many more spoke in tongues.

---

13 Frodsham, *With Signs Following*, 107–108: CC 156–157.

14 Minnie Abrams, *The Baptism of the Holy Ghost and Fire* 2nd ed. (Kedgaon, Maharashtra: Pandita Ramabai Mukti Mission, 1906), 3–4: CP 249.

Abrams wrote this in 1907: "Then the great outpouring of the Spirit came upon us, and today we have 400 Spirit-filled young women, and they are saying, 'Here I am; send me.'"[15]

Alfred and Lillian Garr, the first missionaries from Azusa Street, also arrived in Calcutta in 1907 before traveling on to Hong Kong and Sri Lanka, where a thousand reportedly spoke in tongues. They would later visit the Mukti Mission. Stanley Burgess wrote, "The Mukti revival stands as one of the most outstanding outpourings of the Holy Spirit in history."[16] Today Pandita Ramabai is known as the "Mother of the Pentecostal Movement in India," even having an Indian postage stamp printed in her honor in 1989, and Ramabai's Mukti Mission continues to this day. Currently India has about 33.5 million Pentecostals—the fifth largest Pentecostal population in the world.[17]

Pandita Ramabai (in large chair) Minnie Abrams (above her to the left) and staff at the world-famous Mukti Mission near Mambai, India. In June 1905, nearly a year before the Azusa Street Revival, a matron from one of the girls' dorms reported to Administrator Abrams that one of the girls had been baptized with visible tongues of fire in the middle of the night. Immediately, revival spread as others reported experiencing similar signs, visions, and dreams. Many repented, sang, danced, prayed, wept aloud, spoke in tongues, and were slain in the Spirit. Today Ramabai is known as the "Mother of the Pentecostal Movement in India." Source: columbia.edu. Photo: Wikimedia/Sridharbsbu.

---

15 Gary B. McGee, "Baptism of the Holy Ghost and Fire! The Revival Legacy of Minnie F. Abrams," *Assemblies of God Enrichment Journal:* enrichmentjournal.ag.org/199803/080_baptism_fire.cfm (Accessed 2 March 2013).

16 CP 244.

17 G.B. McGee and S.M. Burgess, Global Survey "India": DPCM 118.

CHILE

[handwritten marginal annotations: "Interesting the origin's watchman is not named." "as in the N.T." "Persecution helped to fan the flames and spread Pentecostalism"]

When Minnie Abrams sent a copy of her book *Baptism of the Holy Ghost and Fire* to her friend and former classmate Mary Anne Hoover and her husband Dr. Willis C. Hoover (1858–1936), Methodist missionaries to Chile, their hearts were stirred to seek God for revival. About that same time, a night watchman had a vision in which Jesus told him, "Go to your pastor and tell him to gather the most spiritual people in the congregation. They are to pray together every day. I intend to baptize them with tongues of fire." Hoover immediately organized special times to pray for revival, some of which lasted all night. Finally, at one of the all-night prayer meetings in 1909, the floodgates of heaven opened and the atmosphere became electrified with the Holy Spirit. People were falling on the floor speaking in tongues. Others reportedly sang in perfect harmony in the Spirit "as if led by an invisible chorister."[18] But when the Methodist officials caught wind of this, they charged Hoover with being "unscriptural, irrational, and anti-Methodist" and expelled him and his followers from the church. Hoover then organized the Pentecostal Methodist Church of Chile, instructing his 440 followers to preach in the streets every Sunday proclaiming, "Chile sera para Cristo" (Chile shall be for Christ). Today, Hoover is recognized as the "Father of Pentecostalism in Chile," and Pentecostals make up the largest non-Catholic group in Chile with about 2 million members, which represent about 13 percent of the population.[19] When charismatics and neo-charismatics are added to

---

18   Frodsham, With Signs Following, 177–178: CC 158.

19   "International Religious Freedom Report: Chile" United States Department of State. 2008. "Pentecostal Revival Movement in Chile," *Wikipedia: en.wikipedia.org/wiki/Pentecostal_revival_movement_in_Chile* (Accessed 3 March 2013).

the mix, the number rises to about 5.5 million or about 30 percent of the population.[20] A popular saying in Chile today makes this claim: "In every village throughout Chile there is sure to be a post-office and a Pentecostal Methodist church."[21] Missiologist Peter Wagner wrote, "Many Methodists who blamed the devil for what happened in 1909 have since wondered out loud on whose side the devil might really have been."[22]

Dr. Willis C. Hoover led the Pentecostal Revival in Chile in 1909, founded the Pentecostal Methodist Church of Chile, and became known as the "Father of Pentecostalism in Chile." Source: The Methodist Pentecostal Church of Chile.

ARGENTINA

In 1907, Italian immigrant Luigi Francescon (1866–1964) received the baptism in the Holy Spirit at William Durham's North Avenue Mission in Chicago. After Durham prophesied that he was called to bring the gospel to the Italian people of the world, he and his friend Pietro Ottolini founded the first Italian-American Pentecostal congregation in America, "Assemblea Cristiana" (Christian Assembly), with several churches in Chicago, Los Angeles, St. Louis, and Philadelphia. Today these churches are part of the International Fellowship of Christian

---

20   David Barrett, *World Christian Encyclopedia*, 2nd edition (New York: Oxford, 2001); D.D. Bundy, Global Survey "Chile": DPCM 55.

21   Ignacio Vergara, *El Protestantismo en Chile* (Santiago, 1962), 110–111: HPT 137.

22   Vinson Synan, *In the Latter Days* (Ann Arbor, Mich.: Servant, 1984), 60: CC 159.

Assemblies. Giacomo Lombardi, another associate of Francescon's, went to Italy and organized several other churches as part of the Italian Pentecostal movement there. Then in 1909, the two traveled together to Argentina, where they founded "Iglesia Cristiana Pentecostal de Argentina" (Pentecostal Church of Argentina) and in 1910 went to São Paulo, Brazil, where they founded "Congregação Christã no Brasil" (Christian Congregation in Brazil)—the first Pentecostal church of Brazil. Today the Christian Congregation in Brazil has a presence in over 60 countries with 2.3 million members in Brazil alone.[23] Alice C. Wood—a Canadian Methodist-Holiness minister who joined the Christian and Missionary Alliance—also went to Argentina in 1910 and founded a church and Sunday school that would later join the Assemblies of God. Currently there are some 8.4 million Pentecostal-charismatics in Argentina, about 20 percent of the population.[24]

Luigi Francescon and family in 1903. After receiving the Pentecostal experience through William Durham's Chicago ministry in 1907, Luigi became a prolific missionary and pioneer of the Italian Pentecostal movement, founding the Christian Church of North America (International Fellowship of Christian Assemblies), the Christian Assembly in Argentina, the Assemblies of God in Italy, the Christian Congregation in the U.S., and the Christian Congregation in Brazil. Source: Christian Congregation in Brazil.

23 Brazilian Institute of Geography and Statistics *Census* (2010) Accessed August 9, 2012, "Table 1.4.1"; Christian Congreagation in Brazil (August 2012–2013) "Grand Total of Houses of Prayer Christian Congregation in Brazil," Report 76, 03 and 07, support (Statistics), "Congregação Cristã no Brasil," *Wikipedia: pt.wikipedia.org/wiki/Congrega%C3%A7%C3%A3o_Crist%C3%A3_no_Brasil* (Accessed 5 March 2013).

24 Barrett, *World Christian Encyclopedia* (2001); D.D. Bundy, Global Survey "Argentina": DPCM 23.

BRAZIL

In 1909, Swedish Baptist immigrants Daniel Berg (1884–1963) and Gunnar Vingren (1879–1933) received the baptism in the Holy Spirit in South Bend, Indiana, where Vingren pastored a Swedish Baptist Church. When the two men received a prophecy stating they were to go to "Para," they had to go to the Chicago Public Library and search the World Almanac to learn where Para was. Upon discovering it was a province in Brazil, Berg and Vingren immediately made plans to purchase one-way tickets to Brazil. But on their way, they stopped in Pittsburgh and felt led to give all their money to another missionary. The next day, however, as they walked the streets praying, a stranger walked up to them and gave them the exact amount they needed to go to Brazil.

Arriving in 1910, the two men attended a Baptist church, where many received prophecies, tongues, interpretation, and healing through their ministry. However, forbidding such manifestations in the sanctuary, the Baptist pastor allowed them to meet in their basement and before long, most of the Baptist church was meeting in the basement. Thus, the "Missão de Fé Apostólica" (Apostolic Faith Mission) began, later becoming the Assemblies of God in Brazil with more than 22.5 million members. Today the Pentecostal-charismatic population of Brazil remains the largest in the world with 80 million, or an unprecedented 40 percent of the population.[25]

25　Ibid., E.A. Wilson, Global Survey "Brazil": DPCM 35.

Daniel Berg and Gunnar Vingren (right) in 1910. The Lord spoke prophetically to Gunnar at a South Bend, Indiana, prayer meeting that he was to become a missionary in Pará, Brazil. Berg joined him, arriving in Brazil November 19, 1910. The two founded the first Assemblies of God church of Brazil in 1911— now the largest evangelical church in the country with 22.5 million members. Today the Pentecostal-charismatic population of Brazil remains the largest in the world with some 80 million. Source: The Publishing House of the Assemblies of God in Brazil.

SOUTH AFRICA

In 1908, John G. Lake (1870–1935) gave up his seat on the Chicago Board of Trade, a lucrative insurance business, and disposed of his estate and wealth to lead a team of five missionaries to South Africa. When his family arrived in Johannesburg, they were penniless. Since immigration laws required each family to have at least $125, John's wife Jennie asked him, "What are you going to do?" Lake replied, "I am going to line up with the rest. We have obeyed God this far. It is now up to the Lord." As he stood in line, a fellow passenger tapped him on the shoulder and handed him two money orders totaling $200. He said, "I feel led to give you this to help your work." Then another woman approached him on the dock, asking, "How many are in your family?" Lake responded, "My wife, myself, and my seven children." The woman exclaimed, "You're the family!" Then she explained how the Lord had directed her to go to the docks where she was to meet a missionary family from America with two adults and seven children and that she was to provide them with a furnished home.[26] Such stories were common among the early Pentecostal missionaries.

---

26 Lake, *Adventures in God*, 59–69: GG 178–179.

Within days of their arrival, a local minister took a leave of absence and asked Lake to fill his pulpit for him. Over five hundred Zulus, the largest ethnic group in South Africa, attended his first Sunday service. Soon revival broke out as powerful demonstrations accompanied the preaching of the Word and multitudes were saved, healed, and baptized in the Holy Spirit. Lake wrote, "From the very start it was as though a spiritual cyclone had struck."[27] But then the crowds, hungry to hear God's Word and receive healing, followed them to their home and, unwilling to turn any away, Jennie often neglected her own needs to feed those waiting for her husband to return home. When he did return home, their home became like one continuous healing line moving in through the front door and out the back. Those who were instantly healed were dismissed. Those who did not receive their healing were brought into another room where Jennie would reveal to them by the Spirit why they had not received. If they confessed their sins and repented, they would be prayed for again and be healed. If not, they would go home in their affliction. By the end of their first year, the two had become so absorbed in ministry that John had failed to notice Jennie's poor health until she finally died. Lake was devastated.

After a brief return home to garner support for the mission, Lake returned to Africa in 1910 during an outbreak of the plague. The plague was so contagious the South African government was offering one thousand dollars to any nurse who would care for the sick. But Lake and his assistants went to work for free, carrying the dead from their homes and burying them. Seeing this, one doctor asked Lake, "What have you been doing to protect yourself? You must have a secret!" Lake replied, "Brother, it is the law of the Spirit

27   Gordon Lindsay, ed., *John G. Lake: Apostle to Africa* (Dallas: Christ for the Nations, 1979), 25: GG 179.

of Life in Christ Jesus. I believe that just as long as I keep my soul in contact with the living God so that His Spirit is flowing into my soul and body, that no germ will ever attach itself to me, for the Spirit of God will kill it." Then Lake challenged the doctor to conduct an experiment, asking him to take some foam from the lungs of a dead plague victim and look at it under a microscope. The doctor did as instructed and saw masses of living germs. Then to everyone's shock and amazement, Lake extended his hands and asked the doctor to spread some of the deadly foam on them and then look at it again under the microscope. He did. All the germs were dead![28]

John G. Lake (c. 1900-1906). After establishing the Apostolic Faith Mission, South Africa's largest Pentecostal church, Lake also founded Zion Christian Church, South Africa's largest and fastest-growing, and second largest in the continent. Source: John G. Lake Healing Rooms Ministries. Photo: Wikimedia/Mike Hayes.

By the time Lake returned to America in 1912, he had converted some 100,000 Africans and founded two denominations—one black and one white. Today the Apostolic Faith Mission is South Africa's largest Pentecostal church with over a million members, and the Zion Christian Church is South Africa's largest and fastest growing church and second largest in the continent with between 2 and 6 million members.[29]

28 Gordon Lindsay, ed., *John G. Lake Sermons on Dominion Over Demons, Disease & Death* (Dallas, TX: Christ for the Nations, 1949, Reprinted 1988), 108: GG 183

29 Office Bearers of the Apostolic Faith Mission of Africa (Accessed 2 September 2010): "Apostolic Faith Mission of South Africa," *Wikipedia: en.wikipedia.org/wiki/Apostolic_Faith_Mission_of_South_Africa* (Accessed 7 March 2013); Rita M. Byrnes, ed., South Africa: A Country Study, Washington: GPO for the Library of Congress, 1996, "Zion Christian Church," countrystudies.

Upon returning to America, Lake founded several churches and healing homes in Spokane, Washington, and Portland, Oregon. Between 1915 and 1920, a reported 100,000 healings occurred in Spokane alone, and Spokane was declared the "healthiest city in the world" by its mayor, who held a special commemoration in Lake's honor.[30] During this time, Lake had a vision in which an angel opened to him the second chapter of Acts and said, "This is Pentecost as God gave it through the heart of Jesus. Strive for this. Contend for this. Teach the people to pray for this. For this, and this alone, will meet the necessity of the human heart, and this alone will have the power to overcome the forces of darkness."[31]

Though the healing homes would close after Lake's death in 1935, Cal Pierce, a California real estate developer, after praying and fasting in the 1990s, decided to purchase the original property and reopen Lake's healing rooms. Pierce eventually relocated and expanded them to include an entire block in downtown Spokane and founded the International Association of Healing Rooms with more than 3,000 healing rooms in more than 75 countries where people could come to be healed.[32]

KOREA

Mary C. Rumsey received the baptism in the Holy Spirit at Azusa Street in 1907 before returning to Elim Faith Home and Missionary

us/south-africa/54.htm (Accessed 7 March 2013).

30 Gordon Lindsay, editorial note, *The Voice of Healing* (March 1966), 4; David Edwin Harrell, Jr., *All Things Are Possible: The Healing and Charismatic Revivals in Modern America*, (Bloomington: Indiana University, 1975), 15 [hereafter ATP].

31 Wilford Reidt, *John G. Lake: A Man Without Compromise* (Tulsa: Harrison House, 1989), 95: GG 189.

32 Tracy Winborn, "Reopening the Wells: Legacy of Lake's Healing Rooms," May 5, 2014, *The Christian Broadcasting Network: www.cbn.com/cbnnews/us/2014/May/Reopening-the-Wells-Legacy-of-Lakes-Healing-Rooms* (Accessed 25 September 2014).

Society in Rochester, New York. Originally, she had planned to be a missionary in Japan until she received a prophetic word to "go to Korea" instead. Though it took twenty years to raise the necessary funds, by the spring of 1928, Rumsey finally arrived in Japanese-occupied Korea. Immediately, she began ministering at a hospital in Seoul where she conducted Pentecostal services and introduced tongues and the ministry of the Holy Spirit to her friends. Later that year, Rumsey and one of her friends, Hong Huh, cofounded the "Subinggo Pentecostal Church." That same year, Yong Do Lee, a Methodist evangelist, began introducing tongues and healing in his services, founding the famous "Prayer Mountain" ministry. In 1938, Rumsey's church was renamed "Chosun Pentecostal Church and Mission Center." In 1952, it was turned over to the Assemblies of God, whose first project was to open a Bible school. Their charter class included a young Buddhist convert named David (Paul) Yonggi Cho. Six years later, Cho founded Yoido Full Gospel Church—currently the world's largest congregation with nearly a million members.[33] Today there are about 7.5 million Pentecostal-charismatics in South Korea, about 15 percent of the population.[34]

CHINA

William Wallace Simpson (1869–1961) was a Christian and Missionary Alliance (C&MA) minister who learned about Pentecost while serving as a missionary in China in 1908. After his illiterate Chinese cook suddenly spoke in tongues during a convention on the Tibetan border and then interpreted his message in both Mandarin and local

33 "O Come All Ye Faithful," *Special Report on Religion and Public Life* (The Economist), 6. 2007–11–03: "Megachurch,"
    Wikipedia: en.wikipedia.org/wiki/Megachurch (Accessed 10 March 2013).
34 Barrett, *World Christian Encyclopedia* (2001); Yeol Soo Eim, Global Survey "South Korea": DPCM 239.

why so revealed — His burden needed to... (handwritten marginalia)

how shall long... (handwritten marginalia)

dialects, Simpson spent the next four years studying and praying for the baptism in the Holy Spirit with the gift of tongues. Finally, in 1912, he received his Pentecostal experience, forcing him to withdraw from the C&MA. Then without support, Simpson began holding Pentecostal meetings that resulted in many being healed, falling under the power, speaking in tongues, and experiencing visions, dreams, and other manifestations. In 1915, Simpson returned to the U.S., joined the Assemblies of God on their first foreign missions committee, and served as principal of Bethel Bible Institute in Newark, New Jersey. Simpson was attending a camp meeting in 1918 when someone spoke Chinese in tongues, telling him to go back to Taochow on the Tibetan border. Simpson immediately returned, reporting that "the Spirit was poured out in Pentecostal power" upon their arrival and everywhere they went.[35] Unfortunately, such early efforts in China were soon dissolved by the Chinese Civil War in 1927, the Japanese occupation in 1937, and the Communist takeover in 1949. Nevertheless, since Chairman Mao's death in 1976, religious groups have gradually been given more freedom, and today there are an estimated 54 million Pentecostals in China—only Brazil and the U.S. have more.[36]

William W. Simpson (right) returned to Northwest China in 1918 after a woman prophesied to him at an American Pentecostal camp meeting in the Chinese tongue, instructing him to go back. When he departed from China thirty-two years later, he left behind more than 10,000 Chinese believers and fifty churches on the China-Tibet border. Though he had miraculously escaped death countless times, his son, W.E. Simpson (left), was killed at the age of thirty-two by a group of armed bandits. Source: Flower Pentecostal Heritage Center.

35   Edith L. Blumhofer, *Pentecost in My Soul*, (Springfield: Gospel, 1989), 244: CC 161.
36   D.H. Bays and T.M. Johnson, Global Survey "China": DPCM 58, 63.

RUSSIA

Ivan Voronaev's (c. 1885–1937) defection from the state-run Russian Orthodox Church to become a Baptist minister led to a series of relentless persecutions, forcing him and his family to emigrate to the U.S. in 1912. Arriving first in Seattle, Voronaev pastored a Russian Baptist group that happened to meet in an Assemblies of God church pastored by Ernest Williams—an Azusa Street pilgrim and future general superintendent of the Assemblies of God. Williams planted seeds in Voronaev for the baptism in the Holy Spirit before Voronaev moved to New York City to pastor another Russian Baptist Church. While in New York, Vornoaev's teenage daughter, Vera, had been invited by a friend to attend Marie Brown's Glad Tidings Tabernacle, where she received the baptism in the Holy Spirit and spoke in tongues. Now faced with a serious conflict, Voronaev conceded, received the baptism in the Holy Spirit, and resigned his position at the church. After founding the first Russian Pentecostal Church in New York City in 1919, Voronaev received a prophetic utterance at a cottage prayer meeting instructing him to "journey to Russia."[37] Immediately Voronaev left his church and moved his family back to war-torn, famine-ridden, and now, Communist Russia.

Ivan Voronaev, "Apostle of Pentecost to Russia." By 1926, Pentecostal congregations were appearing in almost all regions of Ukraine as well as in the central regions of Russia, the Urals, the Caucasus, and Siberia. Source: Religious Information Service of Ukraine.

---

37 Vinson Synan interview with Peter Voronaev, son of Ivan, in Moscow in November 1991: HPT 139.

After founding the first Pentecostal church of Russia in Odessa near the Black Sea, Voronaev traveled to other Slavic countries, preaching and praying for the sick with signs following. Within six years, he had planted some 350 churches with 17,000 members, earning him the title "Apostle of Pentecost to Russia." But when Joseph Stalin passed a new law denying legal existence to all churches in 1929, Voronaev was arrested, imprisoned, and eventually sent to the infamous Gulag Soviet forced labor camp in Siberia. There he was shot to death in the prison yard after a failed escape attempt in 1937. As one of the Soviet Union's final acts before dissolving in 1991, full freedom of conscience was reinstated for its citizens, replacing the 1929 law. Stalin's attempt to purge the Soviet Union of religion had failed. Today there are about 6.5 million Pentecostal-charismatics in Russia.[38]

EUROPE

Thomas Ball Barratt (1862–1940), a Methodist minister from Norway, was visiting the U.S. in 1906 to raise funds for his city mission in Kristiania (Oslo), Norway, when he received news of the Azusa Street Revival. Immediately recognizing it as the long-awaited latter-day outpouring, Barratt began praying up to twelve hours a day for his own Pentecostal experience. Barratt had planned to travel to Los Angeles, but after receiving the baptism in the Holy Spirit in his New York hotel room, he decided not to make the trip. After some friends had laid hands on him in his hotel room, an unusual brightness like "a tongue of fire" came over his head. Barratt felt filled with light and overcome with a newfound spiritual power and burden for global

38 Barrett, *World Christian Encyclopedia* (2001); S. Durasoff, Global Survey "Russia": DPCM 217.

evangelism as he prayed in heavenly languages. One eyewitness recorded that Barratt not only shouted and spoke in "seven or eight languages" but also burst into "a beautiful baritone solo using one of the most pure and delightful languages" he had ever heard.[39] This continued until 4:00 a.m.

From New York, Barratt wrote to his congregation back home telling them of the wonderful news and a month later returned to Oslo without denominational funding or support. Thus, Barratt rented a gymnasium in Oslo that seated 2,000 and began the first modern Pentecostal meetings in Europe. Barratt reported from Oslo, "Folk from all denominations are rushing to the meetings. A number have received their Pentecost and are speaking in tongues. . . . Many are seeking salvation and souls are being gloriously saved. Hundreds are seeking a clean heart, and the fire is falling on the purified sacrifice. People who have attended the meetings are taking the fire with them to the towns round about."[40]

By 1909, Barratt's membership with the Methodist Church had terminated, leading him to found Filadelfia Church in Oslo, which would soon become Norway's largest church. Barratt also began writing his own publication in six languages while continuing to hold revival meetings throughout northern Europe. Among those attending Barratt's revival meetings were Lewi Pethrus of Sweden and Alexander Boddy, Vicar of All Saints' Parish in Sunderland, England. In 1911, Pethrus became pastor of Filadelfia Church of Stockholm,

39 Thomas Ball Barratt, *In the Days of the Latter Rain* (Oslo, Norway, 1909); T.B. Barratt, *When the Fire Fell: An Outline of My Life* (Oslo, Norway, 1927), 99–126: HPT 130–131.

40 T.B. Barratt, Oslo, 1907: HPT 129.

which soon became Sweden's largest church, complete with a rescue mission, publishing house, periodical, daily newspaper, Bible school, secondary school, savings bank, worldwide radio network, and a host of Pentecostal missionaries being sent to Latin America, Africa, and Europe.

Left to right: Lewi Pethrus, Mrs. Barratt, T.B. Barratt. After meeting Barratt in Oslo in 1907, Pethrus joined the Pentecostal movement. His Baptist-turned-Pentecostal Filadelfia Church in Stockholm, Sweden, soon became the largest Pentecostal church in the world with missions throughout Africa, Latin America, and Europe. Pethrus would also later become active in the Latter Rain and charismatic movements. Source: T.B. Barratt, *When the Fire Fell*. Flower Pentecostal Heritage Center.

Alexander Boddy invited Barratt to speak at his church in Sunderland, England, and soon another revival broke out with thousands attending, making Sunderland a center for British Pentecostalism. Among those who came to Sunderland were George Jeffreys and Smith Wigglesworth. Jeffreys was a young Welsh minister who had recently been saved in the Welsh Revival and would soon preach with signs following in churches, conventions, and camp meetings across the U.K. while planting Elim Pentecostal Churches in the U.K. and Ireland. In 1962, another young minister named Reinhard Bonnke would be vacationing in London when he would "accidentally" stumble on George Jeffreys' home, be invited in for tea, and receive Jeffreys' mantle and anointing for ministry. Though Jeffreys would die the next day, Bonnke would go on to lead some 55 million Africans to salvation with signs following around the turn of the twenty-first century.

After being saved in the 1904-05 Welsh Revival and filled with the Holy Spirit, brothers George (left) and Stephen Jeffreys began preaching. George founded Elim Pentecostal Churches in 1915 and Stephen joined him in 1920. The two then formed an alliance with Aimee Semple McPherson's Foursquare Gospel and began holding massive revival meetings with signs following in tents and meeting halls across the U.K. and Ireland. Stephen later joined the British Assemblies of God, and in 1939, a dispute over church governance led to George's withdrawal from Elim and to the formation of Bible-Pattern Church Fellowship. Today Elim Pentecostal Churches number over 9,000 churches worldwide. Source: Elim Pentecostal Churches/George Jeffreys and Stephen Jeffreys official website.

SMITH WIGGLESWORTH

Smith Wigglesworth (1859–1947) was raised in a poor working-class home in the small town of Menston near Yorkshire, England, where he helped his mother pull turnips in a field from the age of six. Later he worked with his father in a wool mill and attended his grandmother's old-time Wesleyan church, where he received salvation at age eight. At thirteen, his family moved to Bradford, where Smith became involved in the Methodist Church and Salvation Army. When he was seventeen, a godly man at the mill taught Smith the plumbing business. At twenty, he moved to Liverpool, where he ministered in hospitals and on ships, feeding and clothing the hundreds of children who lived on the docks. At twenty-three, Smith moved back to Bradford, where he met and married Mary Jane "Polly" Featherstone—an officer in the Salvation Army. But because of their strict marriage rules, Polly had to leave the Salvation Army to marry Smith, and together they opened a tiny mission on Bradford Street.

Polly did most of the preaching while Smith did altar work, or as Smith put it, "Her work was to put down the net; mine was to land the fish."[41] But over the years, the hard work of the plumbing business seemed to pull Smith further and further away from God as Polly's faith only grew stronger. One night after Polly arrived home late from church, Smith was noticeably irritated and bellowed, "I am the master of this house, and I am not going to have you coming home at so late an hour as this!" to which Polly calmly replied, "I know that you are my husband, but Christ is my master."[42] Indignant, Smith commanded her to go out the back door and locked the door behind her. But in his anger, he had forgotten to lock the front door, so Polly simply walked around and came in through the front door laughing hysterically! Then Smith started laughing with her as his anger melted into repentance and his faith was soon restored.

Smith Wigglesworth's family (c.1900). Top - Alice, Seth and Harold. Bottom - Ernest, Smith, Mary Jane (Polly) and George.
Source: smithwigglesworth.com.

EARLY MINISTRY

One Tuesday after fasting, Smith was traveling to nearby Leeds to pick up some plumbing supplies when he decided to attend a divine

---

41 Stanley Frodsham, *Smith Wigglesworth: Apostle of Faith* (Springfield: Gospel, 1948), 9: GG 203.

42 Ibid., 22: GG 203.

healing service at the Leeds Healing Home. Smith was amazed as he watched people being instantly healed. He began gathering up the sick from all over Bradford—including Polly—even paying their expenses to travel to Leeds every Tuesday. But seeing that Smith did not realize God could also heal people in Bradford, the ministers in Leeds wisely invited him to fill their pulpit while they attended a Keswick Convention. Smith reluctantly agreed, and after he had stood there struggling and stammering for fifteen minutes, fifteen people came forward to be healed—one on crutches. After Smith prayed, the man on crutches was instantly healed and began jumping all over the building. No one was more surprised than Smith. So Smith and Polly began holding healing services and soon had to move their now growing mission to a larger building on Bowland Street. The first night twelve came forward for healing, and all twelve were healed.

During this time Smith also gained an insatiable hunger to learn God's Word. Since he had never finished school and could not read, Polly taught him to read his Bible, which soon became the only book he would ever read or allow in his house. Smith and Polly had also agreed not to allow medicine in their house. However, when Smith contracted an acute case of appendicitis, by the time they called a doctor, his condition had deteriorated so much there was nothing the doctor could do. Then just as the doctor was leaving, an elderly woman and young man who believed in the prayer of faith showed up at their house. The woman prayed while the young man climbed up on Smith's bed laying both hands on him and crying, "Come out, devil, in the name of Jesus!" Immediately Smith was healed and went back to work.

Interior view of Smith and Polly Wigglesworth's mission building on Bowland Street, Bradford, U.K. (c. 1900). Source: smithwigglesworth.com.

THE REAL BAPTISM

When Smith first heard about the Sunderland revival in 1907, like most Methodists and Salvationists, he believed he was already sanctified and baptized and, indeed, had been warned not to go. Nevertheless, not willing to miss anything God might have for him, Smith decided to go anyway. But to his dismay, when he arrived in Sunderland, he found their meetings to be less lively than the ones they were experiencing back home and even disrupted one of their meetings to tell them so! After being removed from the meeting, he was still determined to speak in tongues, so Smith went down the street to the Salvation Army, where he prayed for four more days but received nothing.

Finally, before leaving to return home, he decided to stop by the parsonage to say goodbye and spoke with Alexander Boddy's wife, Mary. As he explained to her that he did not get the tongues, Mary said, "It is not tongues you need, but the baptism."[43] Smith said he already had the baptism but asked if she would lay hands on him before he left. Mary laid hands on him, prayed a simple prayer, and then left the room to tend to business. Suddenly Smith's whole body became filled with light and a holy presence as he saw a vision of an empty

---

43   Ibid., 44: GG 208.

cross with Jesus at the right hand of the Father and then burst forth praising and worshiping God in other tongues! Smith said, "After this, a burning love for everybody filled my soul. I knew then, although I might have received anointings previously, that now, at last, I had received the real Baptism in the Holy Spirit as they received on the day of Pentecost."[44] Smith immediately went next door to join the service already in progress and again disrupted the meeting, but this time to tell them he had been baptized and spoke in tongues! After hearing his testimony, fifty more received and spoke in tongues. Smith could not wait to wire home and tell Polly the good news.

Alexander Alfred Boddy, Vicar of All Saints' Anglican Church in Sunderland, U.K., was influenced by the Keswick Higher Life movement. Boddy visited the 1904-05 Welsh Revival and T.B. Barratt's revivals before making Sunderland a center for British Pentecostalism. Source: smithwiggleworth.com.

WORLDWIDE MINISTRY

When Smith arrived home, he did not get the welcome he was expecting. Polly was adamant: "I want you to understand that I am as much baptized in the Holy Spirit as you are and I don't speak in tongues. . . . Sunday, you will preach for yourself, and I will see what there is in it." That Sunday Smith preached from Isaiah 61: "The Spirit of the Lord God is upon me"—and for the first time ever without stuttering or stammering. Polly said to herself, "That's not my

44 Wendy Brock, "The Legacy of Smith Wigglesworth," *Spiritual Living 360: www.spiritualliving360.com/index.php/the-legacy-of-smith-wigglesworth-30920* (Accessed 12 March 2013); Frodsham, *Smith Wigglesworth*, 44.

Smith!"[45] He preached with such boldness and power that soon the entire congregation—including their son—fell on the floor laughing uncontrollably. Revival hit Bradford as hundreds—including Polly—received the baptism in the Holy Spirit and spoke in tongues.

As news of the revival spread, invitations began coming in from all over the U.K. for Smith to come and minister, eventually forcing him to close down his plumbing business. Then in 1913 while waiting at a train station in Scotland, Smith received news that Polly had had a heart attack and collapsed at the mission. Smith rushed home as fast as he could, but by the time he arrived, she had already been pronounced dead by the doctor. Immediately, Smith rebuked the death and Polly came back for a while saying, "Smith, it is my time, the Lord wants me." He replied, "If the Lord wants you, I will not hold you," and released her.[46] Smith later wrote, "All that I am today I owe, under God, to my precious wife. Oh, she was lovely!"[47] Smith then asked the Lord for a double portion of his Spirit and went back to doing ministry with even greater power. For the next thirty years, he traveled extensively throughout Europe, America, Australia, New Zealand, India, Sri Lanka, and South Africa, occasionally accompanied by his daughter and son-in-law, Alice and James Salter.

In Sweden in 1920, the medical profession forbade Smith to lay hands on the sick, accusing him of practicing medicine without a license. So instead of laying hands on the sick, he asked an outdoor audience of 20,000 to lay hands on themselves and prayed a general

---

45   Ibid., 47: GG 209.

46   J.J. (Dark) Di Pietro, "Smith Wigglesworth," *Cane Creek Church: canecreekchurch. org/what-s-your-legacy/44-smith-wigglesworth* (Accessed 12 March 2013).

47   Frodsham, *Smith Wigglesworth*, 17: GG 201.

prayer of healing as multitudes received instant miracles. Smith called this "wholesale" or "corporate" healing. In Switzerland, he was arrested twice for practicing medicine without a license but each time was released by the police, who found no fault in him—especially when they saw a man they had locked up many times before suddenly and miraculously delivered and in his right mind! As far as Smith was concerned, the only reason people did not receive healing was a lack of faith and often instructed his audiences to "only believe." *Not so.*

Once someone commented on how easily he seemed to be moved by the Spirit. Smith replied, "Well, you see, it is like this. If the Spirit does not move me, I move the Spirit."[48] Smith also believed people could be baptized in the Holy Spirit on their own initiative without having to "tarry." While in California, he once asked everyone in the audience who had not received the baptism in the Holy Spirit to stand. Next he asked everyone to stand who had received the baptism but had not spoken in tongues in the past six months. Then he prayed a simple prayer asking the Lord to baptize them with the Holy Spirit and instructed them to speak in tongues, yelling, "Go!" The sound reverberated throughout the auditorium. Afterward, he instructed them to sing in tongues, again yelling, "Go! Sing!" It sounded like a magnificent choir.

HEALING THE SICK

Smith had a reputation for practicing extraordinary methods of healing and thereby achieving extraordinary results. He was blunt and rough,

---

48   Gordon Lindsay, *John G. Lake: Apostle to Africa* (Dallas: Christ for the Nations, 1981), 126: GG 216.

though sweet and kind. One minister described him as "a lamb outside the pulpit, a lion behind the pulpit."[49] Others said he had a "ruthless" faith, using every and any means imaginable to heal the sick—from anointing oil, handkerchiefs, rebuking demons, and hitting people to pushing and shouting to get people to walk across a platform. But no one ever complained about his methods because they were all healed—except one Irish woman in New York who once threatened to hit him back! When asked why he hit people, he replied, "I don't hit people; I hit the devil, the people just get in the way."[50] Other times, Smith could be seen ministering to the sick with tears streaming down his face. He deeply loved people but was ruthless toward the Devil. Once when Polly was still alive, they were both frightened in the middle of the night. Sensing an evil presence in the room, Polly dared not open her eyes while Smith simply rubbed his eyes and looked across the room. Seeing the Devil, he said, "Oh, it's only you." Then he told Polly that it was "nothing of concern," rolled over, and went back to sleep![51]

Smith Wigglesworth demonstrates healing to a woman at Angelus Temple. Source: *The Bridal Call Crusader*, Los Angeles, September 1927, p. 18. Photo: Flower Pentecostal Heritage Center.

---

49   Roy Harthern, interview with *Charisma* News (Uploaded on Oct. 11, 2011), *YouTube: www.youtube.com/watch?v=McCBrgJEq7s* (Accessed 12 March 2013).

50   JJ Di Pietro, "Smith Wigglesworth," *Cane Creek Church: canecreekchurch.org/what-s-your-legacy/44-smith-wigglesworth* (Accessed 12 March 2013).

51   Ibid.

RAISING THE DEAD

Smith was also known to have raised a number of people from the dead in his lifetime. The first, while Polly was still alive, was a friend named Mr. Mitchell whom a doctor had confirmed dead and then his wife, Polly, who also had been pronounced dead.[52] A five-year-old boy was also raised from his coffin during a home viewing. At another funeral, Smith pulled a man out of his coffin, stood him against the wall, and yelled three times, commanding him to walk in the name of Jesus. The third time, he indicated he would not say it again—and did not have to![53] A Methodist deaconess from America named Mary Pople died in a hospital bed and was pronounced dead by a doctor. Smith likewise stood her against a wall, held her up with his arm, and said, "In the Name of Jesus I rebuke this death!" He then repeated the words as her body began to tremble: "In the Name of Jesus, walk!" The third time, she walked! The woman later testified that she had been with Jesus, who pointed to a door indicating she would have to go back just before she heard the "gruff voice" of Wigglesworth commanding her to live. Then she opened her eyes.[54] Smith rarely spoke of such events, always trying to point people to Jesus and deflect attention away from himself. However, some have since counted fourteen confirmed cases of raising the dead; others, twenty.

---

52 Ibid.

53 Albert Hibbert, *Smith Wigglesworth: The Secret of His Power* (Tulsa: Harrison House, 1982), 34–35; Paul Frederick West, moderator, "Smith Wigglesworth praying in a restaurant" (7/20/2006) *SermonIndex.net*: *www.sermonindex.net/modules/newbb/viewtopic.php?topic_id=11497&forum=35&9* (Accessed 13 March 2013).

54 Di Pietro, "Smith Wigglesworth," *Cane Creek Church*: *canecreekchurch.org/what-s-your-legacy/44-smith-wigglesworth* (Accessed 13 March 2013).

SAVING THE LOST

Smith shared the same compassion for the lost as he did for the sick and the dead. One night as he crawled into bed, he realized he had not led anyone to the Lord that day. So he went outside, found a drunk on the street, and led him to the Lord before getting back into bed. Other times, whether he was in a store, a field, or on a train, people fell under conviction and repented simply by being in his presence. Once while preaching in a small American town, he stayed in the home and slept in the bed of a church member whose husband was unsaved. On the last day, as he was about to leave, the woman cried, "Please don't leave, for my husband is not yet saved." Smith replied, "Just don't change the sheets." That night as her husband lay in bed, he began sweating. Then, feeling the flames of hell coming up over him, he jumped back out of bed and prayed to receive Jesus![55]

THE SECRET OF HIS POWER

Ministers who worked closely with Smith Wigglesworth said you never knew what he was going to say or do at any given moment. One pastor in Sydney, Australia, said he once took Smith to a high society restaurant and while they were being seated, Smith began hitting the side of his glass with a fork until he had the attention of everyone in the restaurant. Then he raised his hand, saying, "Ladies and gentlemen, I have noticed since arriving here that none of you prayed over your food. You resemble a bunch of hogs to me. You just jump in and eat

---

55 "The Tangible Touch," Sermon Outline by Rod Parsley, *Breakthrough* with Rod Parsley: *www.rodparsley.com/MicroSites/PrayerCloth2012/resource/ministrykit/PastorRodParsley-TheTangibleTouch.pdf* (Accessed 13 March 2013).

without giving thanks to the One Who provided it for you. Bow your heads, and I'll pray for you."[56]

Lester Sumrall, who visited Smith in his home on a number of occasions before the battle of Britain in 1939, once asked him how he woke up in the morning. He said, "I jump out of bed! I dance before the Lord for at least ten to twelve minutes—high-speed dancing. I jump up and down and run around my room telling God how great He is, how wonderful He is, how glad I am to be associated with Him and to be His child." Then he said he would take a cold shower, read the Bible for an hour, pray for an hour, and then open his mail to see what God would have him do that day.[57]

SMITH'S FINAL YEARS

In 1932, Smith fought a long, hard battle with kidney stones that nearly ended his life. But then he prayed and asked God to give him fifteen more years of ministry, and God did! For years Smith persisted, sometimes rising out of bed twice a day to pray for hundreds of sick people while he himself was sick, bleeding, and in pain, eventually passing over a hundred kidney stones. Smith had only one fear in life—that people would get their eyes on him instead of on Jesus. One day in 1947 at age eighty-seven, Smith received four invitations from four different nations asking him to come and minister. Then he wept, saying, "Poor Wigglesworth. What a failure to think that people have their eyes on me. God will never give His glory to another; He will take me from the scene."[58] Seven days later while attending a friend's

---

56   Lester Sumrall, *Pioneers of Faith*, (Tulsa: Harrison House, 1995), 173.
57   Ibid., 165.
58   Hibbert, *The Secret of His Power*, 8.

funeral, he kissed the body of his deceased friend and then walked into the vestry, where he saw the father of a young girl he had recently prayed for. He asked how she was doing. The man said, "a little better," indicating that she was still in pain. Deeply disappointed, Smith let out a sigh, bowed his head, and stumbled. He was gone before he hit the floor.

Smith Wigglesworth, "The Apostle of Faith," in 1946 at age eighty-seven. Source: Flower Pentecostal Heritage Center.

By law, an autopsy should have been done to determine the cause of death, but in Smith's case, this law was somehow overlooked. He had once told his wife, "No knife will ever touch this body, in life or in death."[59] John 11:25 was placed on his tombstone at his request: "I am the resurrection and the life." In 2011, international Bible teacher Terry Quinn purchased the Wigglesworths' Bowland Street mission and converted it into an International Training Center and museum to honor the Wigglesworths.

THE APOSTLE OF FAITH

Today Smith Wigglesworth is known as one of the most influential pioneers of early Pentecostalism as evidenced by the multiplied thousands who were saved, healed, and baptized in the Holy Spirit

---

59   Ibid., 9.

the Holy Spirit enables

through his ministry that spanned the globe for several decades. Though he could barely read or write, no less than fifty books have been written comprising his sermons, life, and ministry. And though he lacked refinement and a formal education, he demonstrated to the world what simple childlike faith in God could do when untainted by worldly sophistication. Once again God had chosen the foolish things of this world to confound the wise.[60] His deep intimate relationship with his heavenly Father and unquestioning faith in God's Word brought spectacular results and provided an example to all true believers, earning him the title "The Apostle of Faith."[61]

THE PENTECOSTAL DENOMINATIONS

In the United States, Gaston Barnabus Cashwell (1860–1916), a minister from A.B. Crumpler's Holiness churches in Dunn, North Carolina, visited Azusa Street in 1906, hoping to receive the new Pentecostal experience. But being a white man from the segregated South, he was not comfortable being in a mostly black church led by a black pastor and was considering leaving when a young black man laid hands on him to receive the Holy Ghost. Chills ran up and down his spine, and within days he had received his Pentecostal experience. Not wasting any time, Cashwell returned to Dunn, where he rented a three-story tobacco warehouse and began holding revival meetings. He invited ministers from Crumpler's Holiness churches, Fire-Baptized Holiness churches, and Free Will Baptist churches. Thousands jammed the old warehouse seeking the new experience, including many ministers. One minister reported, "I went to the Holiness Church to services

60 1 Cor. 1:27

61 Frodsham, *Smith Wigglesworth: Apostle of Faith*, title.

here today and heard Brother G.B. Cashwell preach. He has been to California and got Pentecost and speaks in an unknown tongue. Some seeking the same experience here."[62] One Free Will Baptist minister who attended returned home one evening and his children greeted him at the door: "Papa, Papa, have you got the tongues?" "No, but I want it worse than anything in all the world," he replied. A few nights later, he also received "the tongues."[63]

From Dunn, Cashwell toured the South, holding revivals in Tennessee, South Carolina, North Carolina, Virginia, Georgia, and Alabama and firmly established himself as the "Apostle of Pentecost to the South."[64] Huge crowds gathered to hear him preach and to receive the new experience. Then in February 1907, Joseph Hillary King, overseer of the Fire-Baptized Holiness Churches, received the Pentecostal experience. In April, N.J. Holmes, former Presbyterian minister from Greenville, South Carolina, also received the baptism and spoke in tongues. In June, A.J. Tomlinson heard Cashwell in Alabama and invited him to speak at the Church of God General Assembly in Cleveland, Tennessee. At the close of the General Assembly meetings in January 1908, Tomlinson slipped out of his chair "in a heap on the rostrum . . . at Cashwell's feet" and received his Pentecostal experience. The Church of God was now an official part of the Pentecostal movement.[65] Also by 1908, most of Crumpler's

---

62   Thurman Carey, Dunn, North Carolina, December 30, 1906: HPT 107.

63   Florence Goff, *Tests and triumphs: being a sketch of the life of Rev. J.A. Hodges, coupled with some of the Lord's dealings with H.H. Goff and wife, evangelists of the Cape Fear Conference of the Free-Will Baptist Church*, (Falcon, N.C: n.p. c. 1924), 51: HPT 115.

64   HPT 113.

65   Homer A. Tomlinson, *Diary of A.J. Tomlinson*, vol. 1 1901–1923 (Church of God World Headquarters, 1949), 27–29: HPT 124.

Holiness Church ministers had received the Pentecostal experience, except Crumpler, who opposed it and was soon forced to withdraw from the organization he had founded. "Pentecostal" was also added back to the name that year, reconstructing the "Pentecostal Holiness Church." In 1911, the denomination merged with the Fire-Baptized Holiness Church, and in 1915 with N.J. Holmes's former Presbyterian churches based out of Greenville, South Carolina, each time retaining the title Pentecostal Holiness Church.

G.B. Cashwell, a Holiness minister from Dunn, North Carolina, received his Pentecostal experience at Azusa Street in 1906 and immediately returned home to hold revival meetings in a rented tobacco warehouse before touring the South and converting several Holiness denominations to Pentecostalism. He is known as the "Apostle of Pentecost to the South." Source: Flower Pentecostal Heritage Center.

Charles Harrison Mason (1864–1961) visited Azusa Street in March of 1907 accompanied by two fellow ministers. On the second night, Mason went to the altar when "there came a light which enveloped my entire being above the brightness of the sun. When I opened my mouth to say 'Glory,' a flame touched my tongue which ran down me. My language changed and no word could I speak in my own tongue. Oh! I was filled with the Glory of the Lord. My soul was then satisfied."[66]

But when Mason returned to Memphis with his new Pentecostal experience, he found that Glenn A. Cook, a white minister from Azusa Street, had already preached at his church and many already

---

66 "The Founder & Church History," *The Church of God in Christ:*
   www.cogic.org/our-foundation/the-founder-church-history (Accessed 15 March 2013).

spoke in tongues. However, C.P. Jones, his denominational overseer, did not agree with the new teaching and soon split the church—half going with Mason and half with Jones. After two years of court battles, Mason's group retained the name Church of God in Christ and Jones's group formed the Church of Christ (Holiness) USA. As of 2010, Jones's denomination reported a membership of 14,000, while Mason's church reported 5 million—the only difference was the baptism in the Holy Spirit. *Holy Spirit spoke. For all the wrong reasons today. Worn a a badge of approval uses power to enlarge the Kingdom by doing as Jesus did.*

THE ASSEMBLIES OF GOD

Also between 1907 and 1910, a number of ministers began distancing themselves from Charles Parham's Apostolic Faith movement over questions of Parham's moral character. Now in need of an established church name to ordain ministers and receive clergy railroad discounts, a gentlemen's agreement was made with C.H. Mason to use the name Church of God in Christ. This new "white" Church of God in Christ group included E.N. Bell, Howard A. Goss, D.C.O. Opperman, and Arch P. Collins. Bell was a former Baptist pastor from Fort Worth who had been converted to Pentecostalism under William Durham's Chicago ministry. Others would later join from John Alexander Dowie's Chicago ministry and various denominational backgrounds including Methodist, Presbyterian, and Christian and Missionary Alliance. Meanwhile, a second group of white ministers had formed in Alabama led by H.G. Rodgers, a Cashwell convert. By 1911, Durham's "Finished Work" doctrine had spread through the ranks of these independent ministers, who began voicing a need to unify under the new doctrinal position. Bell and Rodgers' groups merged in Mississippi in 1912, creating a mostly-white body of 352 ministers. The call was

was this separation of these between the white + blacks

made for a general council to meet the first week of April 1914 at the Grand Opera House in Hot Springs, Arkansas. Mason, who called the group "the White work" of the Church of God in Christ, was invited to preach. Mason's choir sang before Mason preached and gave his blessings and prayers to the new organization.

The First General Council of the Assemblies of God, Hot Springs, Arkansas, April 2–12, 1914. The first executive presbyters are kneeling front left to right: J.W. Welch, M.M. Pinson, T.K. Leonard, J. Roswell Flower, Cyrus Fockler, Howard A. Goss, E.N. Bell, and D.C.O. Opperman. Source: Flower Pentecostal Heritage Center.

Their purpose was fivefold: 1) formulate an agreed on Pentecostal doctrine, 2) consolidate Pentecostal works, 3) support Pentecostal missions, 4) establish Pentecostal Bible schools, and 5) preserve the fruit of Pentecost in the nation and the world. A keynote address was given by M.M. Pinson on "the finished work of Calvary," and Bell was elected first general superintendent. A congregational form of government and "Finished Work" doctrine was adopted, clearly defining sanctification as a progressive work. Though no one intended to create a new denomination, in essence, that is what happened. The group soon incorporated under the name General Council of the Assemblies of God. Today the World Assemblies of God Fellowship is the world's largest Pentecostal denomination with over 67 million members and a presence in over 212 countries, making it the sixth largest Christian denomination worldwide overall.[67]

67   "Statistics on the Assemblies of God (USA) 2014 Reports," *Assemblies of God: ag.org/top/About/statistics/index* (Accessed 7 April 2016).

OTHER PENTECOSTAL DENOMINATIONS

Fearing too much denominational control in the Assemblies of God, John C. Sinclair, who had succeeded Durham as pastor of the Chicago North Avenue Mission, formed the Pentecostal Assemblies of the USA in 1916, which would later become the Pentecostal Church of God. When the Church of God (Cleveland, Tennessee) split in 1923 over _____ c rule and alleged misha _____ f God was formed, which _____ f Prophecy. By the 1930s _____ ; and independent grou _____

ON

Duri _____ co near Los Angeles in 19 _____ Camp Meeting, R.E. McA _____ preached that "the apo _____ in the name of Jesus Christ" instead of baptizing in the traditional _____ es of the Father, Son, and Holy Spirit.[68] It was another "shot heard round the world." One man who heard that statement, John G. Scheppe, ran through the camp early the next morning shouting that God had revealed to him the truth of baptism in the name of the Lord Jesus Christ. Another man who heard that statement, Frank J. Ewart—an Australian Baptist minister who had converted to Pentecostalism, assisted William Durham in his Los Angeles ministry, and succeeded him there after

[Handwritten note: 106 – Oneness / John G. Scheppe / R. E. McAlister / Frank J. Ewart]

---

68   Fred J. Foster, *Think It Not Strange: A History of the Oneness Movement* (St. Louis: Pentecostal, 1965), 51–52: HPT 156.

his death, would spend a year formulating his ideas before preaching his first "Jesus Name" sermon in 1914.

It was an age-old argument supposedly settled at Nicaea in 325. According to "Oneness" teaching, "Father" and "Holy Spirit" were mere titles designating different aspects of Christ's personality, thus requiring anyone baptized according to traditional Trinitarian beliefs to be "re-baptized in the Name of Jesus." Ewart also took Durham's "Finished Work" doctrine a step further by declaring that salvation, sanctification, and baptism in the Holy Spirit with speaking in tongues all constituted one event that may be received at water baptism when properly done.

One of Ewart's first converts was Glenn A. Cook—the white minister from Azusa Street who had spoken at Mason's church. Together, Ewart and Cook set out on a campaign to "re-baptize" the entire Pentecostal movement. But when Cook converted Garfield T. Haywood—a leading black pastor and his 465-member church in Indianapolis—shockwaves reverberated through the young movement. However, by 1916, and after much infighting, the Trinitarians had won the day. The Assemblies of God adopted its Statement of Fundamental Truths which unequivocally supported Trinitarianism and 156 Oneness preachers were forced to leave and form their own fellowships. Many of them reformed and reorganized under the Pentecostal Assemblies of the World with Oneness Pentecostal teachings and Haywood as their leader. In 380, these men would have been judged "demented and insane" and excommunicated as heretics, but in 1916, they simply reorganized under a new doctrinal position.[69] In 1924, the Oneness

---

69 In 380, Emperor Theodosius decreed that anyone who did not follow Nicene Trinitarian Christianity had been judged "demented and insane." *Codex Theodosianus XVI 1.2*: CH 96–97.

churches split down racial lines to form an all-white denomination called the United Pentecostal Church, which later merged with another Oneness group in 1945, forming the United Pentecostal Church International (UPCI). It has since become more ethnically diverse. Over the years, at least sixteen other Oneness denominations have emerged, and today Oneness Pentecostals have approximately 24 million adherents worldwide.[70]

Glenn A. Cook (left) rebaptizes L.V. Roberts at a Oneness outdoor baptismal service in Indianapolis, Indiana, March 6, 1915. This is said to have been the first Jesus' Name service east of the Mississippi River. Source: Flower Pentecostal Heritage Center.

F.F. BOSWORTH

In 1910, Fred Francis Bosworth (1877–1958) moved from Zion City, Illinois, to Dallas, Texas, where he pioneered an independent Pentecostal church loosely affiliated with the Christian and Missionary Alliance. During this time, Bosworth was greatly persecuted for befriending blacks and holding racially integrated meetings in the segregated South. Nevertheless, by 1912, Bosworth's church had

---

70   Eric Patterson; Edmund Rybarczyk, The Future of Pentecostalism in the United States (New York: Lexington Books, 2007), 124: "Oneness Pentecostalism," Wikipedia: en.wikipedia.org/wiki/Oneness_Pentecostalism (Accessed 15 March 2013).

become a center for revival as people from all over the country came to hear Maria Woodworth-Etter—now back in public ministry—preach from her yearlong tent meeting at Bosworth's church.

Bosworth joined the Assemblies of God in 1914, becoming both a delegate and executive presbyter at their first general council. But two years later when the Assemblies drafted a formal doctrinal statement declaring tongues as *the* initial evidence of the baptism in the Holy Spirit, Bosworth disagreed, arguing that tongues was only one of many evidences and stating that the initial evidence and gift of tongues were the same. By 1918, when it became clear that despite his arguments there would be no change, Bosworth quietly withdrew and rejoined the Christian and Missionary Alliance.

About that same time, Bosworth began holding healing campaigns in major cities like Pittsburgh, Toronto, Chicago, and Ottawa, where more than 12,000 attended nightly and hundreds received miraculous healings. In 1924, Bosworth published his first edition of *Christ the Healer*, which contained many of his healing sermons and became an instant classic in faith healing. In 1930, he also established himself as a pioneer in Christian radio. Though he had formally left a Pentecostal denomination, F.F. Bosworth never really changed who he was—an independent Pentecostal healing revivalist.

A capacity crowd at an F.F. Bosworth Evangelistic Campaign in Chicago in 1931. Thousands of conversions and hundreds of miraculous healings were recorded at Bosworth's meetings. Photo: Kaufmann & Fabry, Chicago, Ill. Source: Flower Pentecostal Heritage Center.

E.W. KENYON

Another staunchly independent minister who seemed always on the outside looking in was Essek William Kenyon (1867–1948). Though an enigmatic figure for sure, Kenyon appealed to many early Pentecostals—especially Oneness Pentecostals. It is also possible that Kenyon had an early influence on William Durham's "Finished Work" doctrine, which closely resembled his own. He had met with Durham twice before, in Chicago in 1907 and 1908. Kenyon even referred to Durham once as "the highest and most scriptural type" of Pentecostal.[71] But he also met with many other early Pentecostal leaders including John Alexander Dowie, Charles Fox Parham, John G. Lake, F.F. Bosworth, Maria Woodworth-Etter, and Aimee Semple McPherson. He even sought licensing credentials with the Assemblies of God at one point but was turned down.

Kenyon was never quite willing to work within the confines of Pentecostalism, feeling instead that the young movement should join him. One historian likened placing Kenyon in the Pentecostal movement to "a soccer game where everyone" played by one set of rules while another player decided "to follow the rules of rugby."[72] Kenyon was truly a multifaceted figure in the body of Christ. He founded a publishing company, a shirt business, two Bible colleges, two radio shows, and several churches. Besides being associated with Pentecostals, he was also identified at one time or another with the

---

71 Dale H. Simmons, *E.W. Kenyon and the Postbellum Pursuit of Peace, Power, and Plenty* (Lanham, Md.: Scarecrow, 1997); Douglas Jacobsen, *Thinking in the Spirit: Theologies of the Early Pentecostal Movement* (Bloomington: Indiana University, 2003), 313, 397.

72 Jacobsen, *Thinking in the Spirit*, 319.

Methodists, Free Will Baptists, A.J. Gordon, A.B. Simpson, D.L. Moody, the Higher Life movement, the YMCA, George Müller, Andrew Murray, and Frank Sanford, among others.

E.W. Kenyon's teachings appealed to many early and Oneness Pentecostals and later to many charismatic and Word of Faith followers worldwide. Source: Flower Pentecostal Heritage Center.

What made Kenyon controversial is the fact that during the two and a half years he allegedly backslid (between 1891 and 1893), he took a year of acting lessons at Boston's Emerson School of Oratory, which at the time was a breeding ground for metaphysical "New Thought" teachings. Then add to that the fact that Kenyon's teachings had some similarities to New Thought teaching (though both he and his publishing society vehemently denied this) and he was suspect at best. But at least one Kenyon biographer believed it was more likely that evangelical faith cure and early Pentecostal teachers such as A.J. Gordon and A.B. Simpson had a greater influence on Kenyon's theology.[73] As for Kenyon, he felt that traditional "Dogmas and Doctrines" had become stale and ineffective and that "new" teachings were needed to lift people "from the mire of traditional unbelief into the deep, rich treasures" of their "redemption in Christ."[74] This clearly

73 Joe McIntyre, *E.W. Kenyon: The True Story* (Lake Mary, Fla.: Charisma, 1997): "Word of Faith," *Wikipedia: en.wikipedia.org/wiki/Word_of_Faith* (Accessed 16 March 2013).

74 E.W. Kenyon, *Identification: A Romance in Redemption*, 16th ed. (Seattle: Kenyon's Gospel, 1968; originally published in 1941), 63: Jacobsen, *Thinking in the Spirit*, 352; Quotation from *Kenyon's Gospel Publishing Society: www.kenyons.org* (Accessed 16 March 2013).

resonated with many early Pentecostals who were on parallel paths of discovering "new" doctrines. Kenyon's books and teachings also contained seeds that would later open the door for more extreme elements within the movement.

AIMEE SEMPLE MCPHERSON

Aimee Semple McPherson (1890–1944) was born on a farm near Ingersoll, Ontario, Canada, to James and "Minnie" Kennedy. Minnie was a Salvation Army worker who had responded to a newspaper ad to care for the ailing Mrs. Kennedy. But after Mrs. Kennedy's death, James, who was fifty, married his live-in nurse, who was only fifteen. Feeling she had failed God as a minister, Minnie prayed, "If you will only hear my prayer, as you heard Hannah's prayer of old, and give me a little baby girl, I will give her unreservedly into Your service, that she may preach the Word I should have preached, fill the place I should have filled, and live the life I should have lived in Thy service."[75]

Aimee grew up watching her mother work in Salvation Army soup kitchens, playing "Salvation Army" with her classmates, and lining up her dolls to preach to them. As an only child, she was spunky, dramatic, headstrong, and not easily intimidated. As a teenager, Aimee rebelled against her mother's teachings by reading novels and going to movies and dances, which were strictly forbidden. In high school, Darwin's theory of evolution was being taught, which Aimee opposed while at the same time scoffing at churches for their dead formalism and for forsaking the teachings and miracles of the Bible.

---

75   Daniel Mark Epstein, *Sister Aimee: The Life of Aimee Semple McPherson* (Orlando: Harcourt Brace, 1993), 10: GG 231.

Aimee Elizabeth Kennedy was born on a farm near Ingersoll, Ontario, Canada, in 1890—the only child of James and Minnie Kennedy. Here she is in her Salvation Army uniform (c. 1896). Source: International Church of the Foursquare Gospel.

MARRIED TO ROBERT SEMPLE

At seventeen, Aimee attended Irish evangelist Robert Semple's Holy Ghost revival meetings. She later wrote, "From the moment I heard that young man speak with tongues, to this day, I have never doubted for the shadow of a second that there was a God, and that he had shown me my true condition as a poor, lost, miserable, hell-serving sinner."[76] Aimee married Mr. Semple the following year, and they moved to Chicago, where Robert was ordained in 1909 and began working with William Durham at his North Avenue Mission. During this time, Aimee fell down a flight of stairs and broke her ankle. The doctor ordered her to stay off her feet for a month, but the pain became so unbearable during one of Durham's meetings that she had to hobble on crutches back to her room a block away. Then she heard a voice say, "If you will . . . go over to North Avenue Mission to Brother Durham and ask him to lay hands on your foot, I will heal it."[77] Aimee did, was instantly healed, and began dancing around the church.

Feeling a call to do missions work in China, Robert took Aimee, who was now pregnant, and set sail for China in 1910, visiting his

---

76   Ibid., 47: GG 237.
77   Ibid., 58: GG 240.

family first in Ireland. While in London, Aimee was asked to preach for the very first time—she was not yet twenty. Nervous, she opened her Bible and her eyes fell on Joel 1:4. After she read it, she closed her eyes and felt her tongue begin to move like when she first spoke in tongues. Only this time, it came out in English! Aimee preached prophetically for more than an hour on the Latter Rain restoration of the church throughout the ages. When finished, she looked out at a sea of people clapping and wiping their eyes. But only two months after arriving in Hong Kong, Robert suddenly died of malaria and Minnie sent money for Aimee and baby Roberta to return home.

Aimee with husband, Pentecostal evangelist Robert Semple, in Chicago in 1910. Source: International Church of the Foursquare Gospel.

MARRIED TO HAROLD MCPHERSON

On her way home, Aimee met an accountant, Harold McPherson, in New York, whom she soon married, moving to his Rhode Island home and eventually giving birth to a son, Rolf. Now running from the call of God, Aimee sank into a deep depression, illness, and a series of emotional breakdowns. Repeatedly, she heard the voice of God say, "Go! Do the work of an evangelist." But each time she ignored it to please her husband. Finally, nearing death, Aimee again heard the voice of God, "Now will you go?"[78] Only this time, she responded in the affirmative, the

78   Ibid., 74–75.

pain immediately left, and she was back on her feet within two weeks. Now having chosen to obey God over her husband, Aimee waited till her husband left for work one day, packed up the children, moved to Toronto, and then wired her husband asking him to join her: "I have tried to walk your way and have failed. Won't you come now and walk my way? I am sure we will be happy."[79] There was no response.

Soon Aimee began holding local meetings as Minnie watched the children. Before long, Aimee had to purchase a tent to accommodate the hundreds who were coming to hear her. One night she looked over the crowd and there was her husband, Harold! He had come to hear her preach, and before the night was over, he had received the Holy Spirit and soon joined her in ministry. For the next several years, Aimee crisscrossed the country several times, preaching in more than a hundred cities from her 1912 Packard (which looked more like a traveling church than a touring car) in her distinctive white servant's dress. Aimee also began printing her own newsletter, *The Bridal Call*, during this time. But after about a year of living the vagabond life, Harold had had enough and left, eventually filing for divorce. Minnie soon joined Aimee on the road, bringing Roberta, whom Aimee had not seen in nearly two years, with her.

Left to right: Roberta Semple, Minnie Kennedy, Rolf McPherson, Aimee Semple McPherson, and Harold McPherson at a tent meeting in 1918. Source: Flower Pentecostal Heritage Center.

79   Ibid., 76.

CALIFORNIA, HERE WE COME!

In 1918, a deadly flu virus was sweeping the nation and Roberta contracted it. During this time, Roberta asked her mother why they did not have a home like everyone else. As Aimee prayed for her daughter's healing, the Lord assured her that not only would Roberta live but also they would all live together in sunny Southern California. So after Roberta recovered, they set out for California, stopping in Indianapolis along the way, where Aimee was honored to hear and meet her inspiration and idol—Maria Woodworth-Etter. By the time Aimee arrived in Los Angeles in 1918, the Azusa Street Revival was little more than a memory and its participants scattered. But Aimee was able to re-inspire many of them as she preached her first sermon to a crowd of seven hundred: "Shout! For the Lord Hath Given You the City." Within months, Aimee was packing out the 3,500-seat Temple Auditorium, and the people of Los Angeles could not do enough for Aimee—even volunteering to build a house for her while she went back on the road to raise money to build a new Los Angeles church.

Aimee traveled across America dressed in her white servant's dress, preaching and healing the sick from her 1912 Packard "Gospel Car" with a "Jesus is Coming Soon – Get Ready" sign on the side (1918). Source: International Church of the Foursquare Gospel.

ANGELUS TEMPLE

By the time the press discovered Aimee in 1919, her healing ministry was already in full swing. Actually, according to one biographer, "No one has ever been credited by secular witnesses with anywhere near the number of healings attributed to Sister Aimee from 1919 to 1922."[80] By 1921, Aimee had raised more than enough money to purchase a tract of land in the beautiful Echo Park district of Los Angeles, and construction began on the 5,300-seat Angelus Temple at a cost of 1.5 million dollars. It was the largest church in America at the time.

THE FOURSQUARE GOSPEL

In 1922, Aimee was preaching a message from Ezekiel about the beast with four faces—a man, a lion, an ox, and an eagle—when the Lord gave her a vision showing her the meaning of the four faces: 1) the man represented Jesus as Savior, 2) the lion was Jesus as Baptizer, 3) the ox was Jesus as Healer, and 4) the eagle was Jesus as Coming King. Similar to A.B. Simpson's Four-Fold Gospel of Jesus as Savior, Sanctifier, Healer, and Coming King, The Church of the Foursquare Gospel, based on Aimee's vision, was dedicated on New Year's Day 1923. The *New York Times* gave the event full press coverage, and from then on, the building would fill four times every Sunday with thousands more being turned away, two healing services each week, and a 24-hour prayer tower. The sick and injured came by the tens of thousands. The press clippings and testimonials were extraordinary. But for those who had previously traveled with Aimee, it was ordinary.

As America's first "megachurch," Angelus Temple truly was a church before its time. Aimee felt that churches had grown too cold and formal and wanted to build a church that would reflect joy, encouragement, and laughter. Behind the pulpit was Aimee's theme verse: "Jesus Christ

---

80 Epstein, *Sister Aimee*, 185.

the Same, Yesterday and Today and Forever." The sanctuary was filled with music that emanated from a 100-voice choir, 36-piece orchestra, and Aimee's personal favorite—the great Kimball pipe organ.

Aimee dedicated Angelus Temple on January 1, 1923, as a place of worship and an ecumenical center for all Christian faiths. Methodists, Baptists, The Salvation Army, Presbyterians, Episcopalians, Adventists, Quakers, Roman Catholics, Mormons, secular civic leaders, and critics alike all came and were welcomed. Some even made their way to the podium as guest speakers or preachers. Source: International Church of the Foursquare Gospel.

Sermons were no small events either. Costumes, props, and scenery were created by Aimee's army of carpenters, electricians, artists, and set designers to complement her dramatically illustrated messages. The emphasis was always on salvation, and Aimee wrote many of the skits herself. In one service, Aimee drove on stage in a motorcycle, dressed in a police uniform, blowing a whistle and raising her white-gloved hand to the audience shouting, "Stop, you are going to hell!" In another service, the stage was set like a cotton plantation scene from *Gone with the Wind* as she preached the Foursquare Gospel. In yet another service, she came out dressed in football garb carrying a football called "the Foursquare Gospel" for a touchdown, that is until Jesus called "interference."[81] In yet another service, the stage was set with two miniature airplanes and what looked like the Los Angeles skyline in the background. The first plane had the Devil for the pilot, sin for the engine, and temptation as the propeller. The other plane was piloted by Jesus, who led everyone in the audience to the "Holy City."

---

81   *The Pentecostal Evangel*, June 5, 1926, 1–3; HPT 201; CHS 135.

NO BOUNDARIES

There seemed to be no limit to the variety of people Aimee was able to reach. At one point, it was estimated that 10 percent of the Los Angeles population were members of Aimee's church.[82] The crowds loved her, the press loved her—even famous Hollywood actors like Charlie Chaplin attended her meetings. Actor Anthony Quinn played in her band. Smith Wigglesworth was a frequent guest speaker. A young Quaker boy named Richard Nixon attended her church with his family, while a young evangelist named Kathryn Kuhlman also attended. It seemed the only group that did *not* like Aimee was the religious crowd. One female Holiness preacher called her a "witch," claiming she used creative and crafty methods to draw a crowd.[83] Aimee retorted, "Show me a better way to persuade willing people to come to church and I'll be happy to try your method. But please . . . don't ask me to preach to empty seats. Let's not waste our time quarreling over methods. God has use for all of us. Remember the recipe in the old adage for rabbit stew? It began, 'first catch your rabbit.'"[84]

Aimee Semple McPherson preaching at Angelus Temple (c. 1923). Behind the podium is Hebrews 13:8: "Jesus Christ the Same Yesterday, Today & Forever." Source: *Los Angeles Times*. Photo: Wikimedia/Magnus Manske.

---

82 Roberts Liardon, *God's Generals, Vol. 7: Aimee Semple McPherson* (New Kensington, Penn.: Whitaker House, 2005) DVD.

83 White, *Demons and Tongues*, 112–115: HPT 202.

84 Epstein, *Sister Aimee*, 259: GG 255.

The first Foursquare school of ministry, called the Lighthouse of International Foursquare Evangelism or L.I.F.E Bible College for short (later, Life Pacific College), opened in 1923 featuring Aimee as one of its main instructors. Later that year, Aimee became the first woman to preach a sermon over radio and in 1924 the first pastor to own a radio station. The call letters were KFSG (Kall Foursquare Gospel). Aimee's ministry was huge and growing larger by the day. In 1926, the Angelus Temple Commissary was opened to feed and clothe the poor, and after the Great Depression hit in 1929, the temple fed and clothed more than 1.5 million people in the Los Angeles area.

Believing the gospel had no boundaries, Aimee often showed up at dance clubs, night clubs, pool halls, or boxing matches to announce her meetings. One biographer wrote, Aimee never hesitated "to use the devil's tools to tear down the devil's house."[85] Also fully involved in her community, Aimee served as an honorary member of the police and fire departments, as patron saint at service clubs, and as an official community spokesperson. Aimee launched many personal crusades in social, educational, and political arenas as well—such as the prohibition of alcohol, banning teaching on evolution in public schools, and anything else that seemed to threaten Christian ideals. Aimee was an outspoken supporter of William Jennings Bryan's 1925 Scopes Trial, helping to organize massive church meetings, all-night prayer vigils, parades, and publicly declaring Darwinism as "the greatest triumph of Satanic intelligence in 5,931 years of devilish warfare against the Hosts of Heaven."[86]

---

85   Matthew Avery Sutton, *Aimee Semple McPherson and the Resurrection of Christian America* (Cambridge: Harvard University Press, 2007), 70.

86   Ibid., 37.

KIDNAPPED!

On May 18, 1926, Aimee was preparing a sermon at the beach with her secretary when her secretary briefly left to make a phone call and returned only to find Aimee had disappeared. She immediately contacted authorities, and Aimee's disappearance soon became the hottest item in the press. Minnie, fearing the worst, preached the Sunday service saying, "Sister is with Jesus." Then Minnie received a ransom note for $25,000 and the press went wild. Alleged "Aimee sightings" occurred coast to coast. Later Minnie received another note, this time demanding $500,000 or stating that her daughter would be sold into "white slavery." It was signed "the Avengers." Still fearing the worst, Minnie simply threw the note away.

Then on June 23, as plans were underway for Aimee's memorial service, Aimee suddenly reappeared near the Mexican-Arizona border. After being questioned by police, she told how a couple had approached her on the beach crying and asking if she would come pray for their child, who was dying. She explained that sort of thing happened all the time, so she did not think anything of it. But when she followed the couple to their car, she was shoved in, kidnapped, drugged, tortured, and taken to a shack where she was held for ransom. Then one day, her captors left her alone to go shopping and she was able to escape by cutting through her wrist bands with a tin can, climbing out of a window, and walking for several hours across a desert until she found another cabin and cried for help. The following Sunday, 50,000 people welcomed Aimee back to Angelus Temple. But since the police could neither find her kidnappers nor the shack, the Los Angeles District Attorney charged Aimee with perjury, corruption, obstruction of justice, and conspiracy as a highly publicized Hollywood-style court battle ensued. But Aimee never changed her story, and six months later, all charges were dropped.

Aimee convalescing with her family by her side at a Douglas, Arizona, hospital in 1926, after reemerging from the Mexican desert. From left to right is, mother Minnie, daughter Roberta, and son Rolf. Source: International Church of the Foursquare Gospel.

THE INTERNATIONAL CHURCH OF THE FOURSQUARE GOSPEL

Seemingly unshaken, Aimee founded the International Church of the Foursquare Gospel later that same year. The denomination did not differ theologically from the Assemblies of God she had been a part of but had a more centralized form of government. Showing her Salvation Army roots, Aimee called the parent church the "Salvation Navy" and the satellite churches "lighthouses." Of course, divorced women were allowed to pastor, and to this day about 40 percent of Foursquare ministers in the U.S. are women. Today the denomination boasts a worldwide membership of more than 8 million in over 144 countries.[87]

---

87   "2008 Yearbook of American & Canadian Churches," The National Council of Churches (Retrieved 2009–12–16) "International Church of the Foursquare Gospel," *Wikipedia: en.wikipedia.org/wiki/International_Church_of_the_Foursquare_Gospel* (Accessed 17 March 2013).

In 1932, John R. Richey, concerned over Aimee's kidnapping incident, divorce, and denominational control, led the Foursquare Minnesota and Iowa districts to splinter off and merge with Fred Hornshuh's group of ministers, which had splintered from Florence Crawford's Apostolic Faith Mission in 1919 to form the Open Bible Standard Churches (later, Open Bible Churches). Both Richey and Hornshuh had been influenced by John Alexander Dowie's ministry.

AIMEE'S FINAL YEARS

For years, Minnie had been the backbone of Aimee's ministry—watching her children for her, being her friend and confidante, and serving as financial and administrative overseer for her ever-growing ministry. But the relationship had a price. As her mother, Minnie also became increasingly over protective, not allowing Aimee to have any close personal relationships and was often the reason behind employees quitting or being fired. This caused a strained relationship, which all came to a head in the summer of 1927 when Minnie began publicly accusing Aimee of forsaking her Salvation Army roots by dressing too modern. Then when Minnie showed up one day with what appeared to be a broken nose, the press headlines read, "Ma Says Aimee Broke Her Nose!" But later when the truth came out—that she had had plastic surgery the day before—Minnie denied having the procedure. Aimee had had enough and forced Minnie to retire. But when less capable staff members replaced her and the ministry plunged into debt with numerous pending lawsuits, Minnie briefly returned in late 1929 until continued disagreements led to her final resignation in 1930. A month later, Aimee had a physical and emotional breakdown and was restricted to rest at a beach cottage under doctor's orders. Ten months later, Aimee would return but never with quite the same vigor or vitality.

One of eight showings of Aimee's first sacred opera *Regem Adorate* (Worship the King) at Angelus Temple, Christmas 1939. Aimee's early illustrated sermons were quite elementary compared with their later development. As part of a 1929 temple remodeling project, a beautiful proscenium arch flanked by two choir lofts was installed, allowing for greater presentation of Aimee's illustrated sermons and sacred operas. Source: International Church of the Foursquare Gospel.

Now with no personal friends and desperate for companionship, Aimee married actor and musician David Hutton in 1931. Almost immediately, David was sued by an ex-girlfriend for breach of a marriage promise, while Aimee faced the tenets she herself had put forth regarding ministers remarrying while a previous spouse was still alive. Since Harold was still alive, she was in breach of a trust, and she and David separated in 1933, later divorcing in 1934. Aimee publicly repented of the marriage, saying it had been wrong from the beginning—both personally and theologically.

In 1936, amid financial difficulties, Aimee resigned from many of her personal responsibilities and realigned her staff, which only seemed to lead to more problems and lawsuits—including one from her own daughter, Roberta. Finally, in 1937, Aimee hired Rev. Giles Knight as her new administrator. Rev. Knight kept the ministry out of debt, disposed of some forty lawsuits, and kept the press at bay, allowing Aimee to enjoy her final years in relative peace. During this time, Aimee traveled, trained future ministers, established churches, and sent out foreign missionaries.

In 1942, in true Aimee-like fashion, Aimee led a brass band and color guard through downtown Los Angeles, selling $150,000 in war bonds and organizing prayer meetings for the duration of the war. Believing that military action against the Axis powers was long overdue, Aimee's wartime sermons often linked the church with American patriotism, and the army made her an honorary colonel. In 1944, Aimee appointed her son, Rolf, as vice president as her health continued to deteriorate from a tropical infection she had contracted while overseas. Only Rolf had stuck with her through good times and bad and would remain at the helm for the next forty-four years. Aimee died on September 26, 1944, at the age of fifty-four. Some 60,000 people attended her funeral. In 2001, Matthew Barnett of the Los Angeles Dream Center became pastor at Angelus Temple, where it remains in the Foursquare Gospel family to this day.

By 1943, Aimee had risen to celebrity status, was distributing autographed New Testaments to soldiers, leading prayer meetings, using militaristic sermon themes, and announcing that every soldier would be "right at home at any Angelus Temple service." Source: International Church of the Foursquare Gospel.

AIMEE'S LEGACY

Aimee's death marked the end of the initial thrust of the Pentecostal movement. Nearly single-handedly, Aimee Semple McPherson had propelled Pentecostalism from the backwoods of forest camp meetings to the forefront of American society. The founding of the National Association of Evangelicals (NAE) in 1942 was a major turning point in history because, for the first time in a long time, Pentecostal-like groups were invited and accepted into mainstream Christianity. Though the initial explosive years of the Pentecostal movement were significant and experienced good growth, its total impact worldwide was minimal. It was mainly a time for building momentum, which would accelerate greatly after World War II. OK

this does not make sense

STUDY QUESTIONS

1. What effects of American individualism do you see in American society today? In American churches?

2. What outstanding qualities and commonalities do you find in the early Pentecostal missionaries?

3. What common thread do you find in some of the early testimonies of receiving the Pentecostal baptism in the Holy Spirit? (e.g. T.B. Barratt, Smith Wigglesworth, Evan Roberts, Charles Finney. See also Acts 1:8; 2:36–40; 4:29–31; Psalm 51:11–13; Romans 5:5.)

4. What strikes you most about Smith Wigglesworth's life and ministry?

5. Why is G.B. Cashwell known as the "Apostle of Pentecost to the South?" What Holiness denominations did he convert to Pentecostalism?

6. How was the Assemblies of God founded? What doctrine distinguished them from other Pentecostal denominations of the day? Explain.

7. What is the difference between Oneness and Trinitarian Pentecostals? Explain.

8. Why is E.W. Kenyon considered an enigmatic figure in early Pentecostalism?

9. What was Aimee Semple McPherson's greatest contribution to Pentecostalism?

3

THE HEALING REVIVAL

(c. 1946–1960)

In the beginning, Pentecostals were anti-society. Vinson Synan wrote, "There was hardly any institution, pleasure, business, vice, or social group that escaped the scorn and opposition of Pentecostal preachers"— doctors, lawyers, medicine, life insurance, liquor, Coca Cola, tobacco, dance halls, social events, theaters, movies, state fairs, carnivals, amusement parks, church bazaars, lodges, secret societies, political parties, labor unions, public swimming pools, sports, beauty parlors, jewelry, tattoos, makeup—you name it—they were against it.[1] Likewise, many early Pentecostals faced the scorn and opposition of outsiders who often described them as "repulsive," "fearfully deluded," "demon-worshipers," "Holy Rollers," "tongue-talkers," "snake handlers," "crude Negroes" and "poor white trash." To top it off, Benjamin Warfield's 1918 book *Counterfeit Miracles* claimed to offer final proof that any alleged miracle since the death of the last apostle was a complete fraud.

---

1   HPT 192.

Nevertheless, Pentecostals, like Baptists and Methodists before them, gradually and continually rose from their humble beginnings among the lower classes to a position of suspicious toleration before finally achieving full acceptance in society.

This process was greatly aided by the postwar economic boom. As the lower classes became upwardly mobile, Pentecostals simply climbed the social and economic ladder along with them in a shared prosperity. Thus, Synan wrote, "The social transformation of Pentecostal churches into middle-class institutions" did "not come by converting the middle class, but by entering it *en masse* from below."[2] But such acceptance never comes without a price. As nominal Pentecostals, neo-Pentecostals, and non-Pentecostals began joining Pentecostal churches, many brought with them their worldly and social ways, causing many churches to become "Pentecostal" in name only as their successful rise masked the internal danger of a diminished spiritual presence. Soon many of the old-timers began longing for the days when divine manifestations were regular occurrences while a new generation began hungering for a revival of its own, setting the stage for yet another great movement of God.

Gone were the days when depression era healing evangelists like F.F. Bosworth, Raymond T. Richey, and Charles S. Price could no longer afford large-scale campaigns. Postwar Pentecostals were affluent enough to support mass evangelism, tolerant enough to overlook doctrinal differences, and convicted enough to yearn for the supernatural. When Pentecostal trailblazers like Smith Wigglesworth and Aimee Semple McPherson passed away, the door was left wide

---

2   Ibid., 203.

open for a new breed of innovators that would revive the practice of praying for the sick "on a scale hitherto unknown."[3]

Before there was a healing revival, there were healing pioneers like Charles S. Price. After attending an Aimee Semple McPherson meeting in San Jose, Price, a former Methodist minister from Britain, was baptized in the Holy Spirit and began his own itinerant ministry in 1922 with reports of miraculous healings in Oregon and before capacity crowds in Canada. By 1944, Price was preaching throughout Europe, the Middle East, the U.S., and Canada. Here, Price stands in front of his revival tent in Lancaster, Pennsylvania (c. 1930). Source: Flower Pentecostal Heritage Center.

WILLIAM BRANHAM

William Marrion Branham (1909–1965) was a modern mystic born in a dirt floor log cabin in the hills of Kentucky. On the day of his birth, a light reportedly came whirling in through the window and circled around the bed where he lay. At age seven, after his family had moved to Jeffersonville, Indiana, Branham was sitting under an old poplar tree when he heard the sound of wind coming from atop the tree but nowhere else. Then he heard a voice say, "Never drink, smoke, or defile your body in any way, for I have a work for you to do when you get older."[4] Throughout Branham's youth, he reported having peculiar feelings "like someone standing near me, trying to say something to me, especially when I was alone."[5] In his early twenties, Branham was working at a local gas plant when an accidental chemical exposure led

---

3   John Thomas Nichol, *Pentecostalism* (New York: Harper and Row, 1966), 221: ATP 20.

4   Gordon Lindsay, *William Branham, A Man Sent from God* (Jefferson, Ind.: William Branham, 1950), 30: GG 315.

5   Ibid., 31 GG: 316.

to an illness and eventual appendectomy. After the surgery, Branham momentarily died and again heard a voice say, "I called you and you would not go." Branham said, "Lord, if that is you, let me go back again to earth and I will preach your Gospel from the housetops and street corners. I'll tell everyone about it!"[6] Immediately, he woke up in the hospital room. Still feeling the effects of the exposure, he told the Lord he would have to be completely healed if he were to preach. So after finding an Independent Baptist church that believed in healing, Branham went forward for prayer and was instantly healed.

At age twenty-four, Branham was ordained an Independent Baptist minister and started holding a tent revival that included a baptismal service in the Ohio River. As candidates came forward to be baptized, suddenly that same wind and light he had experienced as a youth came and hung over him. Indeed, many of the 4,000 who stood along the riverbank saw the light and ran in fear. That fall, he built Branham Tabernacle, where he would serve bi-vocationally as pastor and game warden over the next thirteen years, eventually marrying and having two children. During this time, Branham was driving down a road one day when he came across a Oneness Pentecostal camp meeting and decided to stop and check it out. The organizers, realizing Branham was a minister but not realizing he was Baptist, invited him to preach. Immediately, the power of God came on him so mightily that invitations began pouring in from all over the country inviting him to hold revival meetings. But his mother-in-law was adamant. She would not have her daughter among those "Holy Rollers." Branham conceded and cancelled all his meetings. Later he said that decision was the greatest mistake of his life because after

6   Ibid., 40–41: GG 317.

the great Ohio flood of 1937, he lost both his wife and baby daughter to illnesses that Branham believed to be God's direct punishment for not holding those revival meetings. Branham later remarried but only because his wife had wanted him to.

As William Branham baptized new converts in the Ohio River at age twenty-four, that same wind and light he had experienced as a youth came and hung over him, causing many to run in fear. The June 12, 1933, edition of *The Jeffersonville Evening News* reported, "Mysterious Star appears over minister while baptizing." Photo: Voice of God Recordings.

AN ANGELIC VISITATION

On May 7, 1946, Branham was under a maple tree, this time with a friend, when again he heard a rushing mighty wind coming down from the tree. Now determined to know the meaning of these occurrences, Branham went off to a secluded place to pray and read his Bible. At 11:00 that night, a light came in the room where he was staying and then spread across the floor. After this, he heard footsteps and saw what appeared to be a 200-pound man walking toward him dressed in a white robe. As Branham trembled with fear, the man said, "Fear not, I am sent from the presence of Almighty God to tell you that your peculiar life and your misunderstood ways have been to indicate that God has sent you to take a gift of divine healing to the peoples of the world. If you will be sincere, and can get the people to believe you, nothing shall stand before your prayer, not even cancer."[7]

---

7   Ibid., 75–79: GG 324–325.

The messenger went on to say that two signs would be given to him: The first would enable him to discern or detect diseases by a vibration in his left hand, thus building the people's faith. The second would be given in case people did not believe the first sign; he would be able to discern past thoughts and deeds in a person's life that only they themselves knew about. Then the angel made a profound statement, saying, "The thoughts of men speak louder in heaven than do their words on earth." Finally, the angel declared that Jesus was coming soon and if he would be faithful to his call, he would reach the world and shake the nations. The angel also said God was calling his people to come together in the unity of the Spirit with one heart and one accord. The visitation lasted about thirty minutes.[8]

THE HEALING REVIVAL BEGINS

That Sunday, Branham told his congregation about the angelic visitation and they believed him. That same day, he received a telegram from the pastor of a United Pentecostal Church in St. Louis asking him to come pray for his young daughter who had been tormented for months. The church had fasted and prayed and the best doctors in the city could not help her. When Branham arrived at their home, she was skin and bones, clawing at her face like an animal and screaming often. Branham wept and then prayed but to no avail. Branham then asked for a quiet place to seek the Lord and the pastor took him to the church. Three hours later, he returned and prayed but still nothing happened. Then he went out to the pastor's car and prayed some more; this time, he returned knowing exactly what to do. "Do you believe I am God's

---

8   Ibid.

servant?" Branham asked the family. "Yes!" They replied. "Then do as I tell you, doubting nothing." He instructed the father and grandfather to kneel at the foot of the bed and then instructed the mother to fetch a pan of clean water and a white cloth and to stroke her daughter's face, hands, and feet with the damp cloth. Then he prayed, "Father, as thou hast showed me these things so I have done according to the vision that thou hast given me. In the Name of Jesus Christ, Thy Son, I pronounce this child healed." Immediately, the evil spirit left her.[9] As news of the girl's deliverance spread, Branham returned to St. Louis in June and conducted a twelve-day tent revival with many miraculous healings. From there, he was invited to Jonesboro, Arkansas, where 25,000 attended. Many more were healed, including one woman who was raised from the dead inside an ambulance. From there, Branham went to Shreveport, Louisiana, where Jack Moore and Young Brown joined his management team before traveling on to San Antonio, Phoenix, and California.

THE VOICE OF HEALING

In 1947, Jack Moore wrote a momentous letter to his friend Gordon Lindsay (1906–1973) telling him about Branham's incredible ministry. Lindsay was well rooted and widely respected in the Pentecostal community, having been born in Zion City, Illinois, converted under Parham's ministry, and a protégé of John G. Lake prior to joining the Assemblies of God as an Ashland, Oregon, based pastor and evangelist. Moore wrote, "Brother Branham . . . has great success in praying for

---

9   Gordon Lindsay, *William Branham, A Man Sent from God*, 56: *The Midnight Cry: www.williambranhamstorehouse.com/a%20man%20sent%20from%20god.pdf* (Accessed 12 July 2015).

the sick on such a scale as I have never seen before. . . . We haven't found buildings large enough to take care of the crowds."[10] Moore then invited Lindsay to their Sacramento revival. As Lindsay observed, he was immediately convinced an unprecedented movement of God was underway and urged Branham to mobilize his ministry beyond Oneness circles. Branham, recognizing Lindsay as part of the vision the angel had given him, agreed, and Lindsay resigned his position with the Assemblies of God to become Branham's manager. Lindsay immediately gave "voice" to the Branham team as master organizer, publicist, and publisher of the *Voice of Healing* magazine, which both he and Moore edited.

As Branham held a series of meetings in Portland, Oregon, in 1947, Pentecostal missionaries Tommy Lee (T.L.) (1923–2013) and Daisy (1924–1995) Osborn, who had just returned from India feeling dejected because they could not produce any "evidence" for the Indian people that Jesus was the Son of God, saw Branham pray for a deaf-mute girl. "Thou deaf and dumb spirit, I adjure thee in Jesus' Name, leave the child!" Branham exclaimed. Then he snapped his fingers and the girl spoke perfectly. As T.L. watched, he heard what sounded like a thousand voices speaking to him at once saying, "You can do that."[11] The following spring with the help of Gordon Lindsay, the Osborns launched their own healing evangelism campaigns, reaching tens of thousands across the U.S. and Canada before traveling overseas and reaching millions through their healing evangelism campaigns,

---

10   Gordon Lindsay, "The Story of the Great Restoration Revival, Installment II," *World-Wide Revival* (April 1958), 17: ATP 31.

11   T.L. Osborn, "My Life Story and Call to the Healing Ministry, Part II," *The Voice of Healing* (October 1949), 9: ATP 64.

films, publications, and sponsorship of indigenous missionaries. They planted more than 150,000 new churches worldwide.[12]

T.L. and Daisy Osborn teaching faith in one of their first tent crusades in Pennsylvania standing amid crutches, canes, braces, etc., discarded by those miraculously healed. The Osborns' Big Tent Revivals in the U.S. and Canada often numbered over 10,000, while their Latin American, Asian, and African crusades in the 1950s swelled at times to over 100,000. Source: Osborn Ministries International.

Then in Vancouver, British Columbia, Branham added Ern Baxter, another Pentecostal minister to his team. In describing their Northwest tour, Lindsay wrote, "In fourteen days of services, in four cities . . . 70,000 people attended." Despite the fact that nearly all were Pentecostals, Lindsay was amazed that "ninety percent . . . had never previously witnessed a single miracle."[13]

By 1948, the Branham team was holding a series of meetings in Miami, Pensacola, and Kansas City when a young minister named Oral Roberts paid them a visit before they headed back to the west coast. Then just as Branham was beginning to gain worldwide attention, he suddenly had a nervous breakdown and announced his retirement! The long, grueling nights of ministering to the sick had taken their toll. Branham accused Lindsay of overextending him and told Moore and Lindsay they would have to run the *Voice of Healing* without him. Lindsay was shocked. Though he would again work with Branham in

---

12   Tony Cauchi, "Thomas Lee Osborn February 23, 1923-February 14, 2013," (December 2011) *Revival Library: www.voiceofhealing.info/05otherministries/osborn.html* (Accessed 29 September 2014).

13   Lindsay, "Great Restoration Revival," 17: ATP 32.

the future, their relationship would never be the same. To keep the *Voice of Healing* afloat, Lindsay had no choice but to begin including other healing ministers.

Left to right: Young Brown, Jack Moore, William Branham, Oral Roberts, and Gordon Lindsay in Kansas City. Source: Voice of God Recordings.

THE LATTER RAIN MOVEMENT

Meanwhile, inspired by Branham's operating in the gifts of the Spirit at his Vancouver meetings and equally disturbed by the recent lack of spiritual gifts in Pentecostal churches, the faculty of Sharon Orphanage and Schools in North Battleford, Saskatchewan, began directing their students to study, fast, and pray for the gifts of the Spirit. Sharon was part of Global Missions, an independent outreach that had recently had a falling out with the Assemblies of God. Faculty member Ern Hawtin described what happened next on February 12, 1948: "Some students were under the power of God on the floor, others were kneeling in adoration and worship before the Lord. The anointing deepened until the awe of God was upon everyone. The Lord spoke to one of the brethren. 'Go and lay hands upon a certain student and pray for him.' While he was in doubt and contemplation one of the sisters who had been under the power of God went to the brother saying the same words, and naming the identical student he was to pray for. He went in obedience and a revelation was given concerning the student's life and future ministry. After this a long prophecy was given with minute details concerning the great things God was about to do. The pattern for the revival and many details concerning it were given."[14] The next day, students continued searching the Scriptures for confirmation of these events. Then on February 14, Hawtin recorded, "It seemed that all heaven broke loose upon our souls, and heaven came down to greet us. Soon a visible manifestation of gifts was received when candidates were prayed over, and many as a result were healed, as gifts of healing were received."[15]

It was eventually dubbed the "New Order of the Latter Rain," a term previously used by various Holiness and Pentecostal groups, including David Wesley Myland in his 1910 book *The Latter Rain Covenant and Pentecostal Power*—an early apologetic work on the Pentecostal revival.[16] Though Myland was a Christian and Missionary Alliance minister at the time, he later joined the Pentecostal movement when his denomination took a stand against speaking in tongues. The book paralleled the natural seasonal rain cycles in Israel mentioned in Scripture to the church age. Accordingly, the day of Pentecost was believed to be the "early rain" followed by nearly two thousand years of relative drought and culminating in the "latter rain" believed to be the Pentecostal revival. Unfortunately, all latter rain scriptures seem to point to the return of Christ, not to any single event in the church age. The theory also displays an ignorant disregard for nearly two millennia of the Spirit's work in the church by discounting every other

---

14   Richard Riss, "The New Order of the Latter Rain, A Look at the Revival Movement on Its 40th Anniversary," *Assemblies of God Heritage* (Fall 1987), 15-17: CC 172–173.

15   Ibid.

16   Ibid.

major revival before or since. But the theory was re-popularized in 1948 after the United Nations recognized Israel as a state, sparking a renewed interest in prophecy and the imminent return of Christ.

Inspired by William Branham's Vancouver meetings, the faculty of Sharon Orphanage and Schools in North Battleford, Saskatchewan, directed their students to study, fast, and pray for the gifts of the Spirit, launching yet another global "Latter Rain" movement. Source: Sharon Children's Homes and Schools.

A MOVEMENT REJECTED

As news of the "Latter Rain" revival spread, people from many parts of the world came to the North Battleford camp meetings. Soon others joined the movement, including Myrtle D. Beall's Assemblies of God church in Detroit, Ivan Spencer's Elim Bible Institute in Lima, New York, Lewi Pethrus's church in Sweden, and many others. Even Stanley Frodsham, editor of the *Pentecostal Evangel* and a prominent leader within the Assemblies of God, visited Beall's church in Detroit and wrote, "I was moved deeply by scenes of people under great conviction of sin, making confession and finding peace." He also joined the movement.[17] The revival bore many similarities to Azusa Street—widespread brokenness and repentance, tongues, prophecy, holy laughter, healings, late night meetings, heavenly singing, the laying on of hands, the operation of spiritual gifts—and both had been labeled "Latter Rain" movements. But by 1949, officials within the

---

17   W.W. Menzies, *Annointed to Serve: The Story of the Assemblies of God* (Springfield: Gospel, 1971), 232; R.M. Riss, "Latter Rain Movement": DPCM 831.

Assemblies of God and Pentecostal Holiness Church—who owed their very existence to the former—rejected the latter. Now the movement had one more thing in common with Azusa Street—both had been severely reprimanded by the organizations that had founded them. The event was reminiscent of when the Holiness movement rejected the Pentecostals, the Methodists rejected the Holiness movement, the Church of England rejected the Methodists, the Catholic Church rejected the Montanists, and so on. Evidently some complained that their faith had been destroyed after receiving prophecies or having hands laid on them by someone who was inexperienced or who had mixed motives.

Among the major points of contention were the acceptance of present-day apostles and prophets and the bestowing of spiritual gifts through the laying on of hands and prophecy. But behind the scenes, concern for a lack of any centralized leadership also played a major role. As a result, many experienced ministers were dropped from denominational rolls, including Stanley Frodsham, who was forced to resign after twenty-eight years as editor of the *Pentecostal Evangel*. Frodsham was one of the few who had visited both the Azusa and the Latter Rain revivals and attested to their legitimacy. He later commented that a strong atmosphere of the presence of the Lord had been evident at both and stated that it was inappropriate to associate "this new revival which God is so graciously sending, where so many souls are being saved, where so many lives are being transformed, where God is so graciously restoring the gifts of the Spirit, with the fanatical movements of the past forty years."[18] Pentecostal missionary

---

18 Stanley Frodsham, letter to his daughter, Faith Campbell (May 7, 1949); R.M. Riss, "Latter Rain Movement": DPCM 832.

and evangelist Lester Sumrall, who also visited the Detroit Assembly on several occasions, wrote, "They were blessed, happy, rejoicing and dancing. . . . I was grieved because of the way the Holy Spirit was quenched in that move. . . . It was a little fanatical in some places, but it could have been corrected by the leaders loving people and teaching them rather than scolding and beating them down. . . . If the Full Gospel denominations had accepted the Latter Rain movement, they would have enlisted hundreds of thousands of new members because it was the breath of God."[19] Despite their rejection, many of the independent groups continued and eventually became instrumental in spawning yet another great movement of God—the charismatic movement.

GRANVILLE ORAL ROBERTS

Granville Oral Roberts (1918–2009) was born in a two-room shack in the tiny town of Beebe, Oklahoma, the fifth and last child of Ellis Roberts—a Pentecostal Holiness minister, and Claudius Roberts—a Cherokee Indian. A few months before he was born, Claudius "felt the Spirit of the Lord hovering near" and sensed the child she was carrying "was a special child that would have God's anointing upon him."[20] Knowing that he would one day preach the gospel, they named him Oral, which means "spoken word." But growing up, it seemed like a cruel joke because he could not even say his own name without stuttering. He was often taunted by other children, but his mother would pull him up on her lap and remind him, "Oral . . . I gave you to God when you were a baby. You're God's property. . . . Someday he's

---

19 Sumrall, *Pioneers of Faith*, 188.
20 David Edwin Harrell, *Oral Roberts: An American Life* (Bloomington: Indiana University, 1985), 25.

going to heal your tongue, and you will talk. Son, you will preach the gospel."[21] Though born in abject poverty and raised during the Great Depression, Oral had a rich Pentecostal heritage. Despite his speech impediment, he grew up confident, often securing lead roles in school plays and selling more newspapers than all the other kids. His father also encouraged him: "Son, when you are grown you will conduct revivals in the largest auditoriums in the nation and men will go in front of you to make the arrangements and you will go and minister to the people. You will have the greatest revivals of your time."[22] But as a teenager, Oral was not interested in preaching and soon rebelled against his strict upbringing. He hated being called a "Holy Roller," hated being a preacher's kid, but most of all hated being poor. Oral was tall, athletic, and had big dreams of becoming a sports star while pursuing a career in law and politics and maybe even becoming Oklahoma's governor one day.

Granville Oral Roberts (left) with his brother. Source: Oral Roberts Ministries.

Oral's big break came at fifteen when a former junior high teacher invited him to join the high school basketball team he was coaching some fifty miles away in Atoka, Oklahoma. Though his parents begged him not to leave, saying, "You will never be able to go beyond

21 Ibid., 28.
22 Ibid., 29.

our prayers," Oral was defiant.[23] In Atoka, Oral lived "the dream." He was privileged to stay at the home of a local judge, read law books, and studied for school while holding down three part-time jobs, playing basketball, and still finding time for his friends. At seventeen, his health began deteriorating. Then at "the final game of the southern Oklahoma basketball tournament," while "dribbling toward the basket to make the jump-shot that would win the game," Oral collapsed on the floor with blood running from his mouth. The coach drove him home where the doctor pronounced that he was in the final stages of tuberculosis with three to four months to live.

HEALED OF TUBERCULOSIS

For months, Oral lay in bed wasting away. People prayed, doctors treated, but nothing changed. Oral felt his life was over before it began. But when his father knelt at the foot of his bed praying with tears streaming down his cheeks, suddenly he felt a warmth come into his body and a bright light shown as he saw the face of Jesus. He cried, "Save me, Jesus. Save me!"[24] Later his sister Jewel said to him, "Oral, God is going to heal you." Oral said those seven words changed his life forever. Then one evening, his oldest brother Elmer showed up with news of a Brother George Moncey, a healing evangelist, in nearby Ada. Elmer, who was not even a Christian, said, "I believe if I take him there the Lord will heal him."[25] So he borrowed his neighbor's Model

23 Ibid., 30.
24 A Special Miracles Supplement: "Celebrating the Life of Oral Roberts: A Man Who Obeyed God," 3: *Oral Roberts Evangelistic Association: www.oralroberts.com/wordpress/wp-content/uploads/DOC_BIN/miracles_mag/2010/pdf/ORinsertWeb.pdf* (Accessed 29 September 2014).
25 Harrell, *Oral Roberts*, 4.

T, paid his last thirty-five cents for gas, and came by to pick up Oral. Elmer had to help dress and carry his brother on his mattress, laying him across the backseat of the car. Then they loaded up Mama and Papa and drove to the tent meeting.

On the way, Oral was reminded of what his sister had said when suddenly he heard a voice say, "Son, I'm going to heal you. And you are going to take my healing power to your generation." Oral did not know what to make of it. The voice continued, "You are to build me a university. Build it on my authority and on the Holy Spirit." Elmer even brought a rocking chair and some pillows for Oral to sit on at the meeting. After Bro. Moncey preached and laid hands on everyone in the healing line, he approached Oral, who was sitting in the rocking chair. Having already heard about Oral's case, Bro. Moncey began sharing how God had healed another young man of tuberculosis the night before and then asked Oral to stand to his feet. His parents helped him up. The evangelist said, "You foul tormenting disease, I command you in the name of Jesus Christ of Nazareth, come out of this boy. Loose him and let him go free!"[26] Oral felt electricity going through his body, and instantly he could breathe freely with no coughing or blood! Then Bro. Moncey held the microphone up to Oral and said, "Son, tell the people what the Lord has done for you."[27] Oral jumped up on the platform and started shouting, "I'm healed! I'm healed!" And then he ran back and forth praising and testifying without stuttering— apparently God had healed him of that too!

---

26 Ibid., 7.
27 Ibid.

"GOD IS A GOOD GOD"

Soon Ellis and Oral went on the road preaching as a father-and-son team. Still weakened by his condition, however, Oral preached his first sermon from a rocking chair. Oral was also ordained during this time and received the baptism in the Holy Spirit at an Eastern Oklahoma camp meeting (though he later admitted he did not understand it at the time). Oral played guitar in the youth band at the camp meeting and sat next to another preacher's kid—a young female guitarist named Evelyn Lutman. Evelyn wrote in her diary, "I sat by my future husband tonight."[28] Two years and many letters later, Oral drove to Texas with his mother in tow to propose to the young schoolteacher, and Oral and Evelyn Roberts were married on Christmas Day, 1938.

Oral would spend the next eight years pastoring, studying, seeking the Lord, and preaching in small Pentecostal Holiness churches. Then one day while reading his Bible, his eyes fell on 3 John 2: "Beloved, I wish above all things that thou mayest prosper and be in health, even as thy soul prospereth." Oral said to Evelyn, "If this verse is right, then I've been preaching wrong. God is a *good* God . . . and I must preach that to the people." Then God revealed another important truth to Oral about how a farmer plants seeds and expects a harvest and how people could do the same with God's Word. He called it the "seed-faith" principle. And finally, after studying the four gospels and the Book of Acts for thirty days, Oral saw the foundation for his ministry— he was to do the same as Jesus had done . . . come against sin, demons, disease, and fear.

---

28   Ibid., 39.

In 1947, Oral launched his own independent evangelistic organization, his own magazine, conducted his first revival, preached his first healing sermon and reported his first major healing after removing the braces from a young polio victim. Source: Oral Roberts Ministries.

ORAL'S HEALING MINISTRY

In 1947, Oral rented an auditorium in Enid, Oklahoma, inviting people to an interdenominational service to witness the healing power of God. Twelve hundred attended as Oral preached his first healing sermon: *If You Need Healing, Do These Things.* It contained six simple steps: 1) know that it's God's will to heal you, 2) remember that healing begins within, 3) use a point of contact to release your faith, 4) turn your faith loose—now! 5) close the case for victory, and 6) join yourself to companions of faith. The front of the auditorium was flooded for prayer. Many testified of being instantly healed, including one woman who waved her formerly crippled arm around, shouting, "God has healed me!" Oral resigned his pastorate, moved to Tulsa, and soon reported his first notable healing in Muskogee, Oklahoma, when a young polio victim walked without braces for the very first time. Before long, Oral was publishing his own *Healing Waters* magazine with 10,000 subscribers, selling books, and preaching his *Healing Waters Radio Log* on radio.

In 1948, Oral purchased his first "tent cathedral," assembled a revival team, and established Healing Waters, Inc. complete with its own office. Gordon Lindsay announced in the *Voice of Healing* that year, "Brother Roberts has provided himself with perhaps the greatest and most complete equipment ever used by an American evangelist in gospel work," and William Branham testified that Oral's "commanding power over demons, over disease and over sin was the most amazing thing he had ever seen in the work of God."[29] Similar to Branham, Oral felt a manifestation of God's presence in his right hand that enabled him to detect the presence, names, and number of demons and served as a "point of contact" between the believer and God's power.

Oral Roberts' tent was as large as a circus tent but devoted to great revivals and healing campaigns. Thousands were attracted to these meetings and thousands more left both saved and healed. Source: Oral Roberts Ministries.

ORAL'S TELEVISION MINISTRY

In 1949, pioneer Pentecostal television evangelist Rex Humbard began encouraging Oral to film his healing crusades on television for all America to see. However, since television was only in its infancy and Oral was not willing to restrict himself to just healing, he announced in Miami in 1950 that the Lord had instructed him to "emphasize the power and presence of the Holy Ghost and tell the people to have an expectation for Jesus to come during 1950!"[30] Later, of course, he had

---

29 "Visit to Great Roberts Tent Meet at Granite City, Ill.," *The Voice of Healing*, (Sept. 1948), 7: ATP 44; "Branham Visits Roberts Campaign," *The Voice of Healing* (April 1949), 16: ATP 49.

30 G.H. Montgomery, "God's Seven Messages to Oral Roberts," *Abundant Life* (April 1958), 14–15, 25–27: ATP 50.

to retract that statement, declaring simply that people should have an expectation of Jesus' return. By 1953, Oral's tent, which seated 12,500, had become the largest in the world, and his radio network had expanded to over 300 stations as evangelism became the dominant theme. Oral announced a campaign that year to win a million souls within three years. When that goal had been met, he announced another campaign in 1956 to convert 10 million within a decade. But perhaps Oral's greatest contribution to Pentecostalism came in 1955 when he initiated his weekly national television program, bringing his healing crusades into the homes of millions of Americans, most of whom had never seen a healing meeting. Pentecostalism was now reaching its widest audience in history.

A pivotal moment in history occurred when Oral Roberts introduced the motion picture camera into his massive "tent cathedral." Through the medium of television, for the first time millions of Americans could experience a Pentecostal healing revival. Source: Oral Roberts Ministries.

But along with television came a huge budget. Though Oral had been mailing anointed handkerchiefs to the sick since 1948 and courting the business community since 1949, by 1954, he began resorting to more questionable practices such as guaranteeing his followers' gifts would be returned to them "seven-fold" within a year. One rival minister accused Oral of being "a racketeer and a fraud."[31] But Oral always came clean with his audiences, vowing "to touch

---

31   Oral Roberts, "To Touch Neither the Gold Nor the Glory" *Healing Waters* (October 1951), 4–5; ATP 47.

neither the gold nor the glory," and remained more ethical than most.[32] Nevertheless, by early 1958, a shortage of funds threatened to shut down his ministry, and as more and more healing revivalists entered the field whose practices were increasingly unethical, the Pentecostal denominations grew increasingly cold toward the revivalists. Now in danger of losing his base, Oral shut down the old Healing Waters, Inc., with its ties to the Pentecostal churches and immediately reorganized into the new Oral Roberts Evangelistic Association with a much broader ecumenical reach renaming his publication *Abundant Life* and adding a 24-hour prayer line.

BRANHAM RETURNS

As suddenly as Branham had retired in 1948, six months later he was back in the field. In January 1950, accompanied by Moore, Lindsay, Baxter, and now F.F. Bosworth, who had recently come out of retirement to mentor the young revivalists, Branham held a series of meetings in Houston's Coliseum with some 8,000 in attendance. Baxter and Bosworth preached mornings and afternoons. As Baxter preached evangelistic meetings, Bosworth taught how to receive and retain healing in preparation for the evening services. Bosworth's presence was huge because it linked the healing revival to the early Pentecostal movement. During the meetings, Bosworth even held a highly publicized debate with a local Baptist pastor on divine healing. Branham hired two professional photographers to take pictures of the meetings, but strangely, every negative failed to develop—except one depicting Branham with a halo of light over his head. Lindsay

---

32 Oral Roberts, "An Open Letter to Magazine and Newspaper Editors," *Abundant Life* (February 1957), 16–17, 28–29: ATP 47–48.

had the photo professionally examined, and the report came back that the photo had not been "retouched nor was it a composite or double exposed negative."[33] Since then, the photo has become legendary in the postwar healing revival. A copy may be found in the Library of Congress photograph collection.

The famous 1953 photo of William Branham preaching in Houston with the mysterious "halo" of light over his head—caught on camera at last. Source: Voice of God Recordings.

Later that year Branham began traveling overseas. More than 7,000 people filled the largest auditorium in Finland with hundreds and sometimes thousands more standing outside. Branham's miracles spoke for themselves and remain unsurpassed. Bosworth wrote, "When the gift is operating, Brother Branham is the most sensitive person to the presence and working of the Holy Spirit and to spiritual realities of any person I have ever known."[34] But, he qualified, Branham prays for nobody "until God anoints him for the operation of the gift, and until he is conscious of the presence of the Angel with him on the platform. Without this consciousness, he seems to be perfectly helpless."[35] In time, as Branham often reached the limits of his physical strength, he laid hands on fewer people and relied more on the word of knowledge. Swiss Pentecostal theologian and Branham interpreter

33 *Copy of Report and Opinion* by George J. Lacy: "William M. Branham," *Wikipedia: en.wikipedia.org/wiki/William_M._Branham* (Accessed 18 March 2013).

34 "Looking at the Unseen," *The Voice of Healing* (January 1950), 4: ATP 36–37.

35 "Gifts of Healing Plus," *The Voice of Healing* (March 1950), 10: ATP 37.

W.J. Hollenweger wrote, "I am not aware of any case in which he was mistaken in the often detailed statements he made."[36] British Assemblies of God minister and a noted critic of so-called "faith healers," Donald Gee, said Branham was "remarkably accurate" and that it was "impossible to deny something of the Spirit of God in his revelations."[37]

BRANHAM'S FINAL YEARS

By 1950, the Voice of Healing was no longer a magazine but a loose-knit fellowship of healing revivalists who had joined the movement after the early successes of Branham and Roberts. Increasingly, however, Lindsay's time had been taken up with building the young organization, leaving little time for Branham. Conversely, Branham being the intensely spiritual man that he was had little interest in the business side of ministry, rarely giving Lindsay the credit he deserved. Consequently, Lindsay and Branham permanently parted ways, and less capable and less scrupulous managers were soon brought in to replace Lindsay.

F.F. Bosworth (left) came out of retirement in 1947 to help Bro. Branham (right) by traveling and teaching for him in the day sessions so Bro. Branham could be rested for the evening sessions. But after Bosworth passed away in 1958, Branham quit healing and evangelizing and resorted to teaching and prophecy instead. Source: Voice of God Recordings.

By 1955, Branham was faced with mounting financial debt and a tax lawsuit that would haunt him the rest of his life. Then as interest in the

---

36 W.J. Hollenweger, *The Pentecostals*, (Minneapolis: Augsburg, 1972), 354: ATP 38.
37 Donald Gee, *Wind and Flame* (Croydon, England: Heath, 1967), 242: ATP 38.

healing revival began to wane in the late 1950s, unlike Roberts, Branham struggled to reinvent himself, choosing to teach Bible doctrine instead and creating much havoc in the body of Christ. Branham taught strange doctrines on everything ranging from the Trinity to baptism, women, and marriage and divorce to eschatology, which soon led to a cult-like following of "Message Believers" who adopted a belief system known as "Branhamism" based on his bizarre teachings. Before long, Branham's followers were declaring him "Elijah" or the great apostle and prophet of the final church age. By 1964, two prophetic warnings had been issued to Branham—one by Kenneth Hagin, a young prophetic voice within the Voice of Healing, and a second by Anna Schrader, a prophetess. Both were delivered through Gordon Lindsay and warned Branham to stop teaching or face premature death.

Hagin's prophecy declared, "At the end of '65, he who now stands in the forefront of the healing ministry as a prophet will be taken out of the way. He'll make a false step and Satan shall destroy his life, but his spirit will be saved, and his works will follow him. Ere '66 shall come, he shall be gone."[38] Schrader's prophecy was even more direct: "Go warn Brother . . . he's going to die. He's walking in the way of Dowie."[39] Lindsay later wrote, "I begged him not to teach. I said, 'You don't know the Bible, and you're confusing folks. Leave the Bible teaching to the teachers. Just go ahead and preach and exercise the word of knowledge and gifts of healings as the Spirit wills, and be a blessing to the Body of Christ.'" Branham replied, "I know I'm not a teacher, but I want to teach. And I'm going to teach!"[40] On December

---

38 Kenneth E. Hagin, *He Gave Gifts Unto Men*, (Tulsa: Kenneth Hagin Ministries, 1999), 164–170.

39 Ibid.

40 Ibid.

18, 1965, Branham was driving his family through Texas on their way home for the Christmas holidays when a drunk driver swerved out of his lane and struck Branham's vehicle head-on. Branham went through the windshield and back again. Mrs. Branham had no pulse. Bloodied and full of broken bones, Branham realized she was dead. He told his son, "Just lay my hand on her."[41] Instantly, she revived. Branham then went into a coma for six days and died on December 24 at age fifty-six.

As visionary of the healing revival, Branham led the second wave of Pentecost that swept the nation after World War II. The Full Gospel Businessmen's *Voice* wrote in February 1961, "In Bible Days, there were men of God who were Prophets and Seers. But in all the Sacred Records, none of these had a greater ministry than that of William Branham."[42]

THE HEALING REVIVALISTS

By 1949, the *Voice of Healing* was being sent out monthly to some 30,000 subscribers. Gordon Lindsay held the first convention of healing revivalists in Dallas, Texas, that same year. The following year, about a thousand attended the Kansas City convention. Noticeably absent were Roberts and Branham. Lindsay made it clear from the outset: the group would not become a denomination, nor would it ever compete with existing Pentecostal denominations. Actually, the movement contributed greatly to the growth of the Pentecostal denominations both at home and abroad in the 1950s and 1960s. Lindsay believed the

---

41   Roberts Liardon interview with Billy Paul Branham: GG 342.
42   "Concerning Photograph on Front Cover" *Voice* (February, 1961), 3: ATP 161.

healing meetings had been raised up by God to bring about a worldwide revival. By 1952, Lindsay had purchased a new headquarters building in Dallas and laid down some basic rules of admission for the young fellowship: 1) They had to have a mature healing ministry, 2) abide by the rules, 3) have character that was above reproach, 4) practice the values of the organization, 5) labor for unity, 6) help increase the magazine's circulation, and 7) be an evangelist, not a pastor. During its peak between 1950 and 1956, over a hundred evangelists joined the Voice of Healing, but despite Lindsay's best efforts, he was "like the director of an unruly orchestra."[43] Though many of the revivalists owed their very success to Lindsay, they soon began to resent his control and sought independence, which only led to more competition. By 1958, most of the evangelists were encouraging Lindsay to retire. Under pressure, Lindsay changed the publication's name to *World-Wide Revival* with a new emphasis on foreign missions and later to *Christ for the Nations*. In 1970, Lindsay cofounded with his wife, Freda, Christ for the Nations Institute in Dallas to train missionaries to the nations.

But for many middle-class Americans, the healing revival was simply outside the boundaries of respectable religion—the raggedy image of shoddy Pentecostal buildings, holy roller services, long, ecstatic meetings run by seemingly money-hungry "racketeers" and practitioners of "religious quackery" wore on the American conscience. Soon the mortality rate among these independent ministers was such that only the boldest, brightest, and best remained. Among them were William Branham, Oral Roberts, Jack Coe, A.A. Allen, W.V. Grant, T.L. Osborn, Tommy Hicks, William Freeman, Franklin Hall, David Nunn, Kenneth Hagin, and Morris Cerullo. Perhaps the single

43 ATP 57.

most important event of the entire revival was Tommy Hicks' 1954 Argentine Crusade, which reportedly drew 3 million in two months and as many as 300,000 to a single service.[44]

JACK COE

Of all the healing revivalists, no one challenged Oral's leadership in the movement more and no one was bolder than Jack Coe (1918–1956).[45] Jack's father had been a heavy drinker and gambler who literally gambled them out of house and home. Jack's mother, unable to care for seven children alone, left Jack and his brother on the steps of an orphanage. Like his father, Jack grew up to be a heavy drinker until one night he heard a voice say, "This is your last chance." Startled, Jack immediately started attending church. Making his way into Pentecostal circles, Jack became just as zealous for God as he had been about drinking. In the army, he was placed in a psychiatric ward simply because they didn't know what else to do with him. In 1944, Jack contracted malaria and nearly died, but again, the voice spoke: "I've called you to preach the Gospel. Go out and preach it!" Suddenly, he felt a warm sensation going through his body and he was instantly healed.

Jack Coe (c. 1951). Oral Roberts, speaking on behalf of all the healing revivalists, once said of Coe, "He was the boldest evangelist of us all. He was a man of reckless faith in God." Source: Flower Pentecostal Heritage Center.

44   Tony Cauchi, "Tommy Hicks 1909–1973," (January 2012) *Revival Library: www.voiceofhealing.info/05otherministries/hicks.html* (Accessed 29 September 2014).

45   David Harrell interview with Juanita Coe: ATP 59.

By 1947, before beginning his own itinerant ministry, Coe had become an ordained Assemblies of God minister and co-editor of the *Voice of Healing* and had purchased his own tent. Besides being the consummate "faith healer," Coe had a dynamic stage presence and personality. Coe also became the first healing revivalist to attract a large number of African Americans to his meetings. Many appreciated his bold, feisty, tell-it-like-it-is style of preaching combined with his daring ways of challenging people to walk by faith—hitting, slapping, jerking, and even picking people up out of their· wheelchairs. In one Alabama meeting, sixty-three reportedly rose up at once and walked out of their wheelchairs.[46] Coe also began his *Herald of Healing* publication in 1950, eventually reaching over 250,000 subscribers. In 1951, mirroring his upbringing, he built The Herald of Healing Children's Home.

Besides being bold, Coe was extremely competitive, never walked away from a fight, and even created a few enemies of his own. In 1951, he attended an Oral Roberts meeting just so he could measure his tent, order one slightly larger, and then rub it in—publicly! At one of Coe's tent meetings in Little Rock, the governor estimated an attendance of over 20,000.

It was larger than Oral's and larger than the Ringling Brothers'. Jack Coe claimed his 22,500-seat gospel tent was the "largest in the world." Source: Jack Coe International Ministries.

46   Ibid.

Then in 1952, Coe announced he was starting his own independent congregation in Dallas. Tired of the criticisms coming from his own denomination against his healing ministry, Coe wrote an audacious letter to denominational headquarters suggesting they replace their current leadership with men who actually believed in the miraculous power of God. Coe was expelled in 1953 but not without a fight. At one point, he considered starting his own rival denomination called the Fundamental Assemblies of God but later decided his best reprisal would be to complete construction of the Dallas Revival Center. Opening day looked like a "Who's Who" in the Voice of Healing, and within two years, it was one of the largest churches in the area. Coe also opened a faith home where the sick could come and be taught the Word of God until they received their healing. Then in 1954, Coe held a month-long tent revival in Pittsburgh—his largest yet. Some 30,000 were reportedly saved, and 75 percent of those who came on "stretcher night" reportedly rose up and walked. To top it all off, Coe announced the beginning of a new television network.

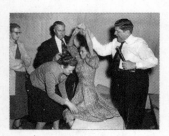

Jack Coe helping a woman rise from her bed of affliction at the Dallas Revival Center. Kenneth Hagin, a prophetic voice within the Voice of Healing, said, "Jack Coe carried the strongest healing anointing of anyone in my lifetime." Source: Jack Coe International Ministries.

Coe's schedule and itinerary were as bold and reckless as his faith. His eating habits were also irregular and unhealthy, causing him to become overweight. In 1956, Coe was preaching in Miami, Florida—a city notorious for persecuting "faith healers"—when he was arrested for practicing medicine without a license. Though later released on bond, Coe decided to stay and fight, inviting all his evangelist friends to come to Miami and support him. Many, including Gordon Lindsay and Raymond T. Richey, came and testified on his behalf. After an intense two-day trial, the judge dismissed the case stating that he could not "condemn the defendant or anyone who in good faith advocates and practices Divine Healing"—a great victory for divine healing had been won![47] However, later that year when Coe was preaching in Hot Springs, Arkansas, he suddenly became critically ill, was diagnosed with polio, and three weeks later, he was dead at age thirty-eight. According to family members, Coe reportedly knew about his death a full year before it happened, but this only drove him to work harder and push himself even more to spread the gospel and heal the sick.

A.A. ALLEN

With Coe's passing in 1956, the one evangelist who emerged as the new leader—even building his ministry at a time when most were folding up their tents and going home—was Asa Allen (1910–1970). Allen's father had also been a heavy drinker who made his own home brew, and Allen's mother had lived with a number of men while he was growing up. Allen ran away from home twice and by age twenty-one was a nervous wreck. He couldn't even hold a cigarette in his hand without shaking. He and his mother built their own bootleg operation in Missouri and turned it into a dance hall on Saturday nights. But one night as Allen passed by an old country Methodist Church, he heard loud singing, clapping, and dancing and decided to check it out. Allen

---

47   Jack Coe, *Tried ... But Freed!* (Dallas: Herald of Healing, 1956), 44, 126: ATP 62.

was soon saved and later filled with the Holy Ghost at a Pentecostal camp meeting. In 1936, while in Colorado, he met and married, Lexie, and became an ordained Assemblies of God minister. After pastoring in Colorado for a while, Allen moved back to Missouri, where he traveled as an evangelist for about four years before being offered a large pastorate in Corpus Christi, Texas.

A.A. Allen was one of the most important evangelists to emerge during the early days of the healing revival and one of only a handful to have a substantial following well past the end of the revival—even until his death in 1970. Source: Flower Pentecostal Heritage Center.

In 1949, Allen attended an Oral Roberts meeting in Dallas when he decided that pastoring was not for him and went permanently on the road. From Oakland, California, in 1950, Allen reported his first campaign to the *Voice of Healing*: "Many say this is the greatest revival in the history of Oakland. . . . Night after night, the waves of Divine Glory so sweep over the congregation that many testify of being healed while sitting in their seats."[48] In 1951, he purchased the A.A. Allen Revival Tent. In 1953, he began the *Allen Revival Hour* radio broadcast, which ran on numerous stations across America, Mexico, and Cuba. And in 1954, he published *Miracle Magazine* with an eventual circulation of 340,000.

In 1955, Allen was arrested in Knoxville, Tennessee—another city notorious for persecuting "faith healers"—on suspicion of drunk

---

48   Lexie E. Allen, *God's Man of Faith and Power: The Life Story of A.A. Allen* (Hereford, Ariz.: A.A. Allen, 1954), 165: GG 397.

driving. Though nothing was ever proven, R.W. Shambach, who had just joined the Allen team, said he was in the car with Allen when he was arrested and Allen was not drunk.[49] Don Stewart, another Allen associate, however, claimed that Allen occasionally drank after Knoxville and that his staff often covered for him.[50] Allen believed it was all part of a conspiracy to ruin his ministry as he was soon forced to resign from both the Assemblies of God and the Voice of Healing. Undaunted, Allen organized his own independent ministry called Miracle Revival Fellowship for the purpose of licensing ministers and supporting overseas missions. Then in 1958, he announced the development of a 1,250-acre tract of land near Tombstone, Arizona, which he called "Miracle Valley." By the 1960s, the property had doubled in size and become a thriving community complete with tent revivals, its own airfield, a 4,000-seat domed church, a Bible college, dormitories, a large warehouse, and administrative buildings that housed Allen's overseas operations, radio programs, publications, and national television ministry.

Despite the Knoxville incident, Allen remained extremely popular throughout the 1950s and 1960s mostly because of the supernatural signs, wonders, and miracles that remained at the forefront of his meetings. Moreover, Allen himself represented the last of a dying breed of "old-time religion" preachers. Though people from all backgrounds attended Allen's meetings, he was particularly popular among African Americans and the poor, often preaching against what

---

49   Roberts Liardon interview with R.W. Shambach (March, 1996): GG 399–400.
50   Don Stewart, *Only Believe: An Eyewitness Account of the Great Healing Revivals of the 20th Century* (Shippensburg, Pa.: Revival, 1999), 131.

he called dead, formal, denominational religion. In many ways, Allen's revivals resembled old-time camp meetings complete with foot-stomping, tambourine shaking, shouting, shrieking, sobbing, crying, speaking in tongues, jerking, and dancing.

An Allen Revival meeting with A.A. Allen superimposed in the photo. Known as "God's man of faith and power," A.A. Allen became one of the most well-known evangelists of the twentieth century and among the last of the "old time" Pentecostal preachers to see thousands converted amid dramatic public displays of healing and deliverances from evil spirits. Source: voiceofhealing.info.

Allen's revivals were also reminiscent of Azusa Street, complete with apparitional flames of fire appearing above the tent, a sign of the cross that allegedly appeared on Allen's forehead, and "miracle oil," which reportedly flowed from the heads and hands of individuals who attended his meetings.[51] But above all, it was the miracles of deliverance that remained the hallmark of Allen's ministry. Allen never shied away from hard cases either, being described by one Pentecostal historian as "the leading specialist at driving out demons."[52] Others reported notable miracles including new skin appearing, an overweight woman shrinking, and a man who received a new lung, new ribs, new bone, and new toe—all while listening to Allen's radio broadcast in his car! Allen also displayed an amazing ability to raise funds and was among the first to teach that God could heal not only physically but also financially, perform "financial miracles" and deliver his children from a "spirit of poverty."

51 Liardon interview with Shambach: GG 400–401.
52 Hollenweger, *The Pentecostals*, 377: ATP 88.

In 1967, Allen separated from his wife, Lexie, faced a major tax lawsuit, and in 1969 had surgery on an arthritic knee. However, the pain only worsened after surgery. In 1970, Allen went to San Francisco to discuss the possibility of a second knee surgery. But the night before his scheduled doctor's visit, he was found dead in his hotel room at age fifty-nine. The cause of death was an apparent heart attack. For many, Allen's death represented the end of "old-time" Pentecostal religion. Since Allen's death, Miracle Valley has continued to operate under a variety of Pentecostal and Christian ministries.

STUDY QUESTIONS

1. What was the cost of social acceptance in many postwar Pentecostal churches after the initial thrust of the Pentecostal movement had ended? Do you find this often repeated throughout history?

2. What qualified William Branham as a "modern mystic"?

3. Describe the legacy of T.L. and Daisy Osborn's worldwide healing ministry.

4. Why did the Pentecostal denominations reject the Latter Rain movement? Do you feel this was justified? Why or why not?

5. What is considered Oral Roberts' greatest contribution to Pentecostalism and why?

6. How did William Branham's later years resemble John Alexander Dowie's? What led to this? Do you see a pattern?

7. What role did the Voice of Healing play in the postwar healing revival?

8. What parallels can you find in Jack Coe and A.A. Allen's lives and ministries?

9. Why did A.A. Allen's death signify the end of "old-time" Pentecostal religion?

4

THE CHARISMATIC RENEWAL

(c. 1951–1980)

By the latter half of the twentieth century, individualism had firmly taken root in America, showing its fruit in the countercultural movement and social revolution of the 1960s. Notorious for its excessive, flamboyant, and irresponsible behavior, the sixties introduced many radical, subversive, and disturbing trends that continued to develop throughout the seventies, eighties, nineties, and beyond. As a new generation came of age, the established norms of American conservatism, liberalism, modernism, and materialism were being severely tested and challenged by the formation of a postmodern counterculture. Postmodernists taught that any claim to absolute or universal truth by any one group, culture, religion, or race was to be rejected in favor of a more relativistic, individualistic, and pluralistic truth. Out of this arose the "hippie" culture, the Black Power movement, the peace and antiwar movement, the environmentalist movement, the civil rights movement, the women's liberation movement, the gay rights movement, the sexual revolution, the drug culture, pop culture, the "Me Decade" of the seventies, the "yuppie" got-mine-get-yours decade of the eighties, and the moral decadence of the nineties.[1]

POSTMODERNISM

The secularization of Europe and North America accelerated at an alarming rate in the second half of the twentieth century. Religion no longer encompassed life but was seen merely as one competing alternative among many. By 1980, 61 million Americans said they had no religious preference or church affiliation, and by the 1990s, that number had risen to over 78 million with millions more describing themselves as "believers" without "belonging."[2] "Old-time religion" was rapidly moving toward a minority status as most Americans chose to live by the nontraditional values of cohabitation, raising children in nontraditional environments, and fighting for gender, sexual, and individual rights. Soon Americans were treating every major commitment—from marriage and work to family and religion— no longer as a moral obligation but as a means to personal happiness. Before long, public education, pop culture, and pop psychology had successfully transformed America from its traditional roots of selfless morality to the new morality of the liberated self. Children were taught to be expressive and demand their rights as happiness was

---

1   Tom Wolfe, "The 'Me' Decade and the Third Great Awakening," *New York Magazine* (August 1976); Dan Rottenberg, "About that urban renaissance. . . there'll be a slight delay," *Chicago Magazine* (May 1980), 154.

2   CH 472.

purported to be a life rich in experiences and strong feelings of self-expression in a highly privatized culture, leading some historians to label the postmodern age as "The Age of Self."[3]

Other fruits of American postmodern individualism included the removal of prayer and Bibles from public schools in 1963; the legalization of abortion in 1973; the easing of divorce laws; the removal of censorship laws making profanity, violence, and pornography commonplace; the systematic removal of religion from public sectors; and the legalization of gay marriages—all of which introduced a new Age of Tolerance and "equality" for every lifestyle. Television and the media soon replaced Christianity as the new standard for determining what was socially acceptable as the first generation weaned on television presented society with a completely new set of problems. Television masked the symptoms of social deprivation by creating a pseudo-social environment of interaction and acceptance. Then the space and arms race created the computer and Information Age as the Internet, social media, and interactive entertainment were added to the mix. By the mid-1980s, Americans could live, work, eat, shop, and interact socially—all from the privacy of their homes, lending new meaning to the term "cocooning." Firewalls, elaborate security systems, and social networking all served to create a new social barrier of protection from the real world. Then as digital, mobile, and wireless technologies continued to advance, young and old alike could now simply "plug in" and move about—all while remaining behind an invisible technological barrier insulated from society.

---

3   CH 473–475.

PERSONAL CHRISTIANITY

By the 1970s, a new gospel of personal freedom and expression was also finding its way into American churches. Traditional denominational churches began their descent from the mainline to the sideline as independent, evangelical, and Pentecostal-charismatic churches that taught personal Christianity began to flourish. Suddenly "born-again" Christians were showing up in every place from politics and sports to media and entertainment to the White House. But despite this growth and visibility, personal Christianity did little to reshape American ideology, government, politics, education, universities, or culture as sexual perversion, divorce, violence, alcohol, and drug abuse remained at an all-time high.

THE NEO-PENTECOSTALS

Meanwhile, when Pentecostalism began to break into middle-class mainline American denominations, the world stood up and took notice. As early as 1958, both secular and religious observers began speaking of a "Third Force in Christendom" that could one-day rival even Protestantism and Catholicism.[4] This new "force" not only became evident in the latter half of the twentieth century but was also every bit equal in strength to the countercultural revolution taking place in that same period. Donald Gee called it a "new Pentecost" when he began observing Pentecostal blessings and phenomena taking place outside

---

4   Henry P. Van Dusen, "Third Force in Christendom," *Life*, June 9, 1958, 113–124; Gordon Atter, *The Third Force* (Petersborough, Ontario, 1962), 1–9; McCandish, Phillips, "And There Appeared Unto Them Tongues of Fire," *The Saturday Evening Post*, May 16, 1964, 31: HPT 166.

Du Plessis, who was serving as Wigglesworth's interpreter to the Afrikaaners at the time, had come from a family of exiled French Huguenots. His parents came into Pentecostalism through John G. Lake and Thomas Hezmalhalch's Apostolic Faith Mission, of which du Plessis was current general secretary. A few weeks after Wigglesworth's prophecy, du Plessis received a letter from J. Roswell Flower, general secretary of the Assemblies of God in the United States, inviting him to attend their next General Council in Memphis.

Left to right: British Pentecostal Evangelist Fred Squire and his wife; Smith's daughter and son-in-law, James and Alice Salter; Smith Wigglesworth; and David and Anna du Plessis outside the du Plessis's home in South Africa. Source: *Redemption Tidings*, Assemblies of God in Great Britain and Ireland, March 12, 1937, p. 11. Photo: smithwigglesworth.com.

Ten years later, du Plessis would play a major role in the first Pentecostal World Conference in Zurich, Switzerland, teach at the Church of God's Lee College (now Lee University) in Cleveland, Tennessee, then join the Assemblies of God and serve as Gordon Lindsay's secretary for the Voice of Healing. True to his prophetic call, du Plessis may have overextended his reach, however, when he joined the National Council of Churches in 1954. As an unofficial representative of Pentecostal churches, du Plessis attended a number of ecumenical conferences, including the controversial World Council of Churches and the Second Vatican Council in Rome as its only Pentecostal observer in 1962. Though warmly received by all and soon dubbed by them "Mr. Pentecost," he was excommunicated by the Assemblies of God that same year. However, by then du Plessis had already established himself as a leading figure within the charismatic renewal and had become a much sought after speaker at h ndred. of Pentecostal-charismatic conferences worldwide.

In 1974, *Time* magazine listed du Plessis, along with Billy Graham, as one of the leading "shapers and shakers" of Christianity. In 1976, the Catholic Church awarded du Plessis the highly-respected *Pax Christi* (Peace of Christ) medal for his work in the International Roman Catholic-Pentecostal Dialogue—the first non-Catholic to receive the award. Father Kilian McDonnell, who had worked closely with du Plessis, described him as "a national treasure."[11] In 1980, the Assemblies of God reinstated him as an unofficial Pentecostal ambassador-at-large despite his insistence that charismatic believers remain in their traditional churches rather than joining classical Pentecostal churches. Du Plessis was a firm believer in the "ecumenicity of the Holy Spirit." According to one biographer, "No one in the 20th century so effectively linked three of the major movements of the time—the pentecostal movement, the ecumenical movement, and the charismatic movement."[12] For this reason, many consider David du Plessis the "father of the charismatic movement."[13]

After receiving a prophecy through Smith Wigglesworth in 1936 stating that he would play a prominent role in the coming move of God among "old-line" denominations, the rest of David du Plessis's life was like a self-fulfilling prophecy. Du Plessis has been dubbed "Mr. Pentecost" and "father of the charismatic movement." Source: Fuller Theological Seminary.

11   R.P. Spittler, "David Johannes du Plessis": DPCM 592.
12   Ibid., 592.
13   Ibid., 591.

HARALD BREDESEN

One of the first Protestant clergyman to receive the baptism in the Holy Spirit, go public about it, and remain in his historic church was Harald Bredesen (1918–2006). A second-generation Lutheran minister from Minnesota, he was serving as Public Relations Secretary for the World Council of Christian Education in New York in 1946 when he noticed hundreds of people from all denominational backgrounds flocking to a Pentecostal summer camp. Not satisfied with his own relationship with God and curious to know more, Bredesen decided to check it out and soon found himself at the altar seeking the baptism in the Holy Spirit and rising up speaking in other tongues! He described his experience this way: "I tried to say, 'Thank You, Jesus, thank You, Jesus,' but I couldn't express the inexpressible. Then, to my great relief, the Holy Spirit did it for me. It was just as if a bottle was uncorked, and out of me poured a torrent of words in a language I had never studied before. Now everything I had ever wanted to say to God, I could say."[14] Bredesen soon tendered his resignation with the Lutheran Church, but it was refused. During these so-called "wilderness" years, Bredesen continued to receive much encouragement from du Plessis and later from the Full Gospel Business Men's Fellowship.

In 1957, Bredesen became pastor of the historic First Dutch Reformed Church of Mount Vernon, New York. Later Bredesen invited a young seminary student named M.G. "Pat" Robertson to join him as his assistant pastor. Together, along with others who had received the baptism in the Holy Spirit, the two began hosting Pentecostal-style meetings behind locked doors in the old church during off hours.

---

14   Harald Bredesen, *Yes, Lord* (Ventura, Calif.: Gospel Light, 2008): CHS 160.

Robertson later spoke of those early meetings, saying, "Together, Harald Bredesen and I watched God open a new chapter of church history."[15] At one of those meetings in 1959, through Bredesen's lips suddenly came a prophecy: "I am doing a new thing in the earth. Why will you be bound by fear? Hold nothing back. Hold nothing back!"[16]

Harald Bredesen held Pentecostal-like meetings behind locked doors at the old Dutch Reformed Church in Mount Vernon, New York, in 1959 until God spoke through him in prophecy one day saying, "I am doing a new thing in the earth. Why will you be bound by fear? Hold nothing back!" Pat Robertson later wrote, "The new thing God was doing . . . would draw the attention of the world and vastly bless scores of millions." Source: Harald Bredesen, *Yes, Lord*. Photo: Cover portrait from *Trinity* magazine. Fuller Theological Seminary.

Immediately, they knew God was leading them to go public. The next night, Robertson sat at dinner with another Dutch Reformed minister—Norman Vincent Peale and his wife, Ruth Stafford Peale—and told them of their experiences. Since the Peales were founders of *Guideposts* magazine, Mrs. Peale ordered senior editors John and Elizabeth Sherrill to write an article on the new movement. Though skeptical at first, after interviewing Bredesen, the Sherrills also received the baptism in the Holy Spirit and John later wrote about it in his 1964 book, *They Speak with Other Tongues*. Then Bredesen introduced them to a young Pentecostal street preacher in New York named David Wilkerson (1931–2011), which led Elizabeth to coauthor another major work: *The Cross and the Switchblade* (1963). In the book, Wilkerson, founder of Teen Challenge, introduced his "thirty second

---

15   Pat Robertson in Harald Bredesen's, *Yes Lord*: CHS 189.
16   Ibid.

cure" for drug addiction, which he claimed far surpassed any federal drug program—the baptism in the Holy Spirit. In 1977, Catholic priest Father Francis MacNutt addressed a crowd of some 50,000 charismatics at a conference in Kansas City. He said, "The Charismatic renewal in the Catholic Church" (by then, some 30 million strong) "began with two books: *They Speak With Other Tongues* and *The Cross and the Switchblade.*" [17]

After interviewing Harald Bredesen, John and Elizabeth Sherrill not only wrote an article for *Guideposts* magazine on the new movement but also received the baptism in the Holy Spirit. Their books *They Speak with Other Tongues* and *The Cross and the Switchblade* helped launch the charismatic renewal worldwide. Source: elizabethsherrill.com.

In 1960, Bredesen joined forces with Jean Stone—a member of Dennis Bennett's Episcopal Church in Van Nuys, California—and together, they formed the Blessed Trinity Society, which held "Christian Advances" throughout the nation. Through its various publications, it also became the first non-Pentecostal organization for the promotion of the baptism in the Holy Spirit. In 1963, Bredesen formed a mission on the campus of Yale University, leading many students into the Pentecostal experience and attracting national attention to the new movement. Bredesen was featured on ABC's *World News Tonight* and Walter Kronkite's *World Tonight*. *Time*, *Saturday Evening Post*, the Associated Press, and United Press International also reported on the phenomenon. *Time* said of the students, "They do not fall into any mystical seizures or trance; instead,

---

17   Ibid.

onlookers report, they seem fully in control as they mutter or chant sentences that sometimes sound like Hebrew, sometimes like unkempt Swedish."[18] In a letter to the editor of *Eternity* magazine that same year, Bredesen and Stone coined the term "charismatic renewal." Robertson later wrote, "The new thing God was doing ... would draw the attention of the world and vastly bless scores of millions."[19]

Bredesen also led *New York Times* editor Bob Slosser and actor-singer Pat Boone into the Pentecostal experience. Boone said, "Abraham ... Moses ... Gideon ... Elijah ... I think I've known a man like these. His name is Harald Bredesen. Miracles trail him wherever he goes."[20] Slosser called Bredesen a "minister to world leaders" because he touched the lives of so many of the most influential figures of his time. In 1978, Bredesen wrote "a call to prayer" for his friend Egyptian President Anwar Sadat. Sadat then cabled it to Israeli Prime Minister Menachem Begin, American President Jimmy Carter, and other world leaders on the eve of the Camp David Accords. Thirteen days later, Jimmy Carter arose from the historical Egyptian-Israeli peace accords stating, "We began this summit with a call to prayer. The results have exceeded the expectations of any reasonable person. I am a Christian. Jesus said, 'Blessed are the peacemakers.'"[21] Many called Bredesen "Mr.

---

18   *Time*, March 29, 1963, 52: HPT 231.

19   Pat Robertson in Harald Bredesen's, *Yes Lord*: CHS 189.

20   Harald Bredesen, *Yes Lord*, Introduction by Pat Boone, "Harald Bredesen," *Wikipedia: en.wikipedia.org/wiki/Harald_Bredesen* (Accessed 20 March 2013).

21   "Harald Bredesen," *Wikipedia: en.wikipedia.org/wiki/Harald_Bredesen* (Accessed 20 March 2013); "Tribute: Harald Bredesen: A Passion for Christ," by Amy Reid and David Kithcart, The Christian Broadcasting Network: *www.cbn.com/700club/features/Harald_Bredesen0307.aspx* (Accessed 12 July 2015).

Charisma."[22] Others called him "father of the charismatic movement."[23] Today charismatics number in the hundreds of millions.

Known as "Mr. Charisma" for his early efforts in bringing many influential people into the charismatic movement, Harald Bredesen would later be instrumental in founding several major Christian media ministries including the Christian Broadcasting Network, the Trinity Broadcasting Network, and 100 Huntley Street in Canada. Source: Fuller Theological Seminary.

THE PROTESTANT CHARISMATIC RENEWAL

After a congregational study of the second chapter of Acts in 1951, Tommy Tyson, pastor of a United Methodist Church in Durham, North Carolina, received the baptism in the Holy Spirit and spoke in tongues. He also resigned his position but his resignation was refused by his bishop. Tyson went on to lead thousands of other Methodist ministers and layman into the Pentecostal experience and worked closely with Oral Roberts in the 1960s. Then Robert Walker, editor of *Christian Life* magazine, received the baptism in 1952 and began publishing articles about a "fuller life in the Spirit" and Pentecostal outpourings. Episcopal ministers Edgar and Agnes Sanford held "pastoral care" conferences on "the power of the Holy Spirit" throughout

22 "Charisma News—Harald Bredesen Dies" (1/25/2007) *Charisma Magazine: www.charismamag.com/site-archives/570-news/featured-news/3857-* (Accessed 20 March 2013).

23 "Harald Bredesen," *Wikipedia: en.wikipedia.org/wiki/Harald_Bredesen* (Accessed 20 March 2013); "Tribute: Harald Bredesen: A Passion for Christ," by Amy Reid and David Kithcart, *The Christian Broadcasting Network: www.cbn.com/700club/features/Harald_Bredesen0307.aspx* (Accessed 12 July 2015).

the 1950s, and Agnes often afterward shared privately with other ministers about her baptism experience. Over the 1954 Christmas holidays, Gerald Derstine, a Mennonite minister, was leading a youth retreat at the Loman Mennonite Church in Minnesota when several of the children suddenly heard angels singing and fell prostrate on the floor, trembling, speaking and singing in other tongues, and prophesying world events. One said that Billy Graham would one day preach behind Eastern Europe's Iron Curtain (he did—five times, twenty-three years later). Then when Derstine returned home to his church in Strawberry Lake, he was shocked to learn that the same phenomena had occurred there and immediately accepted it as a latter-day fulfillment of Joel's prophecy and spoke in tongues as well. But disavowing their Anabaptist roots, the Mennonite elders forced him to recant, admitting it was demonic activity, or face removal. Since Derstine could not deny it was a genuine movement of God, he resigned, moved to Bradenton, Florida, and began Christian Retreat— an independent charismatic ministry.

Next, Father Richard Winkler of Trinity Episcopal Church in Wheaton, Illinois, received the Pentecostal baptism in 1956 and began holding charismatic prayer meetings in his church. James Brown, a Presbyterian pastor in Parkesburg, Pennsylvania, did the same. Then John Osteen, pastor of Hibbard Memorial Baptist Church in Houston, received a "flow of tongues" in 1958 and was soon charged with "heresy" but was retained by his congregation. He and over a hundred supporters left in 1959 to begin Lakewood Baptist Church in a local feed and seed store and soon dropped the Baptist name. After John's death in 1999, his son, Joel, became pastor of Lakewood Church, which quickly became North America's largest congregation with some 45,000 members. In 1961, Larry Christenson, pastor of Trinity Lutheran Church in San Pedro, California, received his Pentecostal experience after attending a local Foursquare Church, not only sparking a renewal in his own congregation and denomination but also becoming a major leader in the charismatic renewal at-large.

About the time his baby daughter was healed of a birth injury, Pastor John Osteen (left) of Hibbard Memorial Baptist Church in Houston, Texas, received a "flow of tongues" in 1958 and was charged with "heresy." In 1959, he established independent Lakewood Baptist Church for charismatic Baptists and soon dropped the Baptist name. Since John's death in 1999, his son, Joel Osteen (right), has pastored Lakewood Church—the largest Protestant church in the U.S. with over 45,000 members, 20 million monthly television viewers in over 100 countries, a number of world tours in stadiums and arenas, numerous best-selling books, and missionaries in over 111 countries. Source: Lakewood Church.

DENNIS BENNETT

Just as the Azusa Street Revival was not the first of its kind but simply the first to receive international attention, so it was with the charismatic renewal. Most historians link the official beginning of the movement to around 1960 after Dennis Bennett (1917–1991), rector of the 2,600-member St. Mark's Episcopal Church in Van Nuys, California, prayed to receive the Pentecostal baptism. He was at a friend's house in November 1959 at nine o'clock in the morning (the same hour as the original Pentecost), hoping to get "the nearness to God" his friends had without the Pentecostal "distraction" of speaking in tongues. Bennett wrote of his experience:

I suppose I must have prayed out loud for about twenty minutes—at least it seemed like a long time—and was just about to give up when a very strange thing happened. My tongue tripped, just as it might when you are trying to recite a tongue twister, and I began to speak in a new language! Right away I recognized several things: first, it wasn't some kind of psychological trick or compulsion. There was nothing compulsive about it. I was allowing these new words to come to my lips and was speaking them out of my own volition, without in any way being forced to do it. I wasn't "carried away" in any sense of the word, but was fully in possession of my wits and my willpower. I spoke the new language because it was interesting to speak a language I had never learned, even though I didn't know what I was saying. I had taken quite a while to learn a small amount of German and French, but here was a language "for free." Secondly, it was a real language, not some kind of 'baby talk.' It had grammar and syntax; it had inflection and expression—and it was rather beautiful. [24]

Finally, on Sunday, April 3, 1960, in an effort to dispel false rumors surrounding his experience, Bennett decided to share his testimony with his congregation. The reaction was subdued in the first service, but in the second service, Bennett's assistant tore off his robe and stormed out of the church. After the service, one member stood on a chair and shouted, "Throw out the damn tongue speakers!" Others said, "We're Episcopalians, not a bunch of wild-eyed hillbillies."[25] Not knowing enough about his new experience to defend it and unwilling to create discord, Bennett promptly resigned. But Jean Stone—one of Bennett's

---

24 Dennis Bennett, *Nine O'clock in the Morning* (Plainfield, N.J.: Logos, 1970), 20–21: CHS 152.
25 Ibid., 61: HPT 229.

parishioners who had also received the baptism in the Holy Spirit—felt Bennett had been treated unfairly and decided to take the story national. *Time* and *Newsweek* each wrote articles. *Time* wrote, "Now glossolalia seems to be on its way back in U.S. churches—not only in the uninhibited Pentecostal sects, but even among Episcopalians, who have been called 'God's frozen people.'"[26] Soon Bennett was offered St. Luke's Episcopal Church in Seattle. The church had already been shut down twice and was currently facing permanent closure, so denominational officials figured he could do little damage there and gave him full freedom to conduct charismatic services. But within a few short years, Bennett had converted the failed parish into the largest Episcopal Church in the region, ministering to over 2,000 including many Catholics, Baptists, Methodists, Presbyterians, and Lutherans and turning St. Luke's into an international center for charismatic renewal.

Dennis and Rita Bennett. Dennis Bennett, rector of St. Mark's Episcopal Church in Van Nuys, California, was baptized in the Holy Spirit and spoke in other tongues at nine o'clock (same hour as Pentecost) on a November 1959 morning. On Sunday, April 3, 1960, Bennett decided to go public with his experience, announcing it to his congregation and marking the official beginning of the charismatic movement. By 2008, a Barna study showed that nearly half (46 percent) of adults in America who attended a Protestant church were charismatic. Source: "Is American Christianity Turning Charismatic?" (January 7, 2008) Barna Group: *www.barna.org/ barna-update/congregations/52-is-american-christianity-turning-charismatic#.VRq5N_10xLM* (Accessed 20 October 2014). Photo: Rita Bennett Ministries.

Before long, informal charismatic prayer groups were springing up in mainline denominations all over the country. Vinson Synan wrote, "Within a decade of Bennett's experience, it was estimated

---

26   Ibid., 52–55: HPT 229.

that 10 percent of the clergy and a million lay members of the mainline churches had received the baptism and had remained in their churches."[27] Meanwhile, classical Pentecostals, though grateful for their new comrades, remained cautious and skeptical about how long the movement would last or how long these new recruits could escape the persecutions that had befallen them only a generation before. Others remained wary of tongue-talkers who could still drink, smoke, or attend "dead" churches. In noting some of the differences between classical and neo-Pentecostals, Jean Stone wrote in *Trinity* magazine that charismatics displayed "less emotion in receiving the gift of tongues," considered "their private use" of tongues to be "more important than public" use, seemed to be "more oriented to clergy and professional classes," and believed themselves to be less "separatist" and their meetings to be "more orderly . . . with strict adherence to Pauline directives" and with "less emphasis on tongues." She described their practices as "more Bible-centered" than "experience"-oriented.[28]

THE CATHOLIC CHARISMATIC RENEWAL

Though hardly anything new since most Catholic authorities recognize charismatic movements as "a quasi-permanent, or ever-recurrent, feature of the life of the Catholic Church,"[29] according to noted Notre Dame Theology Professor Edward O'Connor, "the most important preparation for the charismatic renewal within the Catholic Church

---

27 HPT 233.

28 Frank Farrell, "Outburst of Tongues: The New Penetration," *Christianity Today*, September 13, 1963, 3–7: HPT 232.

29 Louis Bouyer, "Some Charismatic Movements," Edward D. O'Connor, C.S.C. ed., *Perspectives on Charismatic Renewal* (Notre Dame/London: University of Notre Dame, 1975), 113 [hereafter PCR].

was the 1897 encyclical letter *On the Holy Spirit* published by Pope Leo XIII. In it, the pope bemoaned the fact that the Holy Spirit was little known and appreciated, and summoned the people to renew their devotions to Him."[30] The letter had been inspired by Elena Guerra (1835–1914), an obscure Italian nun who recommended that the ten days between the annual Feasts of Ascension and Pentecost be spent like the time the apostles spent in the upper room—in prayer and preparation for the gifts of the Spirit. Guerra had also suggested that the pope dedicate the twentieth century to the Holy Spirit by singing "Come Holy Spirit" on the first day of the century. Guerra wrote in one of her private letters to the pope, "Pentecost is not over. In fact it is continuously going on in every time and in every place, because the Holy Spirit desired to give himself to all men and all who want him can always receive him, so we do not have to envy the apostles and the first believers; we only have to dispose ourselves like them to receive him well, and He will come to us as he did to them."[31]

Both of Guerra's requests were granted. The latter was invoked on January 1, 1901—the same day Charles Fox Parham laid hands on Agnes Ozman—marking the official beginning of the Pentecostal movement in the twentieth century. Some fifty years after her death, Elena Guerra became the first woman to be beatified by Pope John XXIII, who called her a modern-day "Apostle of the Holy Spirit."[32] Though Guerra did

---

30 Edward O'Connor, *New Covenant*, (The Pentecostal Movement Indiana: Ave Maria Press, 1975), 171: CHS 213

31 Domenico M. Abbrescia, o.p., *Elena Guerra, Prophecy and Renewal*, Society of Saint Paul Inc., Makati, Philippines, 1982: CP 231; R.V. Burgess, "Elena Guerra": DPCM 682.

32 "Elena Guera," *Wikipedia: https://pt.wikipedia.org/wiki/Elena_Guerra* (Accessed 10 December 2015).

not live to see her dream fulfilled, it was at least realized in part when Pope John XXIII called the Second Vatican Council (1962–1965) into session praying, "Lord renew your wonders in this our day as by a new Pentecost."[33] In one fell swoop, the church abandoned its age-old fortress mentality by recognizing, for the first time, the existence of other churches outside of Catholicism, opening the door to an exchange of ideas, theologies, and practices. The implications were enormous. For the first time in history, a movement with Protestant or Pentecostal origins could not only enter Roman Catholicism but also be widely accepted and received by Catholic authorities.

Called a modern-day "Apostle of the Holy Spirit," Elena Guerra (1835-1914), an Italian nun and founder of the Congregation of the Oblate (Lay) Sisters of the Holy Spirit, increasingly felt called to spread devotion to the Holy Spirit by publishing dozens of tiny booklets and making numerous direct appeals to the pope to rediscover the work of the Holy Spirit. Her relentless efforts paid off in prayers and preparations for the gifts of the Holy Spirit and in Pope Leo XIII's dedication of the twentieth century to the Holy Spirit. Source: newsaints. com. Photo: Wikimedia/Caulfieldh.

VATICAN II

Calling it a "sudden inspiration" of the Holy Spirit toward Christian unity, Pope John XXIII spoke of a "new Pentecost" and "the hope of our yearning" as he directed Catholics around the world to pray daily for the three-year council.[34] Unfortunately, Pope John died a year later

---

33   HPT 236.

34   Edward O'Connor, "Roots of Charismatic Renewal in the Catholic Church," *Aspects of Pentecostal-Charismatic Origins*, Vinson Synan, ed. (Plainfield, N.J.: Logos, 1975), 183: CC 176.

without seeing the fulfillment of those prophetic words. Nevertheless, as some 2,500 Catholic bishops and superiors from all over the world gathered, along with 100 delegates and official observers from other churches, they spoke openly for the first time since Trent of a "new Reformation" that may even include a reformulation of doctrines. However, what took place over the next three years was more of a revolution than a reformation. Mass was to be spoken in the language of the people instead of Latin, priests were required to face the congregation during services, hymns were to be sung by congregations instead of chanted by priests and choirs, the Scriptures were to be read by laity as well as clergy, informal guitar services were allowed, nuns were permitted to wear conventional attire, and Catholics were encouraged to pray and interact with other Christians who were no longer called "heretics" but "separated brethren." Catholic priests could now participate in Protestant services, and Protestant ministers could speak in Catholic services. Martin Luther's Reformation song *A Mighty Fortress is our God* could now be sung in Catholic churches! But the revolution did not stop there.

GIFTS AND CHARISMS

As the council progressed, many documents reflected an emphasis on the Holy Spirit and the charismatic nature of the church. Leading this effort were the bishops from Chile, who had been experiencing a mighty surge of Pentecostalism since 1909. When the question of charismatic gifts surfaced, the council came down squarely on the side of present-day manifestations. Cardinal Ruffini expressed the traditional cessationist view that such gifts "are extremely rare and altogether exceptional," but then Cardinal Suenens, who shared Pope John's vision for renewal and was appointed by Pope Paul VI as one of four council moderators, offered his response.[35] It has since become the "Magna Carta" for Catholic charismatics everywhere.

"We are [not] dealing here with a phenomenon that is merely peripheral and accidental to the life of the Church" he said. "But it is now time to bring out more explicitly and thoroughly the vital importance of these charisms for the building up of the Mystical Body. We must at all costs avoid giving the impressions that the hierarchal structure of the Church is an administrative apparatus with no intimate connection with the charismatic gifts of the Holy Spirit which are diffused throughout the Church. To St. Paul, the Church of Christ does not appear as some administrative organization, but as a living, organic ensemble of gifts, charisms, and services. The Holy Spirit is given to all Christians, and to each one in particular; and He in turn gives to each and every one gifts and charisms 'which differ according to the grace bestowed upon us' (Rom 12:6)."[36] Suenens petition prevailed, laying the groundwork for the Catholic Charismatic Renewal. Vinson Synan wrote, "With this foundation in place . . . it was nearly inevitable that Pentecostalism . . . break out in the Roman Church."[37]

---

35   Francis A. Sullivan, *Charisms and Charismatic Renewal: A Biblical and Theological Study* (Ann Arbor, Mich.: Servant, 1982), 4: CC 177.

36   Edward O'Connor, "The Hidden Roots," *On the Holy Ghost* (New York, 1944), 185–186: HPT 245.

37   Vinson Synan, *In the Latter Days: The Outpouring of the Holy Spirit in the Twentieth Century* (Ann Arbor, Mich.: Servant Publications, 1984), 109: CC 177; HPT 245.

At Vatican II (1962-65) Cardinal Leo Joseph Suenens obeyed the wishes of Pope John XXIII by rescuing it from deadlock, setting the agenda, and continually steering the council in the direction of renewal. Suenens said in a 1967 Toronto speech, "The Second Vatican Council marked the end of an epoch, or even of several epochs, depending on one's historical perspective. It brought to a close the Constantinian era, the era of 'Christendom' in the medieval sense, the era of the Counter-Reformation and the era of Vatican I. In reference to that past, it marks a turning point in the History of the Church." As for the resulting Charismatic Renewal, Suenens felt it was not so much a movement as a "being moved" by the Spirit. Atila Sinke Guimarães, "Bird's Eye View of the News" June 15, 2012, Tradition in Action: *www.traditioninaction.org/bev/146bev06_15_2012.htm* (Accessed 10 December 2015). Source: myweb.tiscali.co.uk/renewaluk. Photo: Wikimedia/Drex15.

THE DUQUESNE WEEKEND

One year after Vatican II, Ralph Kiefer and Bill Storey, two Catholic lay theology professors at Duquesne University of the Holy Ghost in Pittsburgh, Pennsylvania, read John and Elizabeth Sherrill's books *The Cross and the Switchblade* and *They Speak with Other Tongues*. Then with the help of an Episcopal priest and Presbyterian prayer group, the two men sought and received the Pentecostal experience and spoke in tongues. The professors then planned a weekend retreat at the Ark and the Dove retreat house just north of Pittsburgh for the weekend of February 17–19, 1967. Participants were asked to read the first four chapters of Acts and *The Cross and the Switchblade* in preparation for the retreat. About twenty professors, graduate students, and their wives attended. The first day was devoted to an intensive study of Acts and prayer, as many grew anxious to receive the baptism in the Holy Spirit. A birthday party was planned for one of the professors that evening, but one by one, students began leaving the party to go to the "upper room" chapel and pray. David Mangen, one of the students, entered the chapel and fell prostrate on the floor. He later said, "I cried harder than I ever cried in my life, but I did not shed one tear. All of a sudden Jesus Christ was so real and so present that I could feel Him all around. I was overcome with such a feeling of love that I cannot begin to describe it."[38]

Patti Gallagher Mansfield described what happened next: "That night the Lord brought the whole group into the chapel. . . . The professors then laid hands on some of the students but most of us received the 'Baptism in the Spirit' while kneeling before the blessed sacrament in prayer. Some of us started speaking in tongues, others received gifts of discernment, prophecy, and wisdom. But the most important gift was the fruit of love which bound the whole community together. In the Lord's spirit we found a unity we had long tried to achieve on our own."[39] Some laughed uncontrollably in the Spirit. One man rolled on the floor in ecstasy. Others shouted, praised, wept, and spoke in tongues in what is known in Catholic traditional spirituality as the "presence of God felt."

Students at the now famous Duquesne Weekend at the Ark and Dove retreat house near Pittsburgh in 1967 who helped unleash the Charismatic Renewal in the Roman Catholic Church. God interrupted a Saturday night birthday party as, one by one, students felt led to leave the party and go to the "upper room" to pray. When the presence of God came, many laughed, rolled on the floor, shouted, wept, and spoke in tongues. Source: Patti Mansfield, Catholic Charismatic Renewal of New Orleans. Photo: John Rossmiller.

---

38   Kevin and Dorothy Ranaghan, *Catholic Pentecostals* (1969), 26, 35: HPT 247.

39   Patti Gallagher Mansfield, *As by a New Pentecost: The Dramatic Beginning of the Catholic Charismatic Renewal* (Steubenville, Ohio: 1992): HPT 247.

NOTRE DAME

From there, the movement spread to Notre Dame in South Bend, Indiana—the center of American Catholicism. The students again had to seek outside help since none of the faculty or students had yet received the Holy Spirit. This time they went to Ray Bullard, an Assemblies of God minister and local president of the Full Gospel Business Men's Fellowship. Bert Ghezzi, one of the students, described what happened next in Ray Bullard's basement among eleven Pentecostal ministers: "Very late that evening, sometime after midnight, down in that basement room, the brothers lined us up on one side of the room and the ministers on the other side of the room, and they began to pray in tongues and to walk toward us with outstretched hands. Before they reached us, many of us began to pray and sing in tongues."[40]

Shortly after praying, the students were asked by their Pentecostal friends when they were going to leave the Catholic Church and come join a Pentecostal one. The students assured their friends that being baptized in the Holy Spirit was completely compatible with Catholic beliefs and, though they had great respect for and would continue to fellowship with their friends, they would never abandon the Catholic Church. Ghezzi later commented, "Because we did not . . . the Catholic charismatic renewal became possible."[41] Soon charismatic prayer meetings were springing up all over campus. Candidates for the experience typically received practical instructions before being prayed over and having hands laid on them. Professor Edward O'Connor became a key leader in the movement, as did

---

40 Vinson Synan interview with Bert Ghezzi: HPT 248.
41 Ibid.

Kevin Ranaghan—a teacher at nearby St. Mary's College. A number of scholarly, theological, historical, and ecumenical works on the gifts and charisms of the Holy Spirit soon followed, such as Father Kilian McDonnell's landmark book *Christian Initiation and Baptism in the Holy Spirit: Evidence from the First Eight Centuries.*

"A CHANCE FOR THE WORLD"

Initially, the press dubbed them "Catholic Pentecostals," but by the 1970s, the more neutral term "charismatic" was being used to avoid confusing them with classical Pentecostals. In 1974, the National Catholic Charismatic Conference at Notre Dame drew more than 30,000 participants. In 1977, a similar interchurch conference in Kansas City drew 50,000.[42]

Christianity Today's Sarah Pulliam Bailey asked Pentecostal historian Vinson Synan in an April 21, 2010, interview, what was the high point of the twentieth-century move of God? Synan replied, "The movement reached a climax in America around 1977 during the Kansas City conference, because all the different streams came together. The 50,000 people in the stadium showed the vigor and force that was sweeping the world." Source: Sarah Pulliam Bailey, "Yes, We Have a Witness," April 21, 2010, *Christianity Today*, vol. 54, No. 4, p. 67: *www.christianitytoday.com/ct/2010/April/26.67.html* (Accessed 10 December 2015). Photo Source: *New Wine* Magazine, Vol. 9, No. 9, October 1977, p. 26. Photo: Charles Simpson Ministries, Inc./csmpublishing.org.

On October 10, 1973, Pope Paul VI addressed the Catholic Charismatic Renewal in Rome, saying, "The Church and the world

---

42   CHS 218–220.

need more than ever that 'the miracle of Pentecost should be continued in history.' . . . Nothing is more necessary for such a world, more and more secularized, than the testimony of this 'spiritual renewal,' which we see the Holy Spirit bring about today in the most diverse regions and environments."[43]

Then at Pope Paul VI's second address to the Catholic Charismatic Renewal on October 16, 1974, he discarded his prepared text at one point to speak from his heart: "We can but hope that these gifts will come and with abundance, that in addition to grace there are charisms that the Church of today can also possess and obtain. . . . How wonderful it would be if the Lord should still increase an outpouring of charisms in order to make the Church fruitful, beautiful, and marvelous, and capable of establishing itself even to the attention and astonishment of the profane world, of the secularized world."[44]

At the Feast of Pentecost in 1975, 25,000 had gathered at St. Peter's in Rome, and on Pentecost Monday, Cardinal Suenens conducted the first charismatic Mass ever held at St. Peter's. At the end of the Mass, Pope Paul VI once again addressed the crowd, saying, "Nothing is more necessary for . . . a world more and more secularized, than the testimony of this 'spiritual renewal,' which we see the Holy Spirit bringing about today in the most diverse environments. . . . How then could this 'spiritual renewal' not be a 'chance' for the church and for

---

43 Address of Pope Paul VI to the Catholic Charismatic Renewal on Occasion of the Second International Leaders' Conference, Rome, May 19, 1973 (Vatican City: International Catholic Charismatic Renewal Services, 2000), 18–23 reprinted with permission of the ICCRS: CP 276.

44 A translation of Pope Paul VI's actual words taken from a tape recording by the Vatican Radio Station and published in the New Covenant, 4, no. 7 (January, 1975), 20: PCR 176–77.

the world? And how, in this case, could one not take all the means to ensure that it remains so? It ought to rejuvenate the world, give it back a spirituality; a soul, a religious thought; it ought to reopen its closed lips to prayer and open its mouth to song, to joy, to hymns, and to witnessing. It will be fortuitous for our times, for our brothers, that there should be a generation, your generation of young people, who shout out to the world the greatness of the God of Pentecost."[45]

At the twentieth anniversary of the Catholic Charismatic Renewal in 1987, Pope John Paul II made a similar statement, saying, "The vigor and fruitfulness of the Renewal certainly attest to the powerful presence of the Holy Spirit at work in the Church in these years after the Second Vatican Council. Of course, the Spirit has guided the Church in every age, producing a great variety of gifts among the faithful. Because of the Spirit, the Church preserves a continual youthful vitality. And the Charismatic Renewal is an eloquent manifestation of this vitality today, a bold statement of what 'the Spirit is saying to the churches' (Rev. 2:7) as we approach the close of the second millennium."[46]

At the renewal's thirtieth anniversary, an ad hoc committee of U.S. bishops similarly declared, "Thus, we can say again, with great thanksgiving and enthusiasm, that in the Catholic Charismatic Renewal and in the grace of baptism in the Holy Spirit we see God's outpouring of a new Pentecost."[47]

---

45 Address of Pope Paul VI to the International Conference on Charismatic Renewal May 19, 1975 in O'Connor, *Perspectives*, 177; also *New Covenant*, July 1975, 23–25; Kilian McDonnell, *Presence, Power, Praise*, (Collegeville, Minn.: Liturgical, 1980) vol. 3, 70–76: HPT 252.

46 CHS 222.

47 CHS 216.

In 2014, for the first time, a pope addressed a National Convocation of the Catholic Charismatic Renewal at Rome's Olympic Stadium. Dubbed the first "charismatic pope," Pope Francis spoke to a crowd of some 52,000 charismatics representing some 120 million Catholic Charismatics worldwide who believed that the power of the Holy Spirit could be manifested through supernatural signs such as speaking in tongues, miraculous healings, prophecies, and revelations. The pope invited them to join him for the movement's fifty-year jubilee celebration "Pentecost 2017" in St. Peter's Square. Photo: giulio napolitano/Shutterstock.com.

THE FULL GOSPEL BUSINESS MEN'S FELLOWSHIP

Among independents the charismatic renewal began primarily among the Full Gospel Business Men's Fellowship International (FGBMFI). Not only did the fellowship serve as an important link between the postwar healing revival and modern charismatic movement, but it also served as an effective bridge between Catholics, Protestants, Pentecostals, and independents. Its founder and president, Demos Shakarian (1913–1993), was a successful Los Angeles dairy farmer whose Pentecostal family had emigrated from Armenia through Turkey. After an 1855 prophecy warned of an impending holocaust at the hand of the Muslim Ottoman Turks, his family fled Armenia and eventually became owners of the largest private dairy herd in the world. Following Shakarian's sister's miraculous healing at a Charles S. Price evangelistic meeting, Shakarian became an avid supporter of the healing revivalists—even becoming a trustee of the Oral Roberts Evangelistic Association and helping Oral organize his 1951 Los Angeles campaign. During the meetings, Shakarian invited twenty-one local businessmen to come to Clifton's Cafeteria to hear

Oral speak, and soon a loose-knit fellowship had been formed with Shakarian as president and Lee Braxton—another longtime Roberts associate—as vice president. Its founders announced the organization "would be developed as the Lord leads."[48] In 1953, the Full Gospel Business Men's *Voice* was published, and the organization's first convention was held in Los Angeles, featuring Oral Roberts, Jack Coe, Gordon Lindsay, Tommy Hicks, Raymond T. Richey, and others. The second convention, held in Washington, DC, included Roberts, Coe, Branham, and a visit from Vice President Richard Nixon.

By 1972, the FGBMFI had a membership of 300,000 (no women or preachers), eventually organizing into 3,000 local chapters in 117 countries. Though initially made up mostly of Assemblies of God laymen who felt excluded from their denomination's decision making, as the movement progressed, it began attracting a more diverse membership.[49] Oral dubbed them "God's Ballroom Saints" because they took the Pentecostal message of healing, deliverance, and Holy Ghost baptism from churches and brush arbor meetings to America's restaurants, hotels, cafeterias, and convention halls. Ecumenical, nonsectarian fellowship was emphasized as ministers and lay speakers alike unabashedly shared testimonies of God's miraculous intervention in their lives, businesses, and careers, which eventually came to include success and prosperity teaching though all speakers were repeatedly asked not to preach or teach. Meetings typically concluded with prayer for salvation, baptism in the Holy Spirit, and healing. In 1975, with the help of John and Elizabeth Sherrill, Shakarian shared his own testimony in his book, *The Happiest People on Earth*, and began hosting

---

48   Gordon Lindsay, *The Gordon Lindsay Story* (Dallas: The Voice of Healing, n.d.), 272–3: ATP 147.

49

a half-hour television broadcast called *Good News*. Shakarian suffered a stroke in 1984, and his son, Richard, eventually took the helm.

Demos Shakarian, a third-generation Armenian Pentecostal and successful Los Angeles dairy farmer, played major roles in the development of America's postwar healing revival and the modern charismatic movement. Working with such early healing revivalists as Charles S. Price, William Branham, Oral Roberts and Tommy Hicks, Shakarian then launched the Full Gospel Business Men's Fellowship International with an eventual worldwide membership of over 700,000, while assisting other international charismatic leaders including Harald Bredesen, John Osteen, and Paul Crouch. Source: Flower Pentecostal Heritage Center.

ORAL ROBERTS UNIVERSITY

Never forgetting the second part of God's directive to "take my healing power to your generation" and "build me a university . . . on my authority and on the Holy Spirit," Oral often stopped his car at a farm at 81st and Lewis near his Tulsa headquarters and led his family in a prayer for God to hold the property until he could find a way to build the university. Finally, in 1961, God spoke again: "Raise up your students to hear My voice, to go where My light is dim, where My voice is heard small, and My healing power is not known, even to the uttermost bounds of the earth. Their work will exceed yours, and in this I am well pleased."[50]

The university was to be built for the education of the whole person—body, mind, and spirit. After Oral prayed in the Spirit one day, God gave him the knowledge he needed to build the university. Oral's associate Lee Braxton wrote, "I have always believed that nothing can

50 A Special Miracles Supplement: "Celebrating the Life of Oral Roberts: A Man Who Obeyed God," 5–6: *Oral Roberts Evangelistic Association: www.oralroberts.com/wordpress/wp-content/uploads/DOC_BIN/miracles_mag/2010/pdf/ORinsertWeb.pdf* (Accessed 29 September 2014).

hold back an idea whose time has come."[51] The property was purchased in 1961, ground was broken in 1962, a charter was received in 1963, and the school opened in 1965. Billy Graham performed the dedication ceremony in 1967. Initially the subject of scorn in academia, by the 1970s Oral Roberts University (ORU) had become the premier Pentecostal-charismatic university in America with an average student enrollment of 4,600, seven graduate colleges in medicine, nursing, dentistry, law, business, education, and theology, and a nationally ranked basketball team. The 200-foot prayer tower, also completed in 1967, and the 60-foot bronze sculptured praying hands soon became Tulsa landmarks.

Prayer Tower at Oral Roberts University. Source: Flower Pentecostal Heritage Center.

FROM PENTECOSTAL TO CHARISMATIC

In 1966, Billy Graham and Carl Henry (editor of *Christianity Today* magazine) invited Oral to attend the World Congress on Evangelism in Berlin. Though apprehensive at first, Oral attended and was overwhelmed by the reception he received. Oral thanked Billy and Dr. Henry at the conference for helping open his eyes to the mainstream of Christianity and returned home with a renewed commitment to unity that included all of evangelical Christianity. By 1967, Oral began noticing a new emphasis being placed on the power and work of the

51 "ORU Today" *Abundant Life* (February 1970), 21: ATP 153.

Holy Spirit in his crusades as thousands came from all denominations seeking to understand and receive the Pentecostal experience. Then in 1968, in a move that sent shockwaves through the Pentecostal world, Oral suddenly resigned his membership with the Pentecostal Holiness Church to join the prestigious Boston Avenue Methodist Church in Tulsa—even becoming an elder in the Oklahoma Methodist Conference. Oral made it clear he would change neither his Pentecostal theology nor his divine healing methods. Methodist Bishop Angie Smith assured Oral, "We need you, but we need the Holy Spirit more than we need you and we've got to have the Holy Spirit in the Methodist Church."[52] Oral's acceptance had been indicative of Pentecostalism's new status in society, yet many Pentecostals could not help but wonder whether Oral was trying to bring Pentecostalism to mainstream Christianity, or had the most prominent Pentecostal in the world just defected to Methodism? Oral explained, "My concern was to follow the leadership of the Holy Spirit and to be true to the calling of God upon my life. I felt led to share this ministry of healing and to escape the tendency to denominationalize my full gospel experience of the baptism with the Holy Spirit."[53] But in the end, Oral foresaw the divide between Pentecostals and charismatics and believed strongly the new movement could not and should not be channeled into the narrow Pentecostal denominations. Besides, his university and most of his supporters were also moving in a charismatic direction at the time. The graduate school of theology headed by Dr. Jimmy Buskirk was approved by the Methodist Church as a seminary for Methodist ministry in 1982. Then in 1986, Oral founded the International Charismatic Bible Ministries (ICBM) to provide fellowship for charismatic ministry leaders.

52 Harrell, *Oral Roberts*, 294.

53 Oral Roberts, "The President's Report," *Abundant Life* (February 1970), 7: ATP 152.

"SOMETHING GOOD IS GOING TO HAPPEN TO YOU!"

For nearly thirty years, the Sunday morning television broadcast had made Oral Roberts a household name and his program the number one syndicated religious program in the nation. A 1980 Gallup Poll revealed that Oral's name was recognized by a phenomenal 84 percent of Americans.[54] Historian David Harrell wrote, "Two decades of Roberts' slogans had become the shouts of the neo-Pentecostal, charismatic revival. Millions of Americans had learned Oral Roberts' favorite sayings: 'Expect a Miracle,' 'Our God is a Good God,' and 'Something Good is going to Happen to You.' Hundreds of thousands committed themselves to have 'Seed-Faith' and make a 'Blessing Pact.'"[55] Oral had pioneered the concept that "seed-faith" giving could produce financial prosperity in the life of a donor. In addition to his weekly half-hour television broadcast, Oral announced in 1968 that he would begin airing quarterly prime-time specials. They would include an element of entertainment aimed at reaching a new generation with the gospel. Oral's son, Richard, would join his dad as a featured singer. The specials included such well-known celebrities as Billy Graham, Kathryn Kuhlman, Pat Boone, Roy Rogers and Dale Evans, Jimmy Durante, Jerry Lewis, Lou Rawls, Johnny Cash, the Lennon Sisters, Burl Ives, Shari Lewis, and Tennessee Ernie Ford. With such an illustrious guest list, networks were more than eager to carry the broadcasts, and the ratings attested to their popularity—between 10 and 40 million viewers each show. Oral's 1971 Valentine's Special was nominated for several Emmy awards, further attesting to their success.

---

54   P.G. Chappell, "Granville Oral Roberts": DPCM 1024.

55   ATP 159.

By 1980, thirty years of television had made Oral Roberts a household name. Source: Oral Roberts Ministries.

THE CITY OF FAITH

In 1977, Oral said that God had spoken to him again—this time about building a new kind of medical center, one that would merge God's healing streams of prayer and medicine together, the supernatural with the natural, for the treatment of the whole person. The "City of Faith" complex would consist of a thirty-story hospital, a sixty-story medical center, and a twenty-story research facility. As Oral walked the property where the City of Faith was to be completed, he said Jesus had appeared to him first in 1977 and again in 1980, reassuring him of the success of the project. "I felt an overwhelming holy presence all around me," he said. "When I opened my eyes, there He stood . . . some 900 feet tall, looking at me; His eyes . . . Oh! His eyes! He stood a full 300 feet taller than the 600 foot tall City of Faith."[56] When the City of Faith opened in 1981, it was among the largest health facilities of its kind in the world. In 1983, Oral said Jesus had appeared to him yet again and commissioned him to find a cure for cancer. At its peak in the early 1980s, the Oral Roberts Evangelistic Association was spending $120 million a year to employ a staff of 2,300 that spanned a

---

56 "Oral Roberts tells of talking to 900-foot Jesus" (October 16, 1980) Updated May 23, 2014, *Tulsa World: www.tulsaworld.com/archives/oral-roberts-tells-of-talking-to—foot-jesus/article_bbe49a4e-e441–5424–8fcf-1d49ede6318c.html* (Accessed 30 September 2014).

university, medical school, and hospital on a fifty-acre campus valued at 500 million dollars. Unfortunately, the City of Faith attracted neither the funding nor the patients necessary to keep it running, and in January 1987, Oral announced that God would "call him home" if he did not raise 8 million dollars by March. He raised 9.1 million.

The CityPlex Towers as they appear today in Tulsa, Oklahoma at 81st and Lewis. Photo: Wikimedia/Liam Ferguson.

ORAL'S FINAL YEARS

By 1988, both Oral and Richard were being sued for $15 million by City of Faith patients who claimed they were frauds because they never visited nor healed hospital patients. That same year, the Christian world was rocked by the sex-and-money scandals of fellow televangelists Jim Bakker and Jimmy Swaggart, and Oral's ministry suffered along with them. By late 1989, the school and medical center were buckling under the financial strain and a series of major cutbacks followed that forced the medical center to close while the university remained intact. In 1993, Oral was elected ORU chancellor—a role he would retain until his death in 2009. Richard became university president that same year and resigned in 2007 amid allegations of improper use of funds. Before his death, Oral installed former Assemblies of God minister Mark Rutland as ORU's president. Then Church of God minister Billy Wilson assumed the role in 2013. One commentator said at the time of Oral's death, "In conservative Protestant culture, he was second only to Billy Graham."[57] Biographer David Harrell described Oral as "one of the most influential religious leaders in the world in the twentieth century."[58]

KATHRYN KUHLMAN

Yet another major player in the charismatic movement was Kathryn Kuhlman (1907–1976). The tall, gangly, red-haired, freckled-faced girl born to German immigrants in Concordia, Missouri, was saved at age fourteen in a Methodist Church and began traveling with her sister and brother-in-law, Myrtle and Everett, in their tent meetings throughout the Midwest as an evangelist at age sixteen. Helen Gulliford, a concert pianist who wanted to play for the Lord, later joined their evangelistic team. By age twenty-one, Kathryn decided to launch out on her own, taking Helen with her. The two traveled together throughout Idaho, Utah, and Colorado before finally settling and pioneering the 2,000-seat Denver Revival Tabernacle and a radio ministry when Kathryn was only twenty-eight.

A young Kathryn Kuhlman in front of house with family members (c. 1914). Source: Flower Pentecostal Heritage Center.

---

57 Grant Wacker quote in Justin Juozapavicius, "Evangelist Oral Roberts dies in Calif. at age 91," *Associated Press* (Dec. 15, 2009) *Seattle Times: www.seattletimes.com/ nation-world/evangelist-oral-roberts-dies-in-calif-at-age-91/* (Accessed 12 July 2015).

58 Harrell, *Oral Roberts*, Preface vii.

Raymond T. Richey and a number of other lesser known evangelists came and held revivals at the Denver Tabernacle, including Burroughs A. Waltrip, who preached there for two months. Kathryn was so delighted with Waltrip's preaching she invited him to return in the fall. During Waltrip's second trip, his wife, Jessie, and two children joined him but later returned home to Austin, Texas. A month later, Waltrip wrote to his wife and told her he was not returning home, charged her with desertion, and later divorced her. As the Denver revival came to a close, Waltrip traveled north to Mason City, Iowa, where he was asked if he could stay and build a ministry similar to Kathryn's. Waltrip agreed, inviting Kathryn and Helen to come help him raise funds for the new "Radio Chapel." Shortly after their arrival, a romance developed between Kathryn and Waltrip as he lied to her about his wife leaving him. Though Kathryn knew it was a mistake from the start, and many friends and church members had proceeded to tell her so, she reluctantly agreed to marry him—even fainting at one point during the ceremony as Waltrip clutched her arm to help her through the vows.

Evangelist Burroughs Allen Waltrip Sr., with wife, Jessie, and sons, Burroughs A., Jr. and William Reuben Waltrip, in Lake Charles, Louisiana, 1933. Kathryn Kuhlman would later refer to Waltrip only as "Mister." Source: Flower Pentecostal Heritage Center.

Waltrip loved money, loved the extravagant lifestyle, but most of all loved Kathryn's ability to raise money and draw a crowd. After the marriage destroyed her Denver ministry, the two traveled in ministry together. But as Waltrip preached on stage, Kathryn was often crying backstage. Six years later, Kathryn finally left him, refusing even to speak of the marriage or acknowledge him by any other name than "Mister." She said, "I had to make a choice. Would I serve the man I loved, or the God I loved? I knew I couldn't serve God and live with Mister. . . . I finally told him I had to leave, for God had never released me from my original call."[59] Kathryn bought a one-way ticket to Franklin, Pennsylvania—a coal-mining town settled by German immigrants. Waltrip eventually filed for divorce, dying later in a California prison after being convicted of stealing money—from a woman.

By the time the postwar healing revival was in full swing, Kathryn had visited a number of tent revivals in Pennsylvania and later spoke out against some of the "fanaticism" and "fleshly manifestations" she witnessed in those meetings. But nothing appalled her more than what she considered to be the unwise methods of the evangelists themselves who often blamed their attendees' lack of faith for not receiving a miracle. This, she believed, was totally contrary to the marvelous sacred ministry of the Holy Spirit and to the nature of God. "Was this the God of all mercy and great compassion?" she objected. "I left the tent, and with hot tears streaming down my face, I looked up and cried, 'they have taken away my Lord, and I know not where they have laid Him.'"[60]

No doubt, a Kathryn Kuhlman service would be different. Sure enough, Kathryn was soon invited to hold a series of meetings at the 1,500-seat Gospel Tabernacle in Franklin, Pennsylvania—the same

---

59 Jamie Buckingham, *Daughter of Destiny: Kathryn Kuhlman . . . Her Story* (Plainfield, N.J.: Logos, 1976), 88: GG 287.

60 Ibid., 101–102: GG 290.

venue where famed Evangelist Billy Sunday (1862–1935) had once preached. At that point, Kathryn prayed only for the salvation of souls. But on the second night of her meetings, a woman stood up and announced she had been to her doctor and he had confirmed her tumor was gone. She said the miracle had occurred the night before as she listened to Kathryn preach on the power of the Holy Spirit. The following Sunday, a man who had been declared legally blind had his sight miraculously restored. Kathryn soon moved her meetings to a larger renovated roller skating rink called Faith Temple of Sugar Creek and restarted her daily radio program *Smiling Through* in nearby Oil City and Pittsburgh. After a record snowfall caused the roof of Faith Temple to collapse, Kathryn moved to Pittsburgh, where she would live out the remainder of her life preaching before capacity crowds at First Presbyterian Church and Carnegie Hall.

AN INTERNATIONAL STAR

In 1950, *Redbook* magazine assigned Pittsburgh reporter Emily Gardner Neal to write an article on Kathryn's healing ministry. The article told of "startling things . . . happening at Miss Kuhlman's evangelistic services in Pittsburgh." It included testimonials, medical reports, and statements from clergymen, medical professionals, and public officials who supported her ministry.[61] Literally overnight, Kathryn had been catapulted to national fame. In 1952, pioneer Pentecostal televangelist Rex Humbard (1919–2007) invited Kathryn to nearby Akron, Ohio,

---

61   Jamie Buckingham, *Daughter of Destiny* as cited in "Redbook Magazine on Kathryn Kuhlman," Posted: October 27, 2011, *Revival History: www.revivalhistory.com/blog/redbook-magazine-on-kathryn-kuhlman* (Accessed 8 October 2014).

to help him raise funds for his new Cathedral of Tomorrow. Police reported at 4:00 Sunday morning that 18,000 people had gathered outside the tent for the 11:00 a.m. service. Kathryn ministered from 8:00 a.m. until 2:30 p.m. that day.

Redbook's coverage of Kathryn Kuhlman's healing and evangelistic services in Pittsburgh catapulted her to national fame in 1950. Source: Flower Pentecostal Heritage Center.

In 1954, the Kathryn Kuhlman Foundation was founded and soon became a major contributor to religious and benevolent charities around the world. In the 1960s, Kathryn added a weekly half-hour national television show called *I Believe in Miracles*, which she recorded at CBS studios in Los Angeles. Then in 1965, Pastor Ralph Wilkerson invited Kathryn to hold a series of services at Melodyland Christian Center in Anaheim, California. As the crowds quickly grew too large, they had to rent the 7,000-seat Shrine Auditorium in Los Angeles, where Kathryn would return to hold meetings for the next ten years.

During this time, Kathryn also became a frequent guest on Christian and secular television programs like *The Johnny Carson Show* and *The Dinah Shore Show* and published three national best-selling books: *I Believe in Miracles* (1969), *God Can Do It Again* (1969), and *Nothing is Impossible with God* (1974), all comprising miraculous testimonies from her meetings. Even comedian Phyllis Diller once recommended her book to a dying patient. By the 1970s, Kathryn had become an international leader in the charismatic renewal, receiving numerous acclamations ranging from accolades from the pope to receiving ORU's first honorary doctorate degree. Kathryn also ministered abroad in Sweden, Finland, and Israel, speaking at the Second World Conference on the Holy Spirit in Jerusalem in 1975.

Kathryn Kuhlman standing with a boy who just received a miracle of healing after she prayed for him. Photo: Doug Grandstaff Photography.

A CHARISMATIC MINISTRY

Though Pentecostal at heart, Kathryn's charismatic appeal was evidenced by her ordination with the Evangelical Church Alliance in 1968. Always displaying an independent spirit, Kathryn both sought and attracted audiences from all denominations. At home, she often preached in a Protestant church, while requesting prayer at a Catholic Mass for the success of her meetings and allowing priests and nuns to sit on her platform in full clerical attire. Many Pentecostals held her suspect because of her divorce and because she rarely spoke of her personal experience of speaking in tongues, but many more accepted her. As one healing revivalist put it, "She has the baptism, but she don't really preach like we do . . . she softens it down a little."[62]

Kathryn never permitted an outburst of tongues or prophecy in her meetings, feeling it might hinder people's simple belief in God. She

---

62   David Harrell interview: ATP 191.

also never preached against smoking or drinking and never taught that sickness was of the Devil, believing instead that if she could turn people's eyes to Jesus, everything else would fall into place. Once when asked why some were not healed, she simply said her job was sales, not management, and whatever management decided, she would abide by. Kathryn always placed more of an emphasis on the sovereignty of the Holy Spirit than on faith as she was wary of placing any restrictions on her services that might hinder the flow of the Spirit. Also, she would not allow herself or anyone else on her staff to act out in any selfish or fleshly ways, always being careful to give glory to God for everything. Major denominations have described Kathryn as having the purest ministry of the Holy Spirit in her time. In describing Kathryn's relationship with the Holy Spirit in her meetings, Oral Roberts once said, "It was like they were talking back and forth to each other, and you couldn't tell where Kathryn started and the Holy Spirit left off. It was a oneness."[63]

Kathryn's radio broadcasts, like her meetings, were very warm and personable, sounding more like conversation with someone who had just dropped by for coffee than the shouting of a typical radio preacher. A typical Kathryn Kuhlman radio broadcast began with "Hello there, and have you been waiting for me?" Likewise, a "holy hush" would often come over the crowd in her meetings. Kathryn's soft, slow, carefully enunciated speech was a hallmark feature of her ministry and remained a part of her mystique. Once when asked why she spoke this way, she said it was simply her way of overcoming an early speech defect that combined stuttering with her thick, homespun Missouri accent. Kathryn was every bit as theatrical, flamboyant, and eccentric as her

---

63 Wayne E. Warner, *Kathryn Kuhlman: The Woman Behind the Miracles* (Ann Arbor, Mich.: Servant Publications, 1993), 234: GG 296.

hero and mentor Aimee Semple McPherson. Kathryn always appeared in a strikingly sheer and elegant "pulpit dress," waving her long, thin arms with trademark bell sleeves in the air. Kathryn's biographer and friend Jamie Buckingham wrote, "She loved her expensive clothes, precious jewels, luxury hotels, and first class travel."[64]

Kathryn Kuhlman looking upwards with her arms outstretched; pointing at the audience. Photos: Doug Grandstaff Photography.

KATHRYN KUHLMAN MIRACLE SERVICES

Of course, the main components of Kathryn Kuhlman's Miracle Services were the miracles. Kathryn frequently called out specific disorders that were being healed in a certain part of the auditorium. Then all those who were healed would eventually be asked to line up on either side of the stage as ushers would announce their cures to Kathryn over a microphone. Kathryn would often invite them onto the stage, where she would ask them to do calisthenics or something they could not do before to inspire others to receive. Benny Hinn, who often attended Kathryn's Pittsburgh services, would later pattern his miracle crusades after hers. The concept of being "slain in the Spirit" while falling backward into the hands of a catcher after being prayed for or having hands laid on originated in Kathryn Kuhlman's services. Occasionally, however, dozens or even hundreds would spontaneously fall backward as in the camp meetings of old.

---

64 Buckingham, *Daughter of Destiny*, 247.

A typical Kathryn Kuhlman Miracle Service.
Photo: Doug Grandstaff Photography.

A "VERITABLE ONE-WOMAN SHRINE"

In her early years, Kathryn had been diagnosed with an enlarged heart and defective heart valve but trusted the Holy Spirit to keep her well and empower her to maintain a rigorous schedule. She held her last miracle service at the Shrine Auditorium in November 1975. She reportedly stayed behind to watch the crowd as they exited the auditorium on her last night. Three weeks later, she had open-heart surgery at a Tulsa hospital. Oral and Evelyn Roberts were among the few to visit her after the surgery, but as they were about to pray for her, she held up her hands as if to say "stop" and then pointed toward heaven. Evelyn said to Oral, "She doesn't want our prayers. She wants to go home." She was sixty-eight. At her request, Kathryn was buried at the same cemetery as Aimee Semple McPherson.

Time once called Kathryn Kuhlman a "veritable one-woman Shrine," likening her to the French statue of St. Mary believed to possess miraculous healing powers. But Kathryn was always quick to reply, "I have no healing power. It's the power of God that does the healing. The only part I have in it is making Jesus real to the hearts of men and women. Any results there might be in this life of mine, is not Kathryn Kuhlman. It's the Holy Spirit." Source: Jamie Buckingham, *Daughter of Destiny*, 1–2; Kathryn Kuhlman Foundation. Photo: Flower Pentecostal Heritage Center.

Biographer Roberts Liardon wrote, "Kathryn never believed she had been God's first choice for the ministry. She believed a man had been called to do it, but was not willing to pay the price. She was never quite sure if she was even second choice or third choice, but . . . her ministry stands out as one of the leading ministries, if not the leading ministry of the Charismatic Movement."[65] *Time* once called Kathryn Kuhlman a "veritable one-woman Shrine of Lourdes," likening her to the French statue of St. Mary believed to possess miraculous healing powers.[66] Jamie Buckingham called her "the foremost woman evangelist of the 20th century," stating that when she died in 1976, more than fifty invitations from all over the world lay on her desk.[67]

---

65 GG 296.

66 Buckingham, *Daughter of Destiny*, 1–2.

67 Ibid.

STUDY QUESTIONS

1. What were some of the fruits of American individualism evident in the second half of the twentieth century and in America's churches during that time?

2. What is postmodernism, and how has it affected Western thinking and society?

3. What happened when Pentecostalism broke into the American middle class? Explain.

4. What role did David du Plessis play in the charismatic renewal?

5. What earned Harald Bredesen the title "Mr. Charisma"?

6. What events sparked the Protestant charismatic renewal?

7. Name some differences between classical Pentecostals and neo-Pentecostals or charismatics.

8. How did Elena Guerra, an obscure nineteenth-century Italian nun, affect the twentieth-century Catholic Charismatic Renewal?

9. Why was the Second Vatican Council in Rome considered more of a revolution than a reformation?

10. What events sparked the Charismatic Renewal in the Roman Catholic Church?

11. How did the charismatic movement begin among independent groups?

12. Do you see Oral's leaving the Pentecostal Holiness Church to join a Methodist Church as part of an overall effort to bring Pentecostalism to mainstream Christianity . . . or do you see it as defection?

13. What made Kathryn Kuhlman's ministry more charismatic than Pentecostal?

5

The Charismatic Explosion

(c. 1971–2000)

Securing its unique place in history, the charismatic renewal was not a monolithic movement but an explosion . . . a plethora of movements happening all at once that affected Catholics, Protestants, Pentecostals, and most of all, independents. The movement also witnessed a variety of new phenomena from a rootless wandering mass of meeting-hoppers called "cruismatics" to the cassette tape teaching revolution, spiritual warfare and intercessory prayer groups, storefront churches and coffeehouse ministries, the proliferation of home cell groups, and the singing of simplistic praise choruses to a simple rhythmic dance affectionately known as the "charismatic bunny-hop." Larry Christenson wrote, "In the span of less than two decades the movement spread to every continent of the globe and into every major Christian denomination. No other movement in the history of Christianity has spread so fast and so extensively." He added, "What remains at the center of the renewal . . . is the conviction that charismatic experience is a normal, indeed an indispensable, part of Christian life."[1]

Among the independent groups in North America, the movement began primarily on the west coast with the Full Gospel Business Men's Fellowship, Women's Aglow Fellowship, and a "hippie" youth counterculture known as the Jesus movement, "Jesus People" or "Jesus Freaks." These in turn spawned other movements—Jews for Jesus, Jesus Music, the contemporary worship movement, the Calvary Chapel movement, the Vineyard movement, the Signs and Wonders movement, the Church Growth movement, and the Apostolic-Prophetic movement. Then the movement witnessed yet another first: the power of Christian cable and satellite television with CBN, TBN, PTL, and many others following. CBN eventually sponsored the largest gatherings in the history of Washington, D.C., as John and Anne Giminez's "Washington for Jesus" rallies converged in our nation's capital in the 1980s. Later, Sky Angel, God TV, Daystar, INSP, and a variety of other networks joined in. Meanwhile, the movement was observing a phenomenal rise in Christian music from gospel and contemporary to contemporary worship. It also witnessed a dramatic rise in teaching ministries, the burgeoning of Pentecostal and charismatic universities and Bible colleges, and a seemingly endless list of independent, Pentecostal-charismatic churches, parachurch ministries, and church networks. The movement even had its own *Charisma* magazine to track the many evolving trends.

---

1   Larry Christenson, *Welcome, Holy Spirit: A Study of Charismatic Renewal in the Church* (Minneapolis: Augsburg, 1987), 17, 27.

THE SHEPHERDING MOVEMENT

Such an extensive movement covering such an expanse of space and time was bound to have more than its share of controversies . . . and did. One of the biggest controversies to arise within the charismatic movement—even threatening to overtake it at one point—was the so-called "shepherding" or "discipleship" movement. It began in 1970 among four well-known charismatic Bible teachers: Bob Mumford, Derek Prince, Charles Simpson, and Don Basham—all contributing editors of *New Wine* magazine published by the Fort Lauderdale-based Holy Spirit Teaching Mission. Following the moral failure of its ministry founder and leader, Eldon Purvis, the four were asked to step up and take over the publication. However, feeling the sting of moral failure and mutual vulnerability of their own independent ministries, the four men decided to "submit" their lives in "covenant relationship" to one another. Each was from different backgrounds—Mumford had been with the Assemblies of God, Prince was independent, Simpson had been a Southern Baptist, and Basham had been with the Disciples of Christ. Realizing there were hundreds of thousands of other independent charismatics like themselves who had left their respective denominations only to drift aimlessly from one charismatic group to another, they recognized the need for greater accountability, stronger character development, and deeper relationships within the larger charismatic movement. Using the fivefold ministry as a model chain of command and the Catholic model of "spiritual directors" for personal guidance, they devised a vertical pyramid system in which every disciple could be connected to a leader above them and who, in turn, would make disciples of others.[2]

---

2   Eph 4:11–13

Changing their name to Christian Growth Ministries in 1972, the four began spreading their teachings through *New Wine* as well as their own respective ministry newsletters, books, and teaching tapes, and through charismatic conferences worldwide. Together, they stressed the importance of commitment, loyalty, servanthood, submission, and the fact that everyone should have a male "covering" or "shepherd" to direct their spiritual life. Their teachings caught on like wildfire. Before long, *New Wine* was the most widely circulated publication within the charismatic movement with 100,000 adherents and a network of 500 independent churches submitting to their leadership, complete with home cell groups and lay shepherds. Of course, someone had to be at the top of the pyramid, and it was these four men. Their 1974 conference at Montreat, North Carolina, drew over 1,700 pastors and leaders as the four were then joined by Canadian Pentecostal minister and former Branham associate Ern Baxter, creating what became known as the "Fort Lauderdale Five."

THE CONTROVERSY DEVELOPS

Unfortunately, some of the structures they created led to unusual situations such as church members paying tithes to and receiving pastoral care from someone outside their local church. It also opened the door to many abuses of spiritual power. One example was "lay shepherds" who received tithes and controlled intimate, personal decisions in the lives of their followers like directing where they should live or whom they should marry. Suddenly, disobeying one's "shepherd" became tantamount to disobeying God. Though some reports were exaggerated, the movement quickly gained a reputation for being controlling and abusive and was threatening to divide, if not engulf, the entire charismatic movement. Rumors also swirled that a new massive charismatic denomination was in the making as other charismatic leaders began sounding the alarm.

"The Fort Lauderdale Five" from left to right: Ern Baxter, Derek Prince, Charles Simpson, Don Basham, and Bob Mumford. Recognizing the need for greater accountability among a growing charismatic body, they led the discipleship or "shepherding" movement, which resulted in some abuses of spiritual power. Source: Charles Simpson Ministries, Inc./csmpublishing.org.

In 1975, Demos Shakarian issued a directive forbidding anyone connected with the "Shepherding Movement" to speak at a Full Gospel Business Men's chapter or convention. Then Kathryn Kuhlman announced she would not appear on the same platform with Bob Mumford at the Second World Conference on the Holy Spirit in Jerusalem, stating, "If Bob Mumford goes to Israel, I shall not go . . . the man is a heretic."[3] Next, Pat Robertson refused to allow any of the five to appear as guests on *The 700 Club*, ordering all past tapes to be erased and issuing a stinging letter of rebuke to Mumford that he claimed would blow "the lid off the controversy." In the letter, Robertson accused the men of "controlling the lives of their followers with the overuse of spiritual authority," saying that in a recent visit to Louisville, Kentucky, he had encountered "cultish" language being used like "submission" rather than churches, "shepherds" rather than pastors, and "relationships" rather than Jesus.[4] Robertson then

---

3   HPT 265.

4   Edward E. Plowman, "The Deepening Rift in the Charismatic Movement," *Christianity Today* (Oct. 10, 1975), 52–54: HPT 265.

traveled to ORU and found a twenty-year-old "shepherd" who drew tithes from fellow students as part of their submission. Subsequently, he charged the leaders with placing personal revelations on the same level with Scripture, quoting a devotee who had said, "If God Almighty spoke to me, and I knew for a certainty that it was God speaking, and if my shepherd told me to do the opposite, I would obey my shepherd." Later, Robertson used his television broadcast to denounce the movement, likening it to "witchcraft" and to the Jim Jones Cult that in 1978 committed mass suicide by drinking Kool-Aid laced with cyanide. Robertson said the only difference between the Shepherding Movement and Jonestown was "Kool-Aid."[5]

THE CONTROVERSY WINDS DOWN

In an effort to defuse the controversy, twenty-seven leaders within the charismatic movement agreed to meet with the "Fort Lauderdale Five" in Minneapolis in August in what became known as "the shootout at the Curtis Hotel." Among those represented were Catholics, Protestants, and independents, including Kevin Ranaghan, Dennis Bennett, Larry Christenson, Harald Bredesen, David du Plessis, Pat Robertson, Ken Sumrall, Jamie Buckingham, and Thomas Zimmerman, General Superintendent of the Assemblies of God. Tempers flared and charges were hurled back and forth but no clear verdict was reached. After the meeting, however, the controversy seemed to simmer somewhat despite the continued growth of the movement. Evidently the leaders had decided to heed Gamaliel's words: "If this work is of men, it will come to nothing; but if it is of God, you cannot overthrow it."[6] At

5   H.D. Hunter, "Shepherding Movement," DPCM 784; HPT 265.
6   Acts 5:38–39

the 1977 Charismatic Renewal Conference in Kansas City, attended by some 50,000, there were more than 9,000 "shepherding" delegates with more than 12,000 "shepherding" registrants—second only to the charismatic Catholics.

In 1978, Christian Growth Ministries was renamed Integrity Communications when the ministry moved its headquarters to Charles Simpson's home base in Mobile, Alabama. Only Prince remained in Fort Lauderdale. Then in 1980, the five nearly separated over internal differences and accusations of abuse of spiritual power, which led to a number of leaders and followers defecting. Then just as the movement was peaking in 1982, internal conflicts fueled by external pressures ultimately led to the ministry's demise. Prince was first to withdraw in 1983, stating, "We were guilty of the Galatian error: having begun in the Spirit, we quickly degenerated into the flesh."[7] The remaining four dissolved in 1986 when the publication ceased. In 1987, the name was again changed to Charles Simpson Ministries as a much smaller Fellowship of Covenant Ministers and Churches was founded. In 1989, Bob Mumford issued a formal public apology for his role in the movement, stating, "Unhealthy submission resulting in perverse and unbiblical obedience to human leaders" led to families being "split up and lives" being "turned upside down." He added, "Some of these families are still not back together."[8]

---

7   "Bible Teacher Derek Prince Dies at 88" (Sept. 25, 2003) *Religion News Blog: www.religionnewsblog.com/4598/bible-teacher-derek-prince-dies-at-88* (Accessed 24 March 2013).

8   Bob Mumford, "Mumford's Formal Repentance Statement to the Body of Christ" *Ministries Today* (Jan/Feb 1990), 52: "Shepherding Movement," *Wikipedia: en.wikipedia.org/wiki/Shepherding_Movement* (Accessed 24 March 2013).

PAT ROBERTSON

Religious broadcasting was huge in the latter half of the twentieth century, and one of the pioneers in both religious broadcasting and the charismatic movement was M.G. "Pat" Robertson. Son of a U.S. Senator and a first lieutenant in the U.S. Marine Corps, Pat graduated from Yale Law School before attending New York Theological Seminary, where he served as Harald Bredesen's assistant.

CBN AND THE 700 CLUB

After graduating from seminary, Pat moved to Portsmouth, Virginia, where he purchased a defunct UHF television station in 1960 with an initial investment of $70 and established the Christian Broadcasting Network (CBN)—America's first Christian television station. After being ordained a Southern Baptist minister, Pat held his first telethon in 1963, asking 700 viewers to join the "700 Club" by pledging $10 a month. The name caught on, and by 1966, a daily broadcast had been added with a format that included singing, preaching, prayer, ministry, and telephone response. That same year, Pat was joined by Assemblies of God evangelists Jim and Tammy Bakker, who contributed to the growth of the young network by hosting its successful flagship show along with the *Jim and Tammy* children's show that included puppets and interviews. *The 700 Club* has since become the longest running Christian television program and longest running show of its kind in history. By the early 1970s, however, the Bakkers were let go because of "philosophical differences" and headed to California to help pioneer another Christian television network.

A GLOBAL ORGANIZATION

As *The 700 Club* evolved into a talk show format with prayer that included calling out specific disorders in the television audience that were being healed, CBN continued expanding into major markets, installed a satellite transmitter, and in 1977 purchased a local cable access channel called the CBN Cable Network. Pat literally canvassed door-to-door and in local churches asking Christians to buy cable boxes so they could receive the new channel, while Pat's friends John and Anne Giminez of Rock Church in Virginia Beach donated the volunteers. That same year, Pat founded CBN University (later, Regent University) which would become the preeminent Christian university in the world with graduate schools in communications, education, counseling, business, divinity, law, and the Center of Leadership Studies.

The Christian Broadcasting Network (CBN) was founded on January 11, 1960. Pat Robertson took his network on the air on October 1, 1961, from a defunct Portsmouth, Virginia, UHF TV station. It became the first Christian television station in the U.S. Source: patrobertson.com.

In the 1980s, *The 700 Club* again evolved into a "magazine" format, adding news, opinion, and lifestyle segments between talk interviews. Other syndicated shows were added as well. Today CBN can be seen in over 180 countries with broadcasts in 71 languages, a Middle East Television station in southern Lebanon, and CBN Asia in the Philippines. Operation Blessing International Relief and Development

Corporation was added in 1978 and has since become one of America's largest humanitarian relief organizations with operations in over 100 nations providing over $3 billion in goods and services, including a Boeing 757 flying hospital. Pat also founded a conservative Christian advocacy group called the Christian Coalition, a public law firm called the American Center for Law and Justice for pursuing conservative Christian ideals, and the Founders Inn and Conference Center. CBN's Williamsburg-style complex soon spread over a 700-acre campus in Virginia Beach and Chesapeake, Virginia, with an annual budget of more than $200 million and more than 1,000 employees. Pat also authored over a dozen books, several of which became *New York Times* best-sellers.

PAT FOR PRESIDENT

By the 1980s, Pentecostals were beginning to show up in the most unlikely places. James Watt, President Ronald Reagan's Interior Secretary, and John Ashcroft, President George H.W. Bush's Attorney General, were both Pentecostals. Then in 1988, Pat became the first Pentecostal-charismatic to seek a major party's nomination for president of the United States. Giving up his Baptist ordination, Pat placed second in the critical Iowa caucuses but then placed poorly in subsequent primaries, soon ending his campaign. He later spoke at the 1988 Republican National Convention in New Orleans.

The CBN Cable Network also underwent a number of metamorphic changes over the years, becoming the CBN Family Channel, The Family Channel, International Family Entertainment Inc., Fox Family, and finally, ABC Family in 2007. The only condition upon purchase was that *The 700 Club* had to be aired twice daily in perpetuity regardless of who owned it. *The 700 Club* also aired in syndication and on a variety of cable and satellite networks. In 2007, Pat resigned as chief executive of CBN, succeeded by his son, Gordon, while Pat remained on as chairman and university chancellor.

Left to right: Gordon Robertson, co-host Terry Meeuswen, and Pat Robertson. On the air continuously since 1966, *The 700 Club* became one of the longest running programs in broadcast history seen in 97 percent of U.S. markets by an average of one million daily viewers. Source: CBN.

THE TRINITY BROADCASTING NETWORK

After leaving CBN, Jim and Tammy Bakker teamed up with their former Assemblies of God youth pastors, Paul and Jan Crouch, to establish the Trinity Broadcasting Systems in California with Paul and Jan's flagship variety show *Praise the Lord*. The relationship did not last long, however, and by 1974, the Bakkers were off to Charlotte, North Carolina, to begin their own show, retaining the rights to *Praise the Lord's* initials *PTL*. In 1977, Paul Crouch raised $100,000 toward a down payment on a local Fontana, California, television station, which he renamed KTBN-TV. By 1978, programming had expanded to a 24-hour format with national distribution through cable systems. Over the years, Paul continued buying up independent television stations to obtain the coveted "must-carry" cable status. Consequently, the Trinity Broadcasting Network (TBN) became the third largest broadcast group of television stations in the nation with a viewership of 95 percent of American households. Today TBN World Headquarters is based in Costa Mesa, California, with studios in Dallas, Nashville, Birmingham, Tulsa, Atlanta, Miami, Orlando, New York, London, and Jerusalem. TBN is also the world's largest Christian television network, being broadcast on 70 satellites and over 18,000 television and cable affiliates around the world.[9]

Paul and Jan Crouch in an early Trinity Broadcasting Network *Praise the Lord* program. On May 28, 1973, TBN flashed on the air from a tiny rented studio in Southern California with one borrowed camera, two folding chairs, and a Sears shower curtain for a backdrop. Source: TBN.

Besides its flagship show, TBN also produces more original Christian programs—including talk shows, live events, concerts, holiday specials, movies, dramas, features on health and marriage, music videos, and children's shows—than any other religious network. Over the years, TBN has expanded its programing to include a diverse group of ministries ranging from traditional Catholic, Protestant, and Messianic Jewish programs to independent evangelical, Pentecostal, and charismatic interdenominational programs. TBN has also produced a number of full-length feature and faith-based films from their Hollywood studio. They own and operate a number of attractions, including their studio tours and virtual reality theaters in Costa Mesa and Dallas, Trinity Music City USA in Nashville, and The

9   "The TBN Story," *The Trinity Broadcasting Network:* *www.tbn.org/about-us/the-tbn-story* (Accessed 25 March 2013).

Holy Land Experience in Orlando, which features more than forty exhibits, reenactments, live television events, and church services. In 1995, Jan founded the Smile of a Child Foundation—a U.N.-recognized international humanitarian relief organization for underprivileged children. Together, Paul and Jan founded a number of affiliated networks—a children's channel, a youth network, a church channel, and several foreign-language networks. Paul and Jan's son, Matthew Crouch, became vice president in 2010 and president after Paul's death in 2013 and Jan's death in 2016.

TBN founders, Paul and Jan Crouch. In 2014, Paul shared, "God in these last forty years has done exactly what he promised us in those early years to do . . . . We have over 6,000 affiliated television cable stations and 76 satellites covering every square inch of planet earth." Source: TBN.

THE PTL CLUB

After aiding in the establishment of both CBN and TBN, it was time for Jim and Tammy Faye Bakker to launch their own Christian television network. What began as a local TV broadcast in a converted Charlotte, North Carolina, furniture store in 1974 quickly grew into a worldwide Christian satellite and cable television network phenomenon known as the PTL Television Network and carried by nearly a hundred stations with an average viewership of over 12 million. The Bakkers were an overnight sensation, displaying both extraordinary creativity and a seemingly unerring talent for raising money. Their flagship show, *The PTL Club* (originally *Praise the Lord* but later *People That Love*), featured many well-known ministers and Christian recording artists and was soon being broadcast from Heritage Village—the Bakker's ministry complex and Charlotte headquarters. Then in 1978, the Bakkers opened Heritage USA—a 2,300-acre Christian theme park in nearby Fort Mill, South Carolina, complete with a Main Street USA, 501-room Heritage Grand Hotel, shopping complex, church, production studio, amphitheater, water park, skating rink, Bible and evangelism school, prayer and counseling center, campground, housing, timeshares, conference center and recreational facilities. By 1986, Heritage USA had become a top U.S. tourist destination second only to Disneyland and Walt Disney World with nearly 6 million annual visitors and 2,500 employees.[10]

Evangelists Jim and Tammy Faye Bakker (c. 1985) hosted the popular *PTL Club* talk show and flagship television program of the PTL Satellite Network from their Charlotte, North Carolina, and Fort Mill, South Carolina, Heritage Village studios between 1974 and 1987. Source: Flower Pentecostal Heritage Center.

Jim and Tammy had always been publicly truthful about any past marriage failures or ministry crises, but nothing could have prepared their TV audience for what happened in 1987. First, Tammy was admitted to a California drug rehab clinic. Then Jim suddenly announced he was resigning from the Assemblies of God and as PTL's Chairman, claiming he was being blackmailed by a "hostile force" (later

---

10   Stanley Burgess, "James Orsen ('Jim') Bakker": DPCM 353; "Heritage USA," *Wikipedia: en.wikipedia.org/wiki/Heritage_USA* (Accessed 26 March 2013).

revealed to be fellow televangelist Jimmy Swaggart). Swaggart was trying to have Bakker removed from ministry after allegations surfaced of a 1980 sexual encounter and subsequent payment of "hush money" to his former church secretary. Bakker then turned his ministry over to yet another televangelist—Jerry Falwell—in hope of preventing a "hostile takeover" with the agreement that Falwell would later give it back. After the transaction, however, Falwell publicly agreed with Swaggart, calling Bakker a "cancer" on the church that needed to be removed. Independent auditors soon revealed that Bakker had recently paid himself over $3.4 million in bonuses and that PTL was $70 million in debt. PTL lawyers immediately filed bankruptcy and an IRS investigation ensued. A 1987 *New Yorker* article said Jim and Tammy "epitomized the excesses of the 1980s; the greed, the love of glitz, and the shamelessness; which in their case was so pure as to almost amount to a kind of innocence."[11] Others in the press were not so kind, remarking that PTL stood for "Pass the Loot."

In 1988, Bakker was indicted on twenty-four counts of fraud for overselling lodging rights and promising "Lifetime Partnerships" to tens of thousands of people for one 501-room hotel and in 1989 was sentenced to forty-five years in prison and a $500,000 fine (which was later reduced to $8,000). Bakker was released in 1994 after serving less than five years. In his 1996 book, *I Was Wrong*, Bakker blamed the "prosperity message" for his past mistakes and admitted he had read his Bible for the first time from cover to cover while in prison and, in so doing, discovered that most prosperity scriptures were taken out of

---

11   Frances FitzGerald, *The New Yorker* April 1987; "Jim Bakker," *Wikipedia: en.wikipedia.org/wiki/Jim_Bakker.*

context. He wrote, "The more I studied the Bible, I had to admit that the prosperity message did not line up with the tenor of Scripture. My heart was crushed to think that I led so many people astray. I was appalled that I could have been so wrong, and I was deeply grateful that God had not struck me dead as a false prophet!"[12]

Tammy Faye divorced Jim during his imprisonment to marry Heritage USA developer Roe Messner and died in 2007. In 2003, Jim returned to broadcasting with the new *Jim Bakker Show* from his new Studio City Cafe in Branson, Missouri, with his second wife, Lori. In 2008, the Bakker's moved their ministry to a 600-acre development in nearby Blue Eye, Missourri, called Morningside, that resembles Heritage USA, but this time the property is owned by Bakker's associates, not him.

Jim and Lori Bakker on the set of *The Jim Bakker Show*, an hour-long daily broadcast that features prophetic and biblical revelations brought to light in today's world. Filmed at Morningside in the Ozark Mountains, the show is aired through multiple broadcasts that can be seen on satellites throughout the U.S., Canada, and the entire world. Source: The Jim Bakker Show.

Though Falwell initially raised the $20 million necessary to keep Heritage USA afloat with his promised, well-publicized waterslide plunge, after Hurricane Hugo caused severe damage to many of the buildings in 1989, Heritage USA closed. Pentecostal evangelist Morris Cerullo purchased the property in 1991 in partnership with an investment group but then later backed out, retaining only the cable

12   Jim Bakker, *I Was Wrong* (Nashville: Thomas Nelson, 1996), 535: "Jim Bakker," *Wikipedia: en.wikipedia.org/wiki/Jim_Bakker* (Accessed 26 March 2013).

network, which he renamed The Inspiration Network (INSP) and turned it over to his son, David. Most of the remaining property was developed into a residential community and golf course, while other sections were sold off to businesses and other Christian ministries.

JIMMY SWAGGART

Jimmy Lee Swaggart was born in the small town of Ferriday, Louisiana, to a musically gifted and talented family that included cousins rock 'n' roll pioneer Jerry Lee Lewis and country music legend Mickey Gilley. Swaggart himself turned down an early recording career with a major label, stating he had been called to preach the gospel instead. In the 1960s, Swaggart became an ordained Assemblies of God minister, holding camp meetings and crusades in Assemblies of God churches. Swaggart's first encounter with the media came in 1969 when he introduced his fiery brand of preaching and singing on his *Campmeeting Hour* radio broadcast, which was eventually carried by 550 radio stations nationwide. In 1972, Swaggart moved his crusades from local churches to city auditoriums, while remaining intensely loyal to his denomination and, in effect, became the first independent evangelist since the early 1950s to receive his denomination's enthusiastic backing.

After breaking out on his own, however, Swaggart immediately noticed that more than half his audiences were "denominational people hungry for the Holy Spirit."[13] That same year, Swaggart announced he was expanding into television and eventually dropped his radio broadcast to focus exclusively on television. By 1974, his

---

13   Jimmy Swaggart, "Editor's Notes," *The Evangelist*, (December 1972), 2: ATP 215.

television broadcast was being aired on nearly 40 stations nationwide, and Swaggart became yet another seeming overnight sensation. His 1972 album, *There is a River*, became the most requested gospel album in America, and his 1976 *Live from Nashville* album was nominated for a Grammy for Best Gospel Album of the Year. Swaggart received numerous other Christian and secular music awards.

A young Jimmy Swaggart seated at the piano. Throughout the 1970s and 80s, Jimmy Swaggart's award-winning gospel albums and popular television broadcasts brought Pentecostalism's message and music into millions of households in America and abroad. Source: Flower Pentecostal Heritage Center.

By the 1980s, Jimmy Swaggart was probably the most widely known televangelist in the world. Besides being an immensely talented musician and formidable preacher, he had learned to "tone down" some of the old-time Pentecostal message to make his ministry even more appealing to mainstream America. His television audience quickly swelled to more than 8 million nationally and more than 500 million worldwide, making it one of the most widespread mass communications of the gospel in history.[14] With a 3,200-station network in 145 countries, Swaggart's exposure was larger than the three major American television networks combined. And with his monthly magazine, *The Evangelist*, being circulated in over 800,000 households, Swaggart was bringing in more than $150 million a year.

14 "A Brief Biography of Jimmy Swaggart," *Jimmy Swaggart Ministries: www.jsm.org/jimmy-swaggart.html* (Accessed 12 October 2014).

Despite the phenomenal growth, Swaggart was determined to keep his ministry "honest" and "clean," retaining only a small but efficient staff. Most of the monies received were used to build a 5,000-seat Family Worship Center and Bible College in Baton Rouge, with millions more being sent to overseas missions, children's relief efforts, foreign Bible college grants, and denominational programs. Swaggart's financial appeals also remained "low-key" compared with most evangelists, whom he often criticized for "perverting the prosperity message to bilk the unfortunate."[15]

True to his Pentecostal roots, a typical Swaggart crusade was positive and uplifting, while engaging the forces of sin and darkness wherever they may be found. Swaggart often spoke publicly against the formalism of Catholicism and Judaism, as well as the sinful practices of adultery and homosexuality—especially among those in ministry. But starting in 1986, it became personal. First Swaggart went after fellow Louisianan and Assemblies of God television minister Marvin Gorman, who had recently been tapped by the Assemblies for general superintendent. Swaggart reported to denominational officials allegations of sexual misconduct that forced Gorman to resign both his church and ministry. Then in 1987, Swaggart exposed yet another fellow Assemblies of God television minister, Jim Bakker, again informing denominational officials of sexual misconduct. Then just as Swaggart was about to announce the formation of his own Pentecostal fellowship that would have threatened the ranks of the Assemblies of God, rumors began surfacing of Swaggart's own sexual misconduct. This time, Marvin

---

15   David Harrell interview: ATP 216.

Gorman began receiving anonymous telephone tips, and this time, it was Gorman who presented denominational officials with evidence of sexual misconduct. Then in his famous "I Have Sinned" speech, Swaggart confessed before a television audience while crying and apologizing to his family, congregation, followers, and to God. The clip was played repeatedly on international tabloids. One headline read, "The Self-Appointed Judge of America's Televangelists Finds Himself the Penitent."[16] Another commentator said, "I thought he was one of the most honest and sincere preachers I had ever met, but I've seen him change over the years. He really seems to have been seduced by the power and the fame."[17] Pentecostal historian Vinson Synan later called the televangelist scandals of the late 1980s the low point of the twentieth century move of God. He said, "That put a black mark on the movement. It didn't stop the movement from growing, but it was so publicized; the whole world watched. On the other hand . . . these people were household names even before the scandals. In spite of some of the problems, they still helped spread the movement worldwide."[18]

Initially, the Louisiana Assemblies of God presbytery suspended Swaggart for three months, but then denominational headquarters extended it to the standard two-year suspension for sexual immorality.

16   Joanne Kaufman, "The Fall of Jimmy Swaggart," *People* Vol. 29 No. 9 (March 07, 1988): *Time Inc.: www.people.com/people/archive/article/0,,20098413,00.html* (Accessed 27 March 2013).

17   Ibid., quoted from William Martin, Rice University Sociologist and long-time Swaggart commentator.

18   Vinson Synan interview with Sarah Pulliam Bailey, "Yes, We Have a Witness," April 21, 2010, *Christianity Today*, vol. 54, No. 4, p. 67: *www.christianitytoday.com/ct/2010/April/26.67.html* (Accessed 10 December 2015).

Swaggart returned after three months claiming to be fully restored. But because he showed no signs of repentance or submission to rehabilitative discipline, the denomination pulled his accreditation. Family Worship Center, now an independent ministry, dropped in attendance as many Bible school students departed, and television stations discontinued his program. To avert any further crises, Swaggart's son, Donnie, and wife, Frances, quickly moved into leadership roles. In 1995, Swaggart launched a modest television comeback through the SonLife Broadcasting Network, which aired over a variety of satellite and cable providers and featured various church services and programs hosted by Jimmy, Frances, Donnie, and grandson, Gabriel.

In 2010, Jimmy Swaggart Ministries launched its all-new 24-hour format SonLife Broadcasting Network (SBN) from its Baton Rouge Family Worship Center studio through various satellite and cable TV providers. Source: Wikimedia/Jntracy75.

THE WORD OF FAITH MOVEMENT

Another popular movement that arose within charismatic circles was the Word of Faith movement. It grew exponentially in the eighties and nineties but was not without its share of controversy. Kenneth Erwin Hagin (1917–2003), whom many referred to as "Dad Hagin," "Pappa Hagin," or simply "Brother Hagin," was considered the founder of the movement. Hagin, who was born in McKinney, Texas, with a deformed heart and incurable blood disease, was confined to his bed by the age of fifteen. After dying three times and seeing the horrors of hell, he experienced a dramatic conversion and healing through a "revelation of faith" in God's Word. Then being raised up from the bed of affliction, Hagin began preaching in a small country church made up mostly of Southern Baptists before receiving the Pentecostal baptism in the Holy Spirit. For the next twelve years, Hagin pastored five different Assemblies of God churches in east Texas. In 1949, he resigned his last church to set out as an itinerant preacher, eventually joining Gordon Lindsay's Voice of Healing and later speaking at Full Gospel Business Men's conventions and other charismatic conferences. Hagin's folksy style of storytelling combined with his homespun charm and Texas twang made him a popular speaker.

Hagin also reported receiving eight separate visions of Jesus Christ during this time. In obedience to one of those visions in which Jesus instructed him to "teach My people faith," he resigned from the Assemblies of God in 1962 to establish the Kenneth E. Hagin Evangelistic Association and began distributing his own books and teaching tapes. In 1966, Hagin moved his ministry from Garland, Texas, to Tulsa, Oklahoma, where he began his *Faith Seminar of the Air* radio broadcast. Two years later, he began his monthly newsletter, *The Word of Faith*, and in 1974, founded Rhema Bible Training Center (now Rhema Bible Training College), moving to nearby Broken Arrow, Oklahoma. Today Rhema has training centers in 17 nations with 40,000 alumni in over 100 countries and more than 1,000 affiliated churches.[19] In 1979, Hagin also founded the Prayer

19   "Introduction to RBTC," *Kenneth Hagin Ministries: www.rhema.org*: "Kenneth Erwin Hagin," *Wikipedia: en.wikipedia.org/wiki/Kenneth_E._Hagin* (Accessed 28 March 2013).

and Healing Center, where the sick could come twice daily, free of charge, to have their faith built up for healing. In 1992, Rhema Bible Church was completed on the Rhema campus. By 2000, Hagin and his son, Kenneth W. Hagin, were distributing more than 53 million copies of 125 Faith Library Publications (mostly transcribed sermons), 58,000 teaching tapes, and 540,000 monthly newsletters in addition to holding their crusades, seminars, and annual Camp Meeting.[20] Since Hagin's death in 2003, his son and daughter-in-law, Ken and Lynette, and grandson, Craig, have continued to run the ministry.

By 1973, Hagin's ministry was being augmented by a number of other "faith" teachers. Charles Capps began his itinerant ministry that year. Frederick K.C. Price founded Crenshaw Christian Center in Los Angeles that year and was later ordained by Hagin's ministry, beginning his *Ever Increasing Faith* television broadcast in 1978 and completing his FaithDome in 1989. Kenneth Copeland also began *The Believer's Voice of Victory* that same year. After listening to Hagin's teaching tapes from his garage, Copeland took the "faith" message global through his Believers' Conventions and television and satellite broadcasts.

In 1978, Frederick K.C. Price gained international renown through his Ever Increasing Faith television broadcast, completing the 10,000-seat FaithDome in Los Angeles in 1989 and founding the Fellowship of International Christian Word of Faith Ministries (FICWFM) in 1990. Source: Crenshaw Christian Center.

The roots of the "faith" message lay deep in classical Pentecostalism, the postwar healing revival, and the charismatic movement, holding

20   R.M. Riss, "Kenneth E. Hagin" DPCM 687.

many doctrinal similarities to such ministers as Smith Wigglesworth, F.F. Bosworth, E.W. Kenyon, John G. Lake, William Branham, Oral Roberts, and A.A. Allen. Its roots can also be traced to the various Holiness and Higher Life movements of the nineteenth century that taught that a holy lifestyle was a path to prosperity and that God-ordained hard work would bring blessing. In more recent years, however, the doctrine has come under attack because of its affiliation with Kenyon, whose alleged exposure to the metaphysical cults while taking a year of acting lessons at Boston's Emerson College of Oratory made him suspect. However, evangelical author Robert M. Bowman Jr., whose *Word-Faith Controversy* book has been acclaimed as one of the most thorough, objective, and balanced examinations on the subject, concluded that while similarities do exist between Kenyon's teachings and the metaphysical cults, evangelical faith cure and early Pentecostal teachers like A.J. Gordon and A.B. Simpson probably had greater influence on Kenyon's theology.[21] Bowman, who described the movement as "neither soundly orthodox nor thoroughly heretical" encouraged charismatic believers to distinguish between acceptable Pentecostal teachings and distorted offshoots by pursuing "a rich, mature, and biblically sound Pentecostalism."[22]

PROSPERITY TEACHING

The main points of controversy with Word of Faith teaching seem to center on five statements: 1) Positive confession can bring things

---

21   Robert M. Bowman, Jr., *The Word-Faith Controversy* (Grand Rapids, Mich.: Baker, 2000), back cover: Reviewed by Tim Chaffey, *Midwest Apologetics:* www.midwestapologetics.org/reviews/wordfaithcontroversy.htm (Accessed 28 March 2013).

22   Ibid.

into existence. 2) Physical healing is part of Christ's atonement. 3) God wants his people to prosper financially, not suffer. 4) God made humans in his image, which makes us "little gods." And 5) Jesus died both physically and spiritually to atone for man's sins. While some within the movement may wholeheartedly agree with some or all those statements, many others have taken issue, preferring, as Hagin often quipped, "not to get in the ditch on one side of the road or the other." Bowman also noted that although extreme teachings abound even among some of the bigger names in the movement, they do not represent the whole. In fact, many Word of Faith ministers, churches, and followers have since distanced themselves from the so-called "prosperity teachers." Some even consider them a separate sect or movement distinct from Word of Faith.

Hagin's 2000 book, *The Midas Touch: A Balanced Approach to Biblical Prosperity*, sharply criticized the extremes within the movement, warning the body of Christ against the dangers of greed and explaining that the purpose of financial blessing is for the furtherance of the gospel. Hagin met privately with some of the major "prosperity teachers," including Kenneth Copeland, Creflo Dollar, Jerry Savelle, Jesse Duplantis, and others, and gave them an opportunity to adjust their messages and correct their errors before the release of his book. Some did, while others did not. Most of the errors outlined in the book seemed to center around gimmicks designed to coerce giving—such as claiming a hundredfold return, "naming a seed" or some other specific benefit, claiming to have an "anointing to break debt," teaching people to give in order to get, or suggesting that material wealth is a sign of spirituality.

Kenneth and Gloria Copeland on *The Believer's Voice of Victory* (2011). For nearly fifty years, Kenneth Copeland has taught a message of faith, love, healing, prosperity, and restoration through music, television, books, multimedia, and Believers' Conventions. Source: Kenneth Copeland Ministries. Photo: Wikimedia/Adrignola.

Many disparaging titles have since been assigned to the movement, including "Name it, Claim it," "Gab it, Grab it," "the positive confession movement," "faith-formula theology," and "the prosperity gospel." Meanwhile, many within the movement have argued Word of Faith teaching was never about prosperity but about applying God's uncompromised Word to every area of life. Though prosperity was always a part of it, the message eventually became twisted until it was no longer about God but about man, resulting in a sustained loss of God's power and presence in the movement. In 2007, Senator Chuck Grassley opened an investigation into the finances of six prosperity teachers: Kenneth Copeland, Creflo Dollar, Benny Hinn, Bishop Eddie Long, Joyce Meyer, and Paula White. Only Meyer and Hinn fully cooperated with the investigation, and in 2011, Grassley's commission concluded that self-regulation by religious organizations was preferable to government action.

Despite the alleged errors, both Word of Faith and prosperity teaching remain popular among poor and upwardly mobile Pentecostal, charismatic, and neo-charismatic groups worldwide. But aside from these extreme elements, perhaps the movement's greatest legacy was the restoration of the ever vital, much-needed teaching ministry in the body of Christ. Similar to the printed Bible movement of the seventeenth century or the Sunday school movement of the late eighteenth century, the Bible teaching movement of the late twentieth century brought in-depth Bible teaching once confined to seminaries, universities, and Bible schools into America's pulpits, living rooms, classrooms, and convention halls. For the first time in history, people came to church toting not only Bibles but also pens, pads, tablets, and later, mobile devices, eagerly awaiting the exploration of God's Word. Many took to heart Hagin's oft-repeated exhortation: "Don't believe anything because I said it. Search the scriptures and prove it out for yourself." Before long, Bible translations, software, apps, concordances, and Bible study aids had become global commodities.[23]

In the last quarter of the twentieth century, Kenneth Hagin's influence brought in-depth Pentecostal and charismatic Bible teaching once confined to seminaries, universities, and Bible schools, into America's pulpits, living rooms, classrooms, and convention halls. Source: Wikimedia/Deepdown19.

MANIFESTATION REVIVALS

Just prior to the turn of the twenty-first century, a number of "manifestation" revivals broke out in North America. First there was Rodney Howard-Browne's 14-week "laughing revival" at Carpenter's Home Church in Lakeland, Florida, in 1993, which featured many divine healings, falling, weeping, joyous laughter, and a mass water

23 Kenneth E. Hagin, *How You Can Know the Will of God* (Tulsa: Faith Library, 1980); *The Believer's Authority* (Tulsa: Faith Library, 1985): "Kenneth Hagin," *ReligionFacts: www.religionfacts.com/people/kenneth-hagin* (Accessed 13 July 2015).

baptism. Then there was the "Toronto Blessing" (a term coined by British newspapers that stuck). This began when Randy Clark, who had been influenced by Rodney Howard-Browne's ministry, visited John Arnott's Toronto Airport Vineyard Christian Fellowship for two months in 1994. Daily meetings continued and peaked by the late 1990s, producing many manifestations, including holy laughter, falling, shaking, roaring, and divine healings. This persisted well into the 2000s and later evolved into Catch the Fire Toronto conferences and Spread the Fire conferences globally. The Toronto movement made a significant impact in the U.K. when Nicky Gumbel, a curate at Holy Trinity, Brompton, Church of England parish in London, and an attendee of the original Toronto Blessing meetings, oversaw the revision and expansion of Holy Trinity's evangelistic "Alpha" course. 250,000 reportedly came to Christ through Alpha in the 1990s, with many also reporting receiving the baptism in the Holy Spirit.[24] Alpha is now supported by most major British denominations and has expanded globally to 169 countries and 112 languages, with over 27 million having taken the course.[25] And finally, there was the "Brownsville Revival" or "Pensacola Outpouring," that began in 1995, when evangelist Steve Hill was invited to John Kilpatrick's Brownsville Assembly of God in Pensacola, Florida. As reports of "a mighty wind" blowing through the sanctuary on the first night began to spread, nightly revival meetings continued with Hill preaching several each week for the next five

---

24   Jon Ronson, "Catch Me If You Can," (2000):
     The Guardian: www.theguardian.com/theguardian/2000/oct/21/weekend7.weekend:
     "Toronto Blessing," *Wikipedia: en.wikipedia.org/wiki/Toronto_Blessing* (Accessed 27 August 2016).

25   "Alpha is running all around the globe..." Alpha.org. (Retrieved 23 February 2015): "Alpha course," *Wikipedia: en.wikipedia.org/wiki/Alpha_course* (Accessed 27 August 2016).

years. These meetings also featured a number of manifestations such as supernatural healings, falling, trembling, shaking, laughing, and weeping. By 1998, more than 2.5 million people from all over the world had reportedly visited Brownsville's Wednesday-through-Saturday evening revival services.[26] Though the church continued to hold special Friday-night services until 2006, the main revival seemed to end when Hill left in 2000. In all, 200,000 claimed to have given their lives to Jesus through the Brownsville Revival.[27]

The Toronto Blessing (left) and Brownsville Revival (right). The end of the twentieth century witnessed a series of "manifestation" revivals, each with worldwide impact. Source: Catch The Fire/Brownsville Assembly.

A GLOBAL RENEWAL

Just as the charismatic movement seemed to be winding down in North America, it went global. The last decade of the twentieth century saw a marked growth and expansion of the movement on all continents, particularly among independents in Africa, South America, and Asia, as new trends adopted by charismatics were rapidly impacting

---

26 Margaret M. Poloma and John C. Green, *The Assemblies of God: Godly Love and the Revitalization of American Pentecostalism,* (New York: New York University, 2010), 1: "Brownsville Revival": *Wikipedia: en.wikipedia.org/wiki/Brownsville_Revival* (Accessed 29 August 2016).

27 "Fire From Above," *Charisma Magazine,* June 2005 (Retrieved 12 February 2012): "Brownsville Revival," *Wikipedia: en.wikipedia.org/wiki/Brownsville_Revival* (Accessed 29 August 2016).

all nations and continents. Suddenly large numbers of churches worldwide were singing charismatic praise choruses, praying for healing, and promoting Spirit-empowered worship and intercession—often without even calling themselves Pentecostals or charismatics. *The New International Dictionary of Pentecostal and Charismatic Movements* has defined the charismatic movement as "a worldwide phenomenon affecting millions of believers from an extraordinary range of Christian churches and streams," further stating that "it cannot be regarded simply as a prayer movement, an evangelistic movement, or a healing movement. It is all of these and more."[28] In the end, the charismatic movement was a global revitalization of the power of the Holy Spirit that affected virtually every aspect of Christian life and mission. In fact, it was not until 2009 that *Charisma* magazine editor J. Lee Grady made this official pronouncement: "The charismatic movement as we know it has ended."[29]

---

28 P.D. Hocken, "Charismatic Movement": DPCM 519.

29 J. Lee Grady, ed., "God Has Pushed a Great Big Reset Button," Fire in My Bones (May 05, 2009) *Charisma Magazine: www.charismamag.com/blogs/fire-in-my-bones/4530-god-has-pushed-a-great-big-reset-button* (Accessed 29 March 2013)

STUDY QUESTIONS

1. What was the "Shepherding" Movement, and what led to its ultimate demise?

2. What role did Pat Robertson play in the genesis and growth of the charismatic movement worldwide?

3. How did Christian television broadcasting help transform American Pentecostal and charismatic Christianity into a global renewal by the end of the twentieth century?

4. What led to the collapse of the PTL Television Network and Heritage USA theme park?

5. What made Jimmy Swaggart perhaps the most widely known televangelist in the world by the 1980s?

6. Although Pentecostal historian Vinson Synan referred to the televangelist scandals of the 1980s as the low point of the twentieth-century move of God, why do you think the scandals did not stop the movement from growing and going global?

7. What was the Word of Faith movement, and how did it begin?

8. Why do you think Robert M. Bowman Jr. called Word of Faith teaching "neither soundly orthodox nor thoroughly heretical"?

9. How does "prosperity teaching" differ from Word of Faith teaching?

10. How did the "manifestation" revivals, such as those in Toronto and Brownsville, affect the growth of charismatic Christianity globally by the end of the twentieth century?

INTO THE TWENTY-FIRST CENTURY

(2001 AND BEYOND)

The twentieth century witnessed many revolutionary changes in the way people lived—from religion and ideology to politics and economics to science and technology. The world's population had increased from 1.6 billion in 1901 to 6.1 billion by 2000. Books, computers, public education, and the Internet made knowledge more widely available, as enhanced science, digital communications, and faster transportation transformed the world more widely and more rapidly than in any previous century. Horses and sailing ships, which had been the staples of transportation for thousands of years, were suddenly replaced by automobiles, buses, high-speed rail, cruise liners, and global commercial air and space travel, thanks in part to the exploitation of fossil fuels.

The twenty-first century began in a similar revolutionary fashion when on September 11, 2001, a group of Islamist al-Qaeda terrorists, attempting to strike at the heart of the "Great Satan" (the world's last remaining superpower and still deemed largely Christian), hijacked four commercial jetliners loaded with fuel. Two were aimed at New York's World Trade Center Twin Towers, a third at the Pentagon, and a fourth probably at the Capitol or White House. The fourth did not reach its intended target but was brought down in a remote field near Shanksville, Pennsylvania, after a group of courageous passengers attempted to retake the plane. In all, 3,000 Americans were killed in the largest single loss of life on American soil from a foreign invader. Churches across North America were filled to capacity the following Sunday as many began searching for answers. The terrorists cited U.S. support for Israel, the presence of U.S. troops on "sacred" Arabian soil, and Iraqi sanctions as primary motives for their attacks. Despite the liberal attempt to create a one-world secular society and despite modern advancements in politics and economics, the ancient religions of the Crusaders were alive and well in the twenty-first century.

The secular world was reawakened to radicalized religion on September 11, 2001. Despite every attempt to create a one-world secular society, the ancient religions of the Crusaders were alive and well in the twenty-first century. Photo: Ken Tannenbaum/ Shutterstock.com.

By 2025, scholars expect Christianity to exceed 2.6 billion people, making it by far the largest faith, with a ratio of one-in-three worldwide.[1] Some experts have noted that religion in the new century

---

1   CH 495.

is even showing signs of overtaking ideology once again as the primary animating force in human affairs.[2] The new century is also witnessing a dramatic shift in Christianity to the Southern Hemisphere as evidenced by the stunning 2013 election of Pope Francis—the first Jesuit, evangelical, charismatic, Argentine, American, and Latin American pope.[3] By the dawn of the new century, 480 million Christians were living in Latin America, 360 million in Africa, and 313 million in Asia compared with only 260 million in North America.[4] Even as far back as the 1960s, Pentecostal researcher Walter Hollenweger predicted that by the turn of the twenty-first century, over half of the world's Christians would be non-white, Pentecostal, and from the Third World—he was right! Penn State history and religion professor Philip Jenkins has also noticed a worldwide revolution taking place in Christianity toward supernaturalism—the ancient worldview of the New Testament in which Jesus is seen as the embodiment of power who overcomes evil forces that inflict calamity and sickness upon the human race.[5] Jenkins also quoted Catholic scholar Walbert Buhlmann, who described this revolution as a "Third Church" distinct from Catholicism and Protestantism that is "likely to become dominant in

---

2   Philip Jenkins, "The Next Christianity" (October 2002 Issue)
     Volume 290, No. 3; 53–68, *The Atlantic Monthly:*
     www.theatlantic.com/magazine/archive/2002/10/the-next-christianity/302591/
     (Accessed 30 March 2013).

3   George Weigel, "The First Evangelical Pope" *National Review Online*
     (March 16, 2013) *RealClearReligion:*
     www.realclearreligion.org/2013/03/16/the_first_evangelical_pope_253125.html
     (Accessed 30 March 2013).

4   Philip Jenkins, "The Next Christianity" (October 2002 Issue) Vol. 290, No. 3:53–68,
     The Atlantic Monthly: www.theatlantic.com/past/docs/issues/2002/10/jenkins.htm
     (Accessed 30 March 2013).

5   Ibid.

the faith."[6] Jenkins then cited what he called the "shrinking population in the liberal West and a growing majority of the traditional Rest." No longer could the Southern Hemisphere be referred to as the "Third World" but as the "Majority World." No longer could Africa be called the "dark continent" but the "bright continent." And Latin America was no longer the "forgotten continent" but the "foremost continent," at least where Christianity was concerned.

On June 1, 2014, Pope Francis addressed a crowd of some 52,000 Charismatic Catholics in Rome, saying, "In the early years of the Charismatic Renewal in Buenos Aires, I did not like the charismatics . . . but after I got to know them, I began to understand the good that that Renewal does for the Church . . . and . . . [in] a few months . . . I was appointed by the Conference of Bishops as chaplain of the Renewal in Argentina." Source: VIS/Vatican Radio, "Pope advises Charismatic Renewal: Be stewards not inspectors of God's grace," June 2, 2014: *Independent Catholic News: www.indcatholicnews.com/news.php?viewStory=24875* (Accessed 3 August, 2016) Photo Source: Korea.net/Korean Culture and Information Service. Photo: Wikimedia/Stemoc.

AFRICA

World War I marked the peak of European colonialism and the beginning of Europe's withdrawal from its colonies around the world. This eventually resulted in scores of new nations springing up all over Asia and Africa and changing the face of the globe—both politically and religiously. Meanwhile, a new wave of Pentecostal missionaries from North America was entering Latin America, and today the continent represents the largest population of Pentecostals in the world. Then by the third quarter of the century, as Western colonial occupation

6   Ibid.

of Africa was coming to an end, no less than forty-two new African nations had gained independence and joined the United Nations. Plus, after centuries of Catholic, Protestant, and later Pentecostal missionaries poured into these nations, a new Christian elite arose among the indigenous ranks and eventually became the governmental leaders of these new nations. This opened the door for major Christian revivals in key African nations such as Nigeria, Congo, Ethiopia, South Africa, Kenya, Uganda, and Tanzania as more than a dozen African nations became between 90 and 100 percent Christian.

Along with this increase in African Christian leadership came new opportunities for mass evangelism, allowing men like German-born evangelist Reinhard Bonnke to preach to 120 million with crowds reaching up to 1.6 million in a single service and leading some 55 million to salvation in Christ—often with complete governmental cooperation.[7] Bonnke heard the voice of God declare in a recurring three-night dream, "Africa Shall Be Saved!" Immediately, he began preaching in major cities, open fields, and capacity-filled stadiums the good news of Jesus Christ with miraculous signs following. In 1991, Bonnke was banned from preaching in Nigeria after his rumored "invasion" and "blasphemy" of Islam incited a series of local riots. Nine years later, however, he was allowed to return to Nigeria, leading multiple millions to Christ between 2000 and 2009. In Bonnke's 2000 Lagos Crusade, he preached to six million in six days, and led one million souls to Christ in a single service—the days of mass evangelism were far from over!

---

7   Reinhard Bonnke: Biography, "A Life on Fire," *Christ for all Nations: new.cfan.org/reinhard-bonnke* (Accessed 13 July 2015).

Reinhard Bonnke's Lagos, Nigeria Crusade reached an estimated crowd upwards of 1.6 million in 2000. Source: CfaN.

Meanwhile, in North Africa—a region traditionally hostile to the gospel—a profound and unprecedented spiritual revival was taking place as tens of thousands of Muslims of all ages were coming to Christ. The only difference was this revival was not limited to any isolated area or conventional evangelistic means. Instead individuals from many nations like Libya, Tunisia, Algeria, Morocco, Mauritania, and Western Sahara were claiming to have miraculous encounters such as seeing visions of Jesus in the form of "a light" or having personal conversations with him. Even illiterate people were finding they could suddenly supernaturally read the Bible. Today it is not uncommon in some traditionally Arab nations to find Christians freely talking about their faith in public or on television. Some Algerian Christian groups are even pledging to send 1,000 missionaries by the year 2025.[8] And worldwide, experts are saying that many Muslims, horrified by the recent violent examples of their faith, are converting to Christianity in large numbers. Indeed, more Muslims have converted to Christianity since the 9/11 terrorist attacks than in the fourteen centuries of

---

8   George Thomas, "Dreams and Visions: Revival Hits Muslim N. Africa" (April 22, 2014) *The Christian Broadcasting Network:*
www.cbn.com/cbnnews/world/2014/April/Revival-in-Land-Once-Hostile-to-Christ
(Accessed 24 April 2014).

Islamic history combined.[9] But for obvious safety reasons, many must keep their conversions a secret.

EUROPE

The numbers are staggering: More Christians worship in Anglican churches in Nigeria today than in all Anglican and Episcopal churches in Britain, Europe, and North America combined. The Assemblies of God has ten times more members in Latin America than in the U.S. where it was founded, and more people worship in church every Sunday in Communist China than in all of Western Europe put together.[10] As the numbers continue to pour in, many Western observers are seeing a "reverse flow" or crosscurrent of missionaries coming out of Africa, Asia, and Latin America into Europe and North America. Yesterday's great mission fields have become today's great missionary forces as nations like China, India, Singapore, South Korea, and Indonesia are beginning to overshadow even the great missionary legacies of Europe and North America. Who could have imagined—after centuries of European and North American dominated world missions—that the descended converts of these missionaries would one day return the favor by sending missionaries of their own to save a secular West from impending moral ruin? Yet the apostle Paul once spoke of the propriety of children repaying their elderly parents for previously taking care of them.[11]

---

9   Dale Hurd, "Ex-Muslims Lighting the Way for Islam's Collapse?" (June 5, 2015) *The Christian Broadcasting Network: www.cbn.com/cbnnews/world/2015/June/Ex-Muslims-Lighting-the-Way-for-Islams-Collapse* (Accessed 5 June 2015).

10   CH 491.

11   1 Tim. 5:4.

The twenty-first century may well see such gratitude and generosity on a global scale. For instance, Embassy of God church in Kiev, Ukraine—the largest evangelical and charismatic church in Europe with more than 700 affiliated congregations in more than 45 countries and more than 25,000 members in Kiev alone—was not founded by a European but by Sunday Adelaja, a Nigerian Pentecostal.[12] Also, four of the ten largest churches in the U.K. today are pastored by Africans, including London's 10,000-member Kingsway International Christian Centre pastored by Matthew Ashimolowo—a Muslim convert and Nigerian Pentecostal.[13]

Pastor Sunday Adelaja—an African immigrant and Pentecostal missionary from Nigeria—is senior pastor of the Embassy of the Blessed Kingdom of God to all Nations with headquarters in Kiev, Ukraine. The Embassy is considered the largest evangelical church in Europe and its influence is well noted in Christian and mainstream media around the world. Source: godembassy.org.

NORTH AMERICA

Similar missions are beginning to take root in North America. Redeemed Christian Church of God of North America (RCCG)—a Nigerian Pentecostal denomination with headquarters near Dallas, Texas—has more than 720 churches in virtually every major city in the United States. RCCG is a global Pentecostal denomination with

12 "The Unlikely Ambassador," *Charisma* Magazine (October 2007): "Sunday Adelaja," *Wikipedia: en.wikipedia.org/wiki/Sunday_Adelaja* (Accessed 31 March 2013).

13 Philip Jenkins, *God's Continent: Christianity, Islam, and Europe's Religious Crisis,* (New York: Oxford, 2007), 92 and Table 4.1.

mission outposts in over 147 countries.[14] General Overseer Enoch Adeboye sums up their mission: "Made in heaven, assembled in Nigeria, exported to the world."[15] Nigerian Pentecostals have their own brand of colorful music and worship infused by an intense belief in the supernatural presence of God. They are disciplined, regimented, deliberate, and systematic in their approach to church growth and world evangelization. But they are not alone.

Zenzo Matoga, a missionary from Malawi, is worship leader at one of New England's largest churches—Jubilee Christian Center and founder of United Night of Worship (UNOW)—one of the largest cross-cultural interdenominational gatherings in New England.[16] Matoga gathers thousands of believers annually in Boston's open square near where George Whitefield once preached to thousands in America's First Great Awakening and where many believe America's next revival will begin. Bishop Bart Pierce, a white Pentecostal minister from Baltimore, believes African missionaries will be "the midwife for the next great move of God in America."[17] Hillsong—an Assemblies of God church based out of Sydney, Australia—also has church plants in major European and American cities, including New York, Los Angeles, Phoenix, London, Paris, Barcelona, Stockholm, Kiev, Copenhagen,

---

14 Lisa Miller, "The Newsweek 50: E.A. Adeboye," (December 19, 2008) *Newsweek: www.newsweek.com/newsweek-50-e-adeboye-83039* (Accessed 1 April 2013); Wesley Granberg-Michaelson speech at Symposium on "World Christianity, Immigration, and the U.S.: The non-Western Church Comes to America" (February 26, 2014) *Library of Congress: www.loc.gov/today/cyberlc/transcripts/2014/140226klu0900.txt* (Accessed 21 October 2014).

15 Andrew Rice, "Mission from Africa" (April 8, 2009), *The New York Times: www.nytimes.com/2009/04/12/magazine/12churches-t.html?pagewanted=all&_r=0* (Accessed 21 October 2014).

16 "Zenzo and Michelle Matoga, Founders and Visionaries," *United Night of Worship: www.unitednightofworship.com/our-team* (Accessed 23 October 2014).

17 Ibid.

Amsterdam, and Dusseldorf. In 2013, South African missionary Reinhard Bonnke moved to America, where he believes God is getting ready to save millions, and is saying what he once said about Africa: "All America Shall Be Saved!" Bonnke immediately began holding revivals in auditoriums and arenas across the nation.[18] Rodney Howard-Browne, another South African missionary, has organized similar evangelistic efforts in the U.S., including "Celebrate America," which began as a nationwide 24/7 prayer chain and a series of street-witnessing campaigns and meetings in the nation's capital and across the country. He is also hoping to spark yet another Great Awakening in America.

The Great Lakes Reinhard Bonnke Gospel Crusade at Chicago's Allstate Arena in June 2015. 18,000 attended the two nights, with 2,000 decisions for Christ and hundreds more testifying of being healed by the power of God. The second night, the arena erupted and thundered with the glory of God before Bonnke prayed for all who wanted to receive the baptism in the Holy Spirit. Similar meetings were held in major cities across America. Source: CfaN.

With more missionaries now coming from the Majority Church in the Majority World than from the U.K., U.S., and Canada combined, a common refrain being heard in Cape Town, South Africa, these days is that this century will be a century of missions by "everyone" to "everywhere."[19] And with America now being as much a receiver nation as a sender nation, the American church must recognize her new role

18 Jennifer Leclaire, "Reinhard Bonnke: All America Shall Be Saved!" (Feb. 4, 2013) *Charisma Magazine: www.charismamag.com/spirit/evangelism-missions/16696-reinhard-bonnke-all-america-shall-be-saved* (Accessed 24 October 2014).

19 "Professor Steve de Gruchy to keynote 'Everyone, Everywhere' world mission conference" (November 29, 2007) *The Episcopal Church: www.episcopalchurch.org/library/article/south-african-theologian-steve-de-gruchy-keynote-everyone-everywhere-world-mission* (Accessed 3 April 2013).

in the global church by partnering and cooperating with other vibrant, reproducing, sending churches and assisting them in reaching people groups and cultures that the American church alone cannot reach. Asians are more adept at reaching Asians, Africans are more proficient at reaching Africans, Indians are more skilled at reaching Indians, and Latin Americans are experts at reaching Latin Americans. And with North America now being the largest mission field in the Western hemisphere and fifth largest in the world with 120 million unsaved people, it's only natural that they would come.[20] According to a recent U.S. Census, 43 million residents in the United States were foreign born, and 74 percent of them are Christians![21] America's spiritual landscape can and will change, but American churches must first give up their independence and denominational dependencies, trust the present-day work of the Holy Spirit, and learn to become interdependent on the global church. Clearly, a new era in world missions is underway.

ASIA

When the Communist Party took over China in 1949, many Christian leaders were arrested and given 40-year prison sentences. Among them was Simon Zhao. Zhao was released from prison in 1983, and when other Christians heard his story, they invited him to share it with the "underground" churches. Zhao testified that many nights while in prison labor camps, he turned his face toward the West, toward Jerusalem, and prayed, "God, the vision that you've given us has perished, but I pray you will raise up a new generation of Chinese believers to fulfill the

---

20   George Hunter, "The Rationale for a Culturally Relevant Worship Service," *Journal of the American Society for Church Growth, Worship and Growth 7* (1996), 131: Ed Stetzer, *Planting Missional Churches*, (Nashville: B&H, 2006), 13.

21   Wesley Granberg-Michaelson speech at Library of Congress (February 26, 2014).

vision."[22] Zhao died right after the turn of the century but lived long enough to see the beginnings of his vision fulfilled. The underground church movement, which began in the 1920s and grew gradually despite intense persecution and opposition, had an estimated 70 million members by 2011, permeating virtually every level of society from academia to business, science, provincial governors, judges, lawyers, and even drawing some within the Communist Party itself.[23]

After the infamous 1989 Tiananmen Square massacre in which China's political leaders enforced martial law on student-led popular demonstrations in Beijing, experts said the military crackdown actually helped church growth as many Chinese intellectuals and other elites lost faith in communism and embraced Christianity instead. Since then, China's church has grown so large that the Communist Party fears its influence and, despite the persecution of unregistered house churches, the number of believers continues to grow.[24] The city of Wenzhou, for example, known as "China's Jerusalem," has a population of over seven million with nearly one million Christians and hundreds of churches. And what has become known as "Christianity fever" in China is now spreading beyond China's borders and has become a "Back to Jerusalem" movement in honor of Zhao's generation. Since China considers itself "the ends of the earth," they intend to fulfill the Great Commission in reverse by carrying the gospel west and encircling the globe before finally reaching Jerusalem.

22 Tony Lambert, *China's Christian Millions*, (London: Monarch, 1999): CH 492.

23 Rodney Stark, Byron Johnson, and Carson Mencken, "Counting China's Christians," (May 2011) The Institute on Religion and Public Life, *First Things: www.firstthings.com/article/2011/05/counting-chinas-christians*.

24 "Tiananmen Massacre Still Spurring Church Growth," (June 4, 2014) *The Christian Broadcasting Network: www.cbn.com/cbnnews/world/2014/June/Tiananmen-Square-Massacre-Still-Spurs-Church-Growth*.

Today's Chinese house church movement is hoping to send 100,000 missionaries to the fifty-one unreached people groups between China and Jerusalem, having already planted some 7,000 Chinese churches in Singapore, Hong Kong, and throughout Southeast Asia. South Korea has sent nearly as many, and church leaders in the Philippines are now pledging to send at least one missionary for every two they receive, concentrating on the unreached Muslim nations. One of the largest Christian churches in the Arabian Peninsula today is pastored by a Filipino.

Reinhard Bonnke preaching at Bethany Church of God—a Pentecostal church in Surabaya, Indonesia, with more than 200,000 members, hundreds of additional satellite churches, and new churches being planted throughout the world each year. Bethany is located in the largest Muslim-populated nation on earth and the 40,000-seat worship center is considered the largest public building in Southeast Asia. Source: CfaN.

Millions of Chinese believers are also praying for the 10/40 Window—an area stretching from Southeast Asia to North Africa between 10 and 40 degrees latitude north of the equator that currently comprises 95 percent of the world's unreached people. Islam, Hinduism, Buddhism, and other world religions are major strongholds in this region. Christians are also heavily persecuted in this region—an estimated 100,000–160,000 are martyred each year, more than any other time in history. An estimated 80 percent of Christians in Asia are also Pentecostal-charismatic because of the phenomenal spread of the charismatic movement in nations like Korea, India, the Philippines, Indonesia, and China.[25] Despite the threat of persecution and death, a tsunami of the Holy Spirit is heading for the Muslim world.

25 Wesley Granberg-Michaelson speech at Library of Congress (February 26, 2014).

LATIN AMERICA

Pentecostalism in Latin America is not a religion of the *classes* but of the *masses*. It does not *engage* culture; it *transcends* culture. It *has* no social or political program; it *is* a social program. It does not *invite* unbelievers to *come*; it *seeks* and *goes* to unbelievers. Latin American Pentecostal churches are the only churches in the world currently growing three times faster than the general population. Latin American Pentecostalism is a deeply embedded, indigenous grassroots movement currently in a struggle with Catholicism for the heart and soul of Latin America. Peter Wagner said that their "secret is the power of the Holy Spirit."[26] Latin American Pentecostals firmly believe the baptism in the Holy Spirit and speaking in tongues are an essential part of their movement. A popular saying among them is, "It doesn't matter if you know the Bible well. The important thing is to be filled by the Holy Spirit, and be led by Him," and they are unapologetic about it.[27] The power of Jesus Christ over demonic forces is frequently and openly displayed for all to see with miraculous healings, deliverances, and salvation. They freely speak in tongues, sing and dance during worship, which is culturally relevant, fun, loud, ecstatic, dramatic, participative, and real. Their preaching often focuses on the power of God with the promise of a better life immediately upon conversion. And since their preaching is more of a shared dialogue than a lecture, nobody falls asleep.

---

26 C. Peter Wagner, *Spiritual Power and Church Growth: Lessons from the Amazing Growth of Pentecostal Churches in Latin America* (Altamonte Springs, Fla.: Creation, 1986) back cover.

27 Pedro C. Moreno, "Rapture and Renewal in Latin America" (New York: June/July 1997), 31–34, The Institute on Religion and Public Life, *First Things: www.firstthings. com/article/1997/06/003-rapture-and-renewal-in-latin-america* (Accessed 3 April 2013).

The National Assemblies of God Youth Congress in Cancún, Mexico, in 2010. A Catholic Archbishop of Santiago de Chile once shared a bad dream. He went to the cathedral to say Mass, only to find it had been completely taken over by a huge crowd of charismatic worshipers praying and singing loudly, arms upraised, to the accompaniment of electronic guitars, with many speaking in tongues and laying hands on the sick. This tendency of mainline parishioners to worship at Pentecostal-charismatic churches, known as "Pentecostal drift," has become a global nightmare for many archbishops. Today, an estimated 54 percent of Latino Catholics identify themselves as charismatic. Photo: Wikimedia/Rayttc.

Latin American Pentecostals are equally enthusiastic when they leave church. To them, being a Christian means working for God and being actively involved in "body life" ministry. Not everyone does the *same* thing but everyone does *some* thing, whether they minister in jails or hospitals, pray for the sick, call on church members, preach, or plant new churches. Their leaders also have an authoritarian form of government that church members respect and follow. Many are anti-elitists, anti-intellectual, and anti-educational—especially when it comes to their governmental and religious leaders. Any form of higher education beyond basic Bible literacy is frowned upon—including Bible schools. Why? Modern education and science are seen as opposing the clear truths and teachings of the Bible and have been proven again and again to draw people further away from Christ, separating them socially from the common people and thus diluting the power of the Holy Spirit that is so vital to their spiritual growth. Intellectual pastors are seen as being weakened in their devotion to, dependency on, and faithfulness toward God. For them, revelation is more important than reason, and the ability to relate socially to the commoner is far more treasured than a formal education. They are "the church of the disinherited." Like a populist solidarity movement, they identify with the poor, marginalized, and hurting and offer to raise them up to a new life in Christ. Today the fastest growing segment of Latin American Pentecostals combines elements of classical Pentecostalism with popular religious culture.

PENTECOSTALISM WORLDWIDE

By the turn of the twenty-first century, Pentecostal-charismatics numbered 530 million worldwide and were growing at a rate of 19 million per year, or 54,000 per day.[28] One of twelve people alive today is Pentecostal, and one of four Christians is Pentecostal-charismatic.[29] Though modern Pentecostalism has been around for just over a hundred years, it is already the largest family of Protestants in the world and second largest family of Christians—second only to the Catholic Church. Peter Wagner wrote, "In all of human history, no other non-political, non-militaristic, voluntary human movement has grown as rapidly as the Pentecostal-charismatic movement in the last 25 years."[30]

Most of the largest congregations in the world are Pentecostal: Yoido Full Gospel Church in Seoul, South Korea, has between one-half and one million members. Jotabeche Methodist Pentecostal in Santiago, Chile, has 350,000. Anyang Assembly of God, also in Seoul,

---

28   David B. Barrett, "The Twentieth-Century Pentecostal-Charismatic Renewal in the Holy Spirit, with Its Goal of World Evangelization," (July 1988) No. 3, p. 119, *International Bulletin of Missionary Research:* *www.internationalbulletin.org/issues/1988–03/1988–03–119-barrett.pdf* (Accessed 3 April 2013).

29   Wesley Granberg-Michaelson speech at Library of Congress (February 26, 2014).

30   Vinson Synan, *The Spirit Said "Grow": The Incredible Pentecostal-Charismatic Factor in the Global Expansion of Christianity* (Missions Advanced Research, 1992), ii: HPT 281.

has 150,000. Deeper Life Bible Church in Lagos, Nigeria, has 145,000. Vision Del Futuro in Buenos Aires, Argentina, has 145,000, and Brasil Para Cristo in São Paulo, Brazil, has 85,000.[31] As the new century dawned, no less than one million Pentecostal-charismatic churches had been planted throughout the world comprising 740 Pentecostal denominations, 6,530 independent charismatic networks, and 18,810 independent neo-charismatic denominations and networks.[32] Projections for 2025 are 93 million classical Pentecostals worldwide, 274 million charismatics, and 460 million neo-charismatics.[33] In 2014, a group of leaders called "Empowered 21," led by ORU President Billy Wilson and representing a broad spectrum of Pentecostal and charismatic groups from around the world, met in Jerusalem to worship, pray, and begin a global movement with the goal of seeing every individual touched by a real encounter with the Holy Spirit by the year 2033.[34]

With between one half and one million members, Yoido Full Gospel Church in Seoul, Korea, is the largest Christian congregation in the world. Source: Wikimedia/Jhcbs1019.

31   HPT 287; CHS 374.
32   David Barrett, "The Worldwide Holy Spirit Renewal": CHS 383.
33   Ibid.
34   Chris Mitchell, "World Ready for a Second Pentecost Outpouring?" (May 30, 2014) *The Christian Broadcasting Network: www.cbn.com/cbnnews/insideisrael/2014/ March/World-Ready-for-a-Second-Pentecost-Outpouring* (Accessed 31 May 2014).

THE THIRD WAVE

Theories abound on what the Holy Spirit is doing today or what the next great movement of God will be with each theorist hoping to correctly coin the term or properly identify the current trend or development. As early as the 1980s, Peter Wagner began speaking of a "Third Wave" he saw happening within evangelical mainline churches, which were beginning to receive and exercise the gifts of the Spirit without using Pentecostal or charismatic labels. Some were even discarding elements of the previous movements, such as a subsequent experience and speaking in tongues while embracing ecstatic worship, praying for the sick, and exercising other spiritual gifts, which some argued was not Pentecostalism at all. Unfortunately, unless generally applied to the contemporary worship movement within evangelicalism or the worldwide neo-charismatic movement, Wagner's "Third Wave" concept never really caught on. But it may yet be for an appointed time. David Barrett's 2000 World Christian Encyclopedia has defined the Pentecostal, charismatic, and so-called "third wave" or neo-charismatic movements as part of a "single, cohesive movement into which a vast proliferation of all kinds of individuals and communities have been drawn," like three clearly defined waves moving simultaneously toward the beach but crashing at different times.[35]

THE NEW APOSTOLIC MOVEMENT

In the 1990s, Wagner identified another trend, this one toward the formation of new independent church networks, which he called

---

35 Barrett, "Worldwide Holy Spirit Renewal" in CHS 382; Stanley M. Burgess and Gary B. McGee, ed., *Dictionary of Pentecostal and Charismatic Movements* (Grand Rapids, Mich.: Zondervan, 1988), 818: CC 182.

"non-" or "post-denominationalism." In his book The New Apostolic Churches, Wagner described these new church networks as "new wineskins" for the new church age and then provided numerous examples of independent charismatic and evangelical networks of churches led by pastors with apostolic callings. According to Wagner, virtually any pastor of a church with 700–800 members or more seemed to have an "apostolic gift" for planting and overseeing other churches. Though certainly a growing worldwide trend, it is not unique in history. Many Pentecostal pioneers used similar names or methods including Edward Irving's "Catholic Apostolic Church," John Alexander Dowie's "Christian Catholic Apostolic Church," and Parham's, Seymour's, and Crawford's "Apostolic Faith" churches, leading many observers to believe these new independent church networks are simply "pre-denominations" in the making as opposed to "post" or "non."

C. Peter Wagner (1930-2016) was an evangelical missionary, missiologist, theologian, teacher, and prolific author. He was a leading authority in the Church Growth movement, Apostolic-Prophetic movement, and New Apostolic Reformation—a movement to restore apostolic and prophetic leadership in the church—through his Wagner Leadership Institute and other organizations. Source: Wikimedia/Globalgroningen.

THE THIRD CHURCH

The term "Third Church," which also began in the late twentieth century, is the language of Swiss Catholic theologian and missiologist Walbert Buhlmann. Aside from its simplistic interpretation that Catholicism was the first church, Protestantism the second, and Pentecostalism the third, Buhlmann saw three chronological churches coinciding with the three millennia in which the church has existed. The first was predominantly Eastern, covering the spread of Christianity and expansion from Jerusalem to Rome (AD 1–1000). The second was primarily Western, beginning with the Roman Church, then spreading north and west into Europe before finally going global through the European colonies (1001–2000). The third is largely southern as Africa, Southeast Asia, and Latin America now lead the world as one massive missionary force from the ends of the earth to Jerusalem (2001–3000). The fact that the Third Church consists primarily of former "Third World" nations is purely coincidental. "Third World" was originally a Cold War term used to describe any nation non-aligned with the Western free "first" world or Eastern Communist bloc "second" world. In time, however, it became a term of derision used to describe any nation that was impoverished or politically insignificant. But since most of these nations are no longer considered by some to be poor or insignificant, a more correct term is "Majority World" or "Global South." Buhlmann compared the three chronological churches to the stars, moon, and sun, saying, "A church historian may compare the eastern church to the morning star, silent, glittering, ever full of hope; the western church to the moon, which, after a night almost as luminous as the day, is now growing dim; and the third church to the sun, newly risen on the horizon, ruling the day."[36]

THE CONVERGENCE MOVEMENT

Another term dating back to the previous century and similar to Buhlmann's three chronological churches is Anglican Bishop Lesslie

---

36   Walter Buhlmann, *The Coming of the Third Church: An Analysis of the Present and the Future of the Church* (Maryknoll, NY: Orbis, 1977), 24: McClung, *Azusa Street & Beyond*, 235.

Newbigin's three major types of Christianity, each with its own authentic contribution to the body of Christ.[37] The first is the Catholic tradition, emphasizing continuity, orthodoxy, and sacramental living. The second is the Protestant tradition, emphasizing faith, the preaching of the Word, and the centrality of Scripture. The third is the Pentecostal tradition, emphasizing the present-day ministry of the Holy Spirit through its various gifts and operations. According to Newbigin, the church needs all three to be a powerful force in the modern world. Catholic author Ralph Martin also spoke of the importance of merging these "three streams" of Christianity together in his book *Fire on the Earth,* and Michael Harper echoed his sentiments in his autobiographical book *Three Sisters.*[38] The latter wrote, "One sister (evangelical) taught me the basis of Christian life is a personal relationship with Jesus Christ. A second (Pentecostal) helped me experience the spiritual dynamic of the Holy Spirit. Yet another (Catholic) ushered me into a whole new world where I began to see the implications of Christian community" (parentheses added).[39] Charismatic Episcopal Bruce L. Rose also spoke of the church's need "to preserve in its teaching and worship the best of Catholic tradition, while . . . learning a renewed reverence for and love of the Word of God" from the Protestants and "the empowerment of the Holy Spirit available today as in the days of the Apostles" from the Pentecostals.[40]

Many see the convergence movement as a way of looking into the future church, a combining of three historical streams—liturgical,

---

37 Lesslie Newbigin, *The Household of God,* (New York, 1954); Van Dusen, "The Third Force," *Life,* 113–24: HPT 291.

38 Ralph Martin, *Fire on the Earth* (Ann Arbor, Mich.: Servant, 1975), 30–42; HPT 291.

39 Michael Harper, *Three Sisters* (Wheaton: Tyndale, 1979), 9–15: HPT 291–292.

40 Bruce L. Rose, "Episcopal Church: Catholic-Evangelical-Charismatic," *Acts 29,* (Feb. 1984), 1–6: HPT 292.

evangelical, and charismatic—converging into one mighty river in the new century. Early signs of this included the formation of several new charismatic-evangelical-liturgical denominations with networks in Africa, South America, Asia, North America, and Europe. Other early signs included a number of Pentecostal-charismatic churches joining historic Episcopal and Eastern Orthodox denominations, as well as many liturgical and sacramental elements being incorporated in Pentecostal-charismatic churches.

THE MEMPHIS MIRACLE

Another convergence of sorts that took place in North American Pentecostalism before the turn of the century was a breakthrough in race relations. Despite the fact that all nations and races were invited to participate in the founding of the Pentecostal World Congress in Zurich, Switzerland, in 1947, a similar organization formed in Des Moines, Iowa, in 1948 to promote "ecumenism" among Pentecostal denominations, did not include all races. Instead, an all-white Pentecostal Fellowship of North America (PFNA) was formed along racial lines. This was disbanded in Memphis in 1994 in favor of the more racially inclusive Pentecostal and Charismatic Churches of North America (PCCNA). Leaders of this new organization repented of past racial shortcomings, signed a manifesto pledging to oppose racism in all its forms, and formed a new racially integrated board with Bishop Thiel Clemens of the Church of God in Christ as chairman and Bishop Bernard Underwood of the Pentecostal Holiness Church as vice chairman.

One of the highlights of this historic conference dubbed the "Memphis Miracle" came when Donald Evans—a representative of the Assemblies of God—washed the feet of Bishop Clemmons while begging his forgiveness for past sins, immediately followed by COGIC Bishop Charles Blake washing the feet of Thomas Trask—General Superintendent of the Assemblies of God. Though purely symbolic, given the history of North American Pentecostalism, it was a "miracle" nonetheless. And the idea seems to be catching on as many North American Pentecostal-charismatic churches begin to show signs of cultural diversity, with some even achieving significant diversity (80 percent or less). Others are achieving cultural diversity through Christian television, conferences, leadership forums, and church staffs. Though 90 percent of North American churches remain racially segregated as more and more church leaders refuse to take the "colorblind" approach by ignoring the problem, Rev. Martin Luther King Jr.'s oft-quoted statement "the most segregated hour of Christian America is eleven o'clock on Sunday morning" could soon become a distant memory with Pentecostal-charismatic churches leading the way.[41]

Dubbed the "Memphis Miracle," Assemblies of God pastor Donald Evans washed the feet of COGIC Bishop Ithiel Clemmons as a symbolic gesture of healing the racial divide that plagued early Pentecostalism and set the stage for the new racially inclusive Pentecostal and Charismatic Churches of North America (PCCNA) in 1994. Source: Flower Pentecostal Heritage Center.

41   Martin Luther King, Jr., *Stride Toward Freedom: The Montgomery Story* (New York: Harper & Row, 1958) in *The Quote Garden: www.quotegarden.com/mlk-day.html.*

THE EMERGING CHURCH MOVEMENT

Yet another development gaining traction in the new century and bearing some resemblance to the convergence movement is the emerging church movement. Found primarily among younger independent, evangelical, charismatic, and denominational groups in North America, Western Europe, and other westernized nations, emerging churches are difficult to define because they tend to be quite diverse, eclectic, and fluid. But two things all emerging churches have in common are the language of reform and the wholesale "deconstruction" of modern church paradigms—especially in areas of worship, evangelism, community, and missions. While many emerging churches embrace the power and gifts of the Holy Spirit, a high value is also placed on relationships, discipleship, community involvement, social activism, global justice, and missional living that includes radical displays of hospitality toward fellow emerging individuals.

Emerging churches also reject traditional, imperialistic, patronizing approaches to evangelism in favor of more relational, conversational approaches that make "truth claims" with humility and respect combined with heavy doses of plain old-fashioned good works. Emerging believers feel that people need to freely come to Christ through the Holy Spirit on their own terms by having conversations in a Christian communal setting, not through some confrontational pre-digested formula. For many emerging believers, missional living is not a church program but their life's purpose. And unlike the stereotypical megachurch leader, emerging church leaders are by default transparent and authentic. They do not preach—they have "conversations." Moreover, their churches are often multisite, satellite, or house church models as opposed to the modern "lost-in-the-crowd" megachurch model.

According to missiologist Ed Stetzer, several categories of emerging churches exist, ranging from relevant conservatives to reconstructionist evangelicals to emergent liberal revisionists who question the very relevancy of modern evangelicalism in a postmodern world. A number of emerging churches are also rising out of charismatic communities self-described as "modern monastics" or "mystical communion" models of churches that often create cafes, centers, house churches, or other communal expressions for the express purpose of practicing radical Christian hospitality in a postmodern context. This may involve anything from expressive, neo-charismatic worship and contemporary music and film to ancient mystical and liturgical expressions of contemplative prayer, symbolic multisensory worship, and storytelling. Some have dubbed this the "Ancient-Future church movement." Unsurprisingly, many emerging church activities involve blogging, social media, and decentralized internet communications that may be sacred or secular and local or part of the broader emerging community. In the end, the emerging church movement exists to help people shift from being spiritual tourists to becoming Christian pilgrims.

THE CONTEMPORARY WORSHIP MOVEMENT

Growing right alongside the emerging church movement is the contemporary worship movement. With its roots dating back to the Jesus movement and the singing of charismatic praise choruses, this phenomenon eventually expanded to include all of Western evangelicalism before ultimately affecting nearly every major sect of Christianity. Contemporary worship is distinguished from historic, traditional, or liturgical worship in that it has its own unique style, genre, lyrics, singing, performance, and theology. Because of contemporary worship's vast influence, many mainline churches have begun offering both traditional and contemporary services, while other churches have been torn asunder by the so-called "worship wars." The controversy usually stems from contemporary worship's potentially worldly and immoral influences coming from the secular music and entertainment industry, including pop music, pop culture, and using modern instruments. Others feel contemporary worship lacks the depth and richness that many high church hymns or traditional choruses offer.

What began as Pentecostal-charismatic praise choruses in the twentieth century has become nothing short of a contemporary worship revolution and phenomenon in the twenty-first century. Christian bands are doing worship tours, Christian radio stations are playing worship songs, and top worship songs are selling like hotcakes. The modern "worship set" has even become the primary sacrament within most evangelical churches as contemporary worship remains a dominating force in twenty-first century Christianity. Source: Wikimedia/Kopson.

Contemporary worship also bears some similarities to liturgical worship in that they both transcend denominational lines. In fact, it is becoming increasingly difficult these days to differentiate between denominational and non-denominational, conservative and liberal, and evangelical and Pentecostal-charismatic churches because of similarities in worship styles. For such a diverse group of churches to share a mutual form of worship is quite remarkable and miraculous! And while some like the informal, intimate tone of contemporary worship, others feel it can get a little too personal—especially for men, who may be uncomfortable singing romantic "love songs" to Jesus. At the same time, there seems to be a deepening theological content in contemporary worship that often comes at the expense of timeless catchy tunes and choruses. Just before the turn of the century, contemporary worship again evolved into what some have dubbed the "modern worship movement," while others believed it to be just another passing fad. Regardless, if contemporary worship can inspire a new generation of hymn writers while evoking God's presence, reconnecting people with church (the old through the new), and transforming worship from a Sunday morning experience to an everyday experience—praise God!

THE HOUSE CHURCH MOVEMENT

Also growing alongside the emerging church movement, and not without its own set of controversies, has been the house church movement. Currently popular in China, India, Brazil, and Africa, the movement seems to be picking up steam in North America and Europe. Those wishing to avoid the usual trappings of traditional institutional churches are seeking a return to early New Testament Christianity-type gatherings. The movement seems to be gaining momentum especially among emerging believers who typically reject authoritarian structures. A 2011 Barna Research study found that 11.5 million, or 5 percent, of all American adults said they attend a "house church" as opposed to a traditional congregation.[42] Not to be confused with home groups or cell churches that are mere extensions of local

---

42   "House Church Movement Keeps Growing," Barna Research Group (eNews article: April 26, 2011) *Koinonia House: www.khouse.org/enews_article/2011/1768* (Accessed 4 April 2013).

churches, house churches are mostly autonomous and not connected in any way with local congregations. Though historically, tensions have existed between house churches and traditional churches, more recently a number of North American denominations, including Southern Baptists and Foursquare, have decided to support house church networks within their denominations. This, of course, is in addition to the many independent, interdenominational, and parachurch organizations that have already joined the movement, leading some observers to speak of a "Third Reformation"—the first being a theological movement, the second a spiritual gifts movement, and the third a structural "wineskin" movement.[43]

The house church movement remains a growing worldwide trend, especially in densely populated areas or regions where Christians are persecuted. Recent research reveals that six to twelve million Americans, or nine percent of American Protestants, also attend house churches for a variety of reasons. Photo: David Amsler/AmslerPIX.

THE CHURCH PLANTING MOVEMENT

At a recent global mission strategy meeting for the Redeemed Christian Church of God in North America, Nigerian James Fadele

---

43   Wolfgang Simpson, "Houses That Changed the World" (Madras, 1998)
     TheRealChurch.com:
     www.therealchurch.com/articles/houses_that_changed_the_world.html (Accessed 4
     April 2013); Chris Morrison, M.A. "Historical Roots of the Modern House Church
     Movement": *cmmorrison.files.wordpress.com/2011/12/house-church-roots.pdf*
     (Accessed 4 April 2013); "Third Day Churches," *San Diego Churches:*
     www.sandiegochurches.org/churches/third-day-churches (Accessed 4 April 2013).

asked a simple rhetorical question: "How do we love people? We love people by planting churches."[44] Peter Wagner concurred, "The single most effective evangelistic methodology under heaven is planting new churches."[45] While many mainline local churches were dying in North America each year, as many as 5,000 new churches were being planted—50,000 alone between 1980 and 2000.[46] Evangelical missiologist Ed Stetzer said by 2011 the number of new churches being planted in the U.S. had surpassed the number of church closures, and if the movement continued unhindered, we could see a similar explosion in church growth like when the Baptists and Methodists first began evangelizing America around the turn of the nineteenth century.[47]

The church planting movement is made up mostly of independent evangelical, emerging, and Pentecostal-charismatic networks that offer a nontraditional style of ministry. Southern Baptists lead among mainline denominations, many of which are now recognizing the need and joining the movement. Much like the apostle Paul, who planted churches in major cities along the Mediterranean that soon spread to the surrounding villages, the modern church planting movement is seeing a rapid reproduction and multiplication of churches filling entire cities and nations with homegrown, like-minded churches. Many are planting multisite or satellite churches with one senior pastor or overseer. Others are using the more traditional model of a "mother church" or denomination, while still others are linking

---

44 Andrew Rice, "Mission from Africa" (April 8, 2009) *The New York Times.*

45 C. Peter Wagner, *Church Planting for a Greater Harvest* (Ventura, Calif.: Regal, 1990), 11.

46 Stetzer, *Planting Missional Churches*, 14.

47 J. Lee Grady, "Spiritual Trends to Watch in 2012," (January 1, 2012) *Charisma Magazine: www.charismamag.com/site-archives/1485-0112-magazine-articles/features/14744-spirituai-trends-to-watch-in-2012* (Accessed 5 April 2013).

with independent evangelical organizations such as the Association of Related Churches (ARC), which provides support, guidance, and resources for growth-minded church planters. ARC is currently revolutionizing the historical 90 percent new church failure rate by converting that to a 90 percent success rate—at least among its own churches.[48] ARC, which began in 2000 with a goal of planting 2000 churches, is well on its way toward exceeding that goal.

As many mainline local churches in Europe and North America were closing and their facilities were being converted into homes, schools, offices, museums and concert halls, many more emerging, evangelical, Pentecostal and charismatic networks were effectively planting new multisite, satellite, and campus churches in unconventional venues like homes, schools, theaters, industrial parks, community centers and converted retail and warehouse spaces. Source: Great Lakes Church.

THE AGE OF THE LOCAL CHURCH

One phrase that seems to encapsulate what God is doing in the early twenty-first century is this: "God is building strong local churches."[49] The big-name, larger-than-life celebrity televangelist of the previous century seems to be exactly that—a thing of the past. The authoritarian structures of the early apostolic and prophetic movements also seem to be on the wane. Even the great teaching ministries that so characterized the late twentieth century seem to be a dying breed.

---

48 "Become an ARC Church Planter" *Association of Related Churches: www.arcchurches.com/join/church-planter* (Accessed 5 April 2013).

49 Kenneth E. Hagin, *He Gave Gifts Unto Men: A Biblical Perspective of Apostles, Prophets, and Pastors* (Tulsa: Kenneth Hagin Ministries, 1999) back cover.

Today's rising stars seem to be pastors of local churches but not necessarily pastors of megachurches. Pastors of small- and medium-size churches are also making a comeback these days as many church leaders are beginning to realize "bigger is not always better." Today it is not uncommon to see pastors of small and medium-size churches appearing as regular guests or hosts of national religious talk shows. Today's local churches are receiving support from a variety of sources, including fellow local pastors and many independent evangelical and parachurch organizations that have a huge network of resources to assist small, medium, and large local churches.

THE "WIGGLESWORTH" PROPHECY

If you had asked Kenneth Hagin before his death in 2003 what is God doing today, he would have said, "God is building strong local churches that know how to flow in the Holy Ghost."[50] Of the three types of churches that exist today—traditional mainline, emerging evangelical, and Pentecostal-charismatic—Hagin believed the latter would flourish in the last days. But what of the recent tide of emerging independent and evangelical churches, which also seem to be growing exponentially in these days? They remain strong in the Word yet are often resistant to the "flow of the Spirit." The answer may lie in a little known prophecy believed to have been delivered by Smith Wigglesworth before his death in 1947. Though the prophecy seems to have been directed toward the U.K.—Wigglesworth's native country—local and regional references have been removed to reveal its global significance:

---

50   Ibid.

During the next few decades, there will be two distinct moves of the Holy Spirit across the church. . . . The first move will affect every church that is open to receive it and will be characterized by a restoration of the baptism and gifts of the Holy Spirit. The second move of the Holy Spirit will result in people leaving historic churches and planting new churches. In the duration of each of these moves, the people who are involved will say, "This is the great revival," but the Lord says, "No, neither is the great revival but both are steps towards it." When the new church phase is on the wane, there will be evidenced in the churches something that has not been seen before: a coming together of those with an emphasis on the Word and those with an emphasis on the Spirit. When the Word and the Spirit come together, there will be the biggest movement of the Holy Spirit that . . . the world has ever seen. It will mark the beginning of a revival that will eclipse anything that has been witnessed . . . and . . . will begin a missionary move to the ends of the earth.[51]

A GLIMPSE INTO THE FUTURE

This prophecy is strikingly accurate in that the first two movements have already come to pass, leaving little doubt as to the possibility of "the third move." According to the prophecy, "the first move" would "affect every church that is open to receive it" and be "characterized by a restoration of the baptism and gifts of the Holy Spirit." This is

---

51   R.T. Kendall, *Holy Fire: A Balanced, Biblical Look at the Holy Spirit's Work in Our Lives,* (Lake Mary, Fla.: Charisma House, 2014), 176; Matthew Backholer, *Revival Fires and Awakenings,* (U.K.: ByFaith Media, 2009), 189; "Smith Wigglesworth's 1947 Prophetic Word," by Admin on April 2, 2012 in Reports, *Pray for Scotland: www.prayforscotland.org.uk/?p=1530* (Accessed 5 April 2013).

an astonishingly accurate description of the charismatic movement, which happened "across the church," affecting every denomination. "The second move" would "result in people leaving historic churches and planting new churches." Again, this is a remarkable prediction of the present-day church planting movement. As many local mainline churches close, many more emerging, independent, evangelical, and Pentecostal-charismatic churches are being planted. Yet "neither is the great revival, but both are steps towards it." Thus, the recent charismatic and church planting movements are critical steps toward the next great movement of God. A key phrase in the prophecy states, "When the new church phase is on the wane, there will be evidenced in the churches something that has not been seen before: a coming together of those with an emphasis on the Word and those with an emphasis on the Spirit." As of this writing, the church planting movement in the U.S. was not yet on the wane. Though in the U.K., where this prophecy was believed to have been declared and directed, it was certainly waning. When this present movement of God to plant strong local churches is finally exhausted, according to the prophecy, we will see "the biggest movement of the Holy Spirit . . . the world has ever seen."

As the prophecy indicates, many in the mainline churches who were open to receiving the baptism in the Holy Spirit did so during the charismatic renewal. But one group that remained largely unaffected by the charismatic movement was evangelicals. Yet they remain dedicated to the Word and strategically involved in church planting. Is it possible that the next great movement of God will witness a merging of the evangelical and Pentecostal-charismatic streams of Christianity? "Those with an emphasis on the Word and those with an emphasis on the Spirit" initiating a last, great global thrust of missions before the return of Christ?

A MERGING OF STREAMS

Evangelical Christianity was founded in the Wesleyan revivals and the First Great Awakening, both of which featured mighty outpourings of the Holy Spirit. Pentecostalism, by definition, is a branch of evangelical Christianity.[52] When Pentecostals were invited to join the National Association of Evangelicals in 1942, it marked the first time in a long time a Pentecostal-charismatic group had been accepted in mainstream Christianity. Today Pentecostal-charismatics constitute a majority of the NAE's membership. Billy Graham's invitation to Oral Roberts to speak at the 1966 World Congress on Evangelism was another precursor. Many other examples exist. Additionally, in the faith tenets of many of these newly emerging evangelical church plants are clear statements of belief in the baptism in the Holy Spirit, spiritual gifts, and speaking in tongues, but with less practical application. Ed Stetzer has also observed a recent trend in which many Pentecostal-charismatics "are shying away from the oddities and excesses of Pentecostalism, while evangelicals are moving towards the theology of Spirit-filled and Spirit-led ministries" and thus joining the "continualist" movement.[53] Is it possible God is setting up the present-day church planting movement for an historic and sovereign movement of the Holy Spirit of epic proportions?

---

52 "Pentecostalism," *Wikipedia: en.wikipedia.org/wiki/Pentecostalism.*

53 Ed Stetzer, "3 Important Church Trends in the Next Ten Years" (July 3, 2015) *Pastors.com: pastors.com/3-important-church-trends-in-the-next-ten-years* (Accessed 9 July 2015).

OTHER PROPHECIES

It is believed both Parham and Seymour spoke of last-day movements of God similar to the ones they experienced. Parham is said to have prophesied in the early twentieth century that in about a hundred years there would be another great outpouring of the Spirit of God that would surpass anything that happened in Acts, Topeka, or Azusa.[54] Seymour also reportedly prophesied that in about a hundred years there would be a return of the Shekinah glory and a revival that would surpass the Works of God at Azusa.[55] Kenneth Hagin prophesied in 1983: "In this move that is about to come. . . . It will not be altogether something new that you've never seen. It'll be a combination of everything you've seen . . . plus a little bit more. . . . And there'll be a revival of divine healing such as you have not seen in your lifetime, or read about, or heard about . . . a revival of the supernatural, not only . . . in casting out devils . . . healing the sick . . . speaking with other tongues, but . . . in the . . . seen realm. Men will see the glory of God; a cloud will hang over certain congregations, even the church building for days at a time. And everybody that passes by, sinner and saint alike will say, 'Well what in the world is that? I've never seen anything like that.' . . . But the greatest miracle of all is that there'll be so many fish caught . . . that the nets can't hold them. There won't be church houses enough to hold the people . . ." [despite our best church planting efforts!][56]

---

54 TMTS, Billye Brim's forward, vii.

55 TMTS 102.

56 "Kenneth E. Hagin, Prayer Seminar April, 1983: Prophecies, Words of Wisdom and Prayers" *Trinity Church Jonesboro:* *www.trinityjonesboro.com/files/KHprayerseminar1983.pdf* (Accessed 13 July 2015).

Both David du Plessis and Lester Sumrall heard Smith Wigglesworth deliver similar prophecies. Sumrall recorded a Wigglesworth prophecy saying, "I see the greatest revival in the history of mankind coming on Planet Earth. . . . I see the dead raised. I see every form of disease healed. I see whole hospitals emptied with no one there. Even the doctors running down the streets shouting. . . . Nobody will be able to count those who come to Jesus. . . . It will be a worldwide situation, not local, a worldwide thrust of God's power and God's anointing upon mankind."[57]

---

57   Sumrall, *Pioneers of Faith,* 168–169.

STUDY QUESTIONS

1. After more than half a century of postmodern individualism, relativism, and pluralism, why do you think religion is on the rise globally—even threatening to once again become the primary animating force in human affairs?

2. Explain the dramatic shift in Christianity to the Southern Hemisphere as evidenced by the election of Pope Francis.

3. Though modern Pentecostalism has been around for just over a hundred years, why do you think it is the second largest family of Christians today—second only to the Catholic Church?

4. What factors led to the phenomenal growth of Christianity in Africa?

5. What brought on the "reverse flow" of Christian missions from Africa, Asia, and Latin America into Europe and North America?

6. How did North America go from being the largest sender of missionaries into the world to becoming one of the largest mission fields in the world?

7. All things considered, what are some new lessons for the American churches to learn in the twenty-first century?

8. How are China and Asia fulfilling the Great Commission in reverse? (Acts 1:8)

9. What sets Latin American Pentecostals apart from other Pentecostal-charismatics?

10. What current move of God do you think most accurately describes what God is doing today? Why?

11. How has this series helped you? How can knowing what God has done in the past help you live a more fruitful and abundant life today and help prepare you for what is to come?

CONCLUSION

Throughout history, the Spirit of God has ebbed and flowed. Ever since the Spirit of God "moved" over the face of the waters in Genesis, the Holy Spirit has been moving. Of course, we Pentecostal-charismatic believers love the "times of refreshing" when the Spirit of God is flowing, but we must also learn to appreciate the ebbs of the Spirit, knowing they exist for one purpose and one purpose only—to create the next wave. Indeed, the longer the wait, the stronger the undercurrent and the bigger the next wave will be.

Whenever the gifts and manifestations of the Spirit receded throughout history, a vacuum or void was created, and a need for renewal, revival, and awakening was ignited. But without rest, inactivity, or slumber there can be no awakenings; without apathy or a loss of vivacity there can be no revivals. So if we will learn to appreciate the undercurrents of the Spirit as well as the waves, the winters of the Spirit as well as the spring, and "despise not the day of small things," we will do well.[1] Throughout history, each time the church rejected a movement of God—whether it was the Cathars and Waldensians, or Wycliffe and Hus, or the Latter Rain movement—a vacuum was created. Even when the Shekinah glory finally lifted from Azusa Street, and miracles receded, and tongues diminished, a greater renewal and revival emerged. Now the charismatic movement "has ended." Yet throughout history when similar pronouncements were made, an even stronger swell followed. As the postwar healing revival was cooling down, a more powerful charismatic renewal

1 Zech. 4:10.

was being generated, and no sooner had the initial apostolic thrust waned than the Montanists and Monastics were on the scene. Why? Because inside every great movement of God is the seed for the next revival, just as within every wave is the power to create the next wave. Contained within the Moravian Revival were the seeds of the Wesleyan Methodist revival, and within it were the seeds of the Higher Life and Holiness movements, and within them were the seeds of the Pentecostal movement. Indeed, within every movement of God, the principal players were in some way connected with the previous movement. Wesley was affiliated with the Moravians. Phoebe Palmer was a Methodist. Seymour was a Holiness preacher. Shakarian was a Pentecostal. And no doubt the principal players in the next great movement of God will be charismatic or neo-charismatic.

awesome insight!

MOVE ON WITH GOD

Among the few in history privileged to participate in several movements of God was Lester Sumrall. Sumrall participated in the Pentecostal, Latter Rain, healing, charismatic, and Word of Faith movements. He wrote, "I refuse to get stuck in some place or group where the Holy Spirit is not being poured out. If you are not willing to move with God, then you need to understand that God is moving and you are not. If I had lived in the time of John the Baptist, I would have joined him. If I had lived at the time of Jesus . . . I would have joined him. If I had lived during the time of Martin Luther, I would have become a Lutheran. . . . If I had been living in the days of John Knox, I would have joined the Presbyterians. . . . If I had lived in the days of John Wesley, I would have joined the Methodists. . . . If I had been living in the time when the Salvation Army was founded by William Booth, I would have joined that group."[2]

After being miraculously healed of tuberculosis in New Orleans at age seventeen, Lester Sumrall (1913-1996) began preaching and traveling the world with British Pentecostal pioneer Howard Carter, working as a missionary, evangelist, and later as a pastor, founding Cathedral of Praise—the largest congregation in the Philippines—before God sent him home to become a missionary to his own country in 1957. Founding the Lester Sumrall Evangelistic Association, he moved to South Bend, Indiana, in 1963, where he founded Christian Center Church, Indiana Christian University, and LeSEA Broadcasting. Source: LeSEA.

Unfortunately, most never move beyond their first wave of blessing. They are like children swimming in the ocean, armed with boogie boards and floats, waiting for that perfect wave to come. But when it finally comes, they ride it all the way to the shoreline and then lie there like beached whales instead of jumping back in the water to catch the next wave. Sadly, many Christians spend their entire lives on the spiritual shoreline instead of experiencing the exhilarating waves of the Spirit. Often they sit in churches built on previous revivals and remain there uninvolved with what God is presently doing. However, if we live in the past, we will not only miss out on what God is doing, but we may also miss out on what God is getting ready to do.

One sad footnote to the Azusa Street Revival was that many who experienced it went back to living their lives as if nothing happened. Like Peter on the Mount of Transfiguration, they just wanted to pitch a tent so they could bask in the glories of yesteryear. True, many became missionaries of the one-way ticket and carried the message

---

2   Sumrall, *Pioneers of Faith*, 15–16.

of Pentecost to the ends of the earth. Others moved on and helped Aimee Semple McPherson build Angelus Temple to reach a new generation. However, some remained satisfied living in the faded memories of a bygone era. But like the children of Israel, when the cloud of God moves, we must move on with the cloud. We cannot afford to waste our lives daydreaming or living in the past because, as Smith Wigglesworth once said, "To remain three days in the same place would indicate that you have lost the vision. The child of God must catch the vision anew every day. Every day the child of God must be moved more and more by the Holy Ghost. The child of God must come into line with the power of heaven so that he knows that God has his hand upon him." Again he said, "I appeal to you, you people who have received the Holy Spirit, I appeal to you to let God have His way at whatever cost; I appeal to you to keep moving on with God into an ever increasing realization of His infinite purpose in Christ Jesus for His redeemed ones until you are filled unto all the fullness of God."[3]

God has not called anyone to sit on the sideline or the shoreline. He has a fresh wind and wave for each new generation. Today God is reaching a new and emerging generation with a different wind and a different wave. Creation never stops. God never stops, and we must never stop progressing and moving toward the future. The key is to stay flexible and open to the winds of the Spirit that blow as he wills, not as we will. Every historical movement of God contained elements from previous movements as well as new elements that were often rejected by those in the previous movement. British Bible scholar Burnett Streeter exhorted, "The first Christians achieved what they

---

3   Smith Wigglesworth, "Keeping the Vision," *Revival Library: www.smithwigglesworth.com/sermons/ftp6.htm.*

did because the spirit with which they were inspired was one favorable to experiment. In this—and perhaps in some other respects—it may be that the line of advance for the Church of today is not to imitate the forms, but to recapture the Spirit of the Primitive Church."[4]

The only thing worse than living in the past is sitting around waiting for the next movement of God to come. It is a religious spirit that acknowledges God's work in the past and future but not in the present. Times of refreshing are exactly that—times of respite. Revival historian J. Edwin Orr explained, "In times of evangelism, the evangelist seeks the sinner, in times of revival the sinners come chasing after the Lord." Selwyn Hughes, founder of Crusade for World Revival, added, "Evangelism is the work we do for God; revival is the work God does for us."[5] In a revival, the Spirit draws men to God; in a recession, we lead men to God.

"WE MUST HAVE REVIVAL"

Even in times of revival, not everything that happens is of God. Some manifestations are fleshly, others demonic, but the overwhelming majority come from God. In every revival from Acts to Azusa, there were opportunists and exhibitionists. Simon the Sorcerer was an opportunist who thought he could buy the gift of God with money.[6] The seven sons of Sceva were exhibitionists who frivolously tried to cast out demons.[7] If any had focused on those extreme elements, they would have dismissed Pentecost as a movement of God. But

4   Burnett Hillman Streeter, *The Primitive Church* (Macmillan, 1929), 267–268: CC 191.
5   Backholer, *Revival Fires and Awakenings*, 11.
6   Acts 8:9–13, 18–24.
7   Acts 19:13–17.

the apostle Paul lovingly corrected and confronted such extremes at Corinth while encouraging the continued movement of God stating, "Therefore, brethren, desire earnestly to prophesy, and do not forbid to speak with tongues. Let all things be done decently and in order."[8]

John Wesley once prayed, "Oh, Lord, send us the old revival, without the defects; but if this cannot be, send it with all its defects. We must have revival."[9] Jonathan Edwards similarly said if we "wait to see a work of God without difficulties and stumbling blocks, it will be like the fool's waiting at the river side to have all the water run by."[10] Finney agreed: "Almost all true Christianity in the world has been produced by revivals. . . . And so until the world embraces Christian principles and there are no more anti-Christian excitements, it is futile to promote true Christianity except by counteracting awakenings. This is logically and historically true."[11]

Wesley and Edwards, and Finney and Evan Roberts may have been on opposite sides of the theological spectrum, but they wholeheartedly agreed on the necessity and promotion of revival. Roberts said, "It is certainly beyond my power to instigate a fresh revival, for revival can alone be given by the Holy Spirit of God when the conditions are fulfilled." Roberts believed revivals were a sovereign work of the Spirit predicated by people praying, obeying, and surrendering to God. "Bend the church and save the world!" he

---

8   1 Cor. 14:39–40.

9   Backholer, *Revival Fires and Awakenings*, 165; Bartleman, *Azusa Street*, 45.

10   Henry Rogers and Sereno E. Dwight, Edward Hickman, ed., *The Works of Jonathan Edwards, A.M.* (London: Paternoster Row, 1840), 273; Guy Chevreau, *Catch the Fire* (Toronto, Canada: HarperCollins, 1994), 110: MCH 19–21.

11   Charles G. Finney, *Lectures on Revival* (Minneapolis: Bethany House, 1988), 11, 13.

refrained.[12] Finney believed revival rested entirely on the church's shoulders, saying, "Christians are more to blame for not being revived than sinners are for not being converted."[13] But regarding the Rochester revival, he wrote, "The key which unlocked the Heavens in this revival was the prayer of Clary, Father Nash, and other unnamed folk who laid themselves prostrate before God's throne and besought Him for a divine out-pouring."[14] Clearly, both the Creator and the created have roles to play in producing revivals, while nearly all historical revivals have had a few common threads:

1. *Prayer*—120 Christ-followers prayed daily for ten days in the upper room prior to Pentecost. The Moravians prayed daily for ten years as part of the Moravian Revival and leading up to the Methodist revival and Great Awakening. The Holy Club prayed all night on New Year's Eve prior to the Wesleyan revival. Father Nash and others prayed days in advance of Finney's revivals. The Layman's Prayer Revival of 1857-58 began with a Wednesday noontime prayer meeting. The Holiness movement began with Tuesday prayer meetings in Phoebe Palmer's living room. Evan Roberts prayed daily for years before the 1904-05 Welsh Revival. Pentecostalism began with another New Year's Eve Watch Night Service in Topeka, Kansas and with daily prayer on Bonnie Brae and Azusa streets. The charismatic movement also began with closed-door prayer meetings at the old Dutch Reformed Church in Mount Vernon, New York.

---

12   Evans, *Welsh Revival*, 171–173: RF 202.

13   Ibid., 22.

14   J. Paul Reno, *Daniel Nash: Prevailing Prince of Prayer* (Asheville, N.C.: Revival Literature, 1989), 12.

2. *Unity*—120 gathered in one place and in one accord when a rushing mighty wind entered the room. Count Zinzendorf brought unity to warring factions at Herrnhut prior to another worldwide outpouring. James McGready invited other denominational ministers to join him at his Red River church, leading to a Second Great Awakening. Jeremiah Lanphier organized interdenominational meetings at the Fulton Street Dutch Reformed Church that resulted in a worldwide prayer revival. "The color line was washed away in the blood" at Azusa Street in Los Angeles prior to a worldwide Pentecostal outpouring. And Demos Shakarian led ecumenical, nonsectarian meetings in the same city, sparking yet another worldwide movement.

3. *A grassroots movement*—the 120 were considered simple Galilean Zealots and fisherman. The Monastics, Franciscans, Cathars, and Waldensians were all grassroots efforts, as were Wycliffe's poor priests, Hus's Bohemian movement, and Luther's Protestant uprising. Early Quakers were considered uncouth, uneducated, and lacking refinement. Whitefield's and Wesley's revivals began among coal miners and fishermen. America's Second Great Awakening transpired among rugged frontiersmen. Waldo's "poor of Lyons," Wycliffe's "poor priests," and early Methodist circuit riders were mostly uneducated men preaching to the poor. The Prayer Revival of 1857–1858 was led by laymen. The worldwide Pentecostal revival began among a son of former African slaves and a few "negro washwomen."[15]

---

15   Anderson, *Vision of the Disinherited*, 65.

Smith Wigglesworth and most of the postwar healing revivalists were also considered unrefined and uneducated. Latin American Pentecostalism remains a grassroots phenomenon to this day.

4. *Newness*—speaking in tongues, apparitional flames, and mass evangelism began at Pentecost. Ecstatic prophecies and prophetic signs and wonders were hallmarks of the Montanists. Spiritual power gained through prayer and abstinence was popularized by the Monastics. The Franciscans hosted wandering preachers and all-night open-air meetings. The Mystics initiated fervent laughter, singing, and dancing in the Spirit. The Cathars produced the *consolamentum* for Spirit baptism and holy living. The reformers established the doctrine of justification by faith, congregational singing, and modern church life. The Quakers proposed quietly waiting in God's presence. The Moravians launched intercessory prayer groups and worldwide Protestant missions. The Methodists gave new meaning to jumping, shouting, and hymn singing. Finney instituted protracted meetings, altar calls, and citywide revivals. The Holiness movement commenced with hand raising, swaying, and falling on the floor. The Azusa Street Revival ushered in the Shekinah Glory, rooftop flames, Heavenly Choir, and mass healings. The healing revival produced healing through discernment on a scale "hitherto unknown," and the charismatic movement revolutionized worship, spiritual warfare, and Bible teaching.

PROGRESSIVE PENTECOST

The Spirit of God has progressively moved throughout history with each new generation building upon the next. Every time the Spirit flowed, something new and exciting was added to the church that was desperately needed to help prepare the church for the next great movement of God. Each historical revival introduced new measures, new strategies, new concepts, new emphases, and new priorities. Consequently, the next movement of God will look different. So different, in fact, that many Pentecostals, charismatics, and even neo-charismatics may have a hard time accepting or even recognizing it at first. Though it will certainly contain elements from previous revivals, it will have a new style and flavor all its own.

The Spirit of God did not suddenly show up again in Los Angeles in 1906, nor has Pentecostalism been one continuous movement since. Actually, if history repeats itself and Jesus tarries, modern Pentecostalism as we know it—as a renewal movement that places special emphasis on speaking in tongues as the initial evidence of the baptism in the Holy Spirit—may fade with time. While Pentecostalism as a Christian renewal that believes Pentecost is repeatable, that there were repetitions of Pentecost throughout Christian history, and that any believer can be clothed with the same robe of heavenly power that mantled Jesus and the apostles as they carried out their mission to the world—is likely to remain vibrant and continue until the return of Christ. The Spirit of God is being continually poured out in wave after wave of revival in an ever new Pentecost and will continue to do so until the day of Christ. The Spirit of Pentecost—past, present, and future—is a fire that cannot be charted, contained, or controlled.[16] May we see it in our day as Habakkuk prayed:

> Lord, I have heard of your fame;
> I stand in awe of your deeds, Lord.
> Repeat them in our day,
> in our time make them known.[17]

---

16 Grant McClung, "The Next Charismata," *Azusa Street & Beyond*, 281, 290.
17 Hab. 3:2 (NIV)

INDEX

ALSO AVAILABLE FROM JEFF OLIVER

From Pentecost to the Present: The Holy Spirit's Enduring Work in the Church

Book 1: Early Prophetic and Spiritual Gifts Movements

Jeff Oliver

Contrary to popular belief, miracles did not pass away with the twelve apostles. If anything, the Pentecostal sparks that were lit by them continued to spread throughout the known world.

This first installment explains how Jesus and the apostles established the concept of the Holy Spirit's abiding presence in the church laying the groundwork for a Christian initiation that included salvation and Spirit baptism. How spiritual gifts operated through the twelve apostles as they spread Christianity into the known world. How bold witnesses, supernatural signs, and practical love resulted in massive expansion of the early church despite extreme persecution. How Montanism tried to revive the church from moral decay through strict living and prophetical gifts before it was rejected. How Emperor Constantine I reunited the Roman Empire under a new Christian-friendly regime. How the new state-run churches, overrun with sin, caused many to flee to the wilderness resulting in another intense spiritual revival. How the Middle Ages featured the mass conversion of much of northern Europe through miracle-working missionary monks, followed by a period of great jubilation, mystical faith, and charismatic revivals, and ending with the incredible healing ministry of Vincent Ferrer.

From Pentecost to the Present: The Holy Spirit's Enduring Work in the Church

Book 2: Reformations and Awakenings

Jeff Oliver

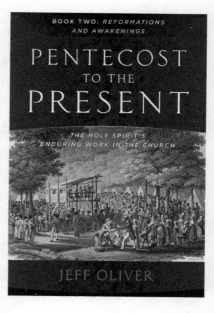

Jesus once spoke of a time when men would sleep and an enemy would come and sow tares among the wheat. The Renaissance, the Enlightenment, and the Modern Age was just such a time.

In this second installment the reader will learn how signs and wonders played roles in the foundations of nearly every new state church, free church, and denomination. How Catholicism countered with its own reformation that included a revival of mysticism, a new army of spiritual soldiers, and the discovery of the New World. How restorationist movements countered the intellectual revolutions of their day with revivals of faith in the supernatural.

How a decade-long prayer meeting shaped the future of revivalism affecting both England's Wesleyan Revival and America's First Great Awakening. How the French Revolution replaced Christianity with liberalism as the world's dominant ideology. How many Americans countered this new revolution with a Second Great Awakening. How Phoebe Palmer began the modern Holiness movement and Jeremiah Lanphier launched a worldwide Laymen's Prayer Revival. How many Americans reunited after the Civil War with a series of Holiness Camp Meetings, followed by a similar "Higher Life" movement in Britain, and later, a new stream of American healing ministries.

Global Wakening
Inform. Inspire. Ignite.

www.globalwakening.com

Visit www.globalwakening.com and help us inspire and equip a new generation with a supernatural Christian worldview that will help ignite a global wakening of God's church!

You can also download companion study tools including a free timeline and summary of the complete trilogy, glossary, sources, pronunciations, abbreviations, and more.